Redeeming the Wasteland

TELEVISION DOCUMENTARY AND COLD WAR POLITICS

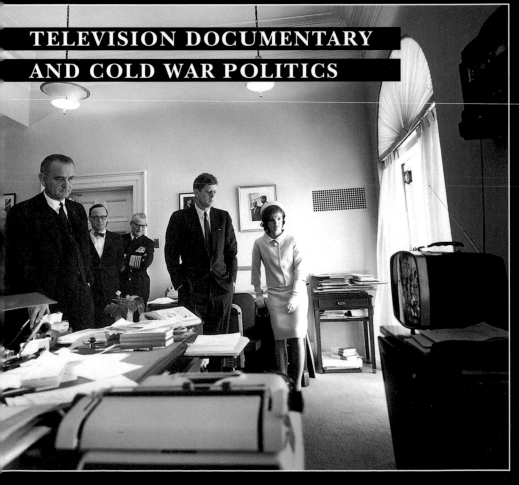

Michael Curtin

Redeeming the Wasteland

Redeeming the Wasteland

Television Documentary and Cold War Politics

Michael Curtin

RUTGERS UNIVERSITY PRESS
New Brunswick, New Jersey

Library of Congress Cataloging-in-Publication Data

Curtin, Michael.
    Redeeming the wasteland : television documentary and Cold War
politics / Michael Curtin.
        p.   cm.—(Communications, media, and culture)
    Includes bibliographical references and index.
    ISBN 0-8135-2221-8 (cloth : alk. paper). — ISBN 0-8135-2222-6
(pbk.)
    1. Television documentary programs—United States.   2. Television
in propaganda—United States.   3. Anti-Communist movements—United
States.   4. Television broadcasting of news—Political aspects—
United States.   5. United States—Politics and
government—1945–1989.   I. Title.   II. Series.
PN1992.8.D6C87   1995
070.1′95—dc20   95-12436
                                                                                CIP

British Cataloging-in-Publication information available

Published by Rutgers University Press, New Brunswick, New Jersey
Manufactured in the United States of America

For Melissa

Contents

and archivists. I especially wish to express my gratitude to staff members at the State Historical Society of Wisconsin, the Museum of Television and Radio, the John F. Kennedy Presidential Library, the Library of Congress, the CBS News Library, and the Billy Rose Theatre Collection of the New York Public Library. I have also received generous support from my colleagues in the Department of Telecommunications at Indiana University. Donald Agostino and Kathy Krendl deserve special credit for bringing me to Bloomington and providing a setting that made it possible to carry this project to conclusion. Similarly, Christopher Anderson played a vital role by carving out a home for cultural studies in our department, making this an especially rewarding place to work. Over the past few years, he also shared many critical insights that helped to shape the manuscript in significant ways. Leslie Mitchner, editor in chief at Rutgers University Press, is to be thanked as well for her critical eye, organizational style, and infectious enthusiasm. Despite the many demands of her job, she never failed to respond to my editorial needs in a timely fashion.

Writing about this period of the Cold War has spurred me to reflect on my childhood years when television played a role in forming some of my first impressions of life outside the family circle. Although I vividly remember my youthful commitment to the struggle against Communism, I also remember that television provided some of the very first images that invited me to question the notion of U.S. global leadership. Such reflections furthermore remind me of how my parents and siblings cultivated these critical inklings in often unexpected ways. I want to thank them for many spirited dinner-table discussions over the years, most of which ended amicably. I also want to thank my parents for the unconditional love and support that fostered in me a self-confidence that made it possible to take on challenges such as this.

Finally, and most important, I must express my appreciation to Melissa, who has put up with me for fourteen years and with this project for almost half as long. Her constructive criticism, good humor, and emotional support are treasures I cannot imagine being without. Words only begin to describe the many ways in which she made this book possible.

Redeeming the Wasteland

Introduction

At nine-thirty on the Friday evening after Thanksgiving in 1960, *CBS Reports* broadcast what would become one of the most famous television documentaries of all time, "Harvest of Shame." This poignant and detailed examination of the exploitation of migrant farm laborers in the United States concluded with reporter Edward R. Murrow's passionate appeal for federal action to cope with the problem. The program stands out in television histories and in the memories of broadcast journalists as one of the shining moments when the medium matched up to its potential to inform and enlighten the American public.

Less well known is the fact that the following Tuesday *NBC White Paper* broadcast an award-winning investigation of the Soviet attack on a U.S. spy plane entitled "The U-2 Affair." And one week after that, ABC's *Bell and Howell Close-Up!* garnered similar kudos from the critics for "Yanki No!" a look at Fidel Castro's expanding influence throughout Latin America. These three broadcasts signaled the rapidly growing presence of informational programming in prime-time television. The change was also reflected in *TV Guide*'s lead article that week, written by producer Fred Friendly, which seemed to sum up the aspirations of network documentarists with the title "Television *Can* Open America's Eyes: The Medium Offers the Hope of Awakening Us to the Truths of a Perilous Age."[1] In the very heart of what would soon be dubbed the "vast wasteland," news workers were staking a claim for probing analysis of important social issues.

These efforts represented a dramatic transformation of network programming practices, for only two years earlier, not a single documentary inhabited the prime-time schedules of the major networks during a similar two-week period. Nor was the early winter of 1958 an exception.

Throughout the fifties, prime-time television was almost exclusively reserved for entertainment programming. Yet at the beginning of the new decade, each network began a dramatic expansion of its television news operations, and documentary would play such a prominent role in this effort that in 1962 alone the three commercial networks produced close to four hundred such programs.[2] At a time when evening newscasts were only fifteen minutes long and at the very moment when opinion polls showed that TV had overtaken newspapers as the public's preferred news source, the three major networks touted their documentaries as one of the most important vehicles of public education in an age of crisis and uncertainty.

It was estimated that some 90 percent of all American homes viewed at least one documentary each month, and the increasing prominence of the genre was nurtured by critical acclaim as well.[3] *Variety* cited the actuality boom as the most exciting program development of the early 1960s.[4] And in 1962 the genre would snag three of the five Emmy Award nominations for program of the year. One year later, a documentary would succeed for the first time in capturing the top honor with Reuven Frank's program about an escape from Communist East Berlin entitled "The Tunnel."[5]

The genre was being promoted as an important new addition to the television syndication market as well. All three networks now used documentaries to distinguish their overseas program catalogs. By 1962 NBC boasted that it was distributing informational fare to more than fifty countries. In addition, the network contended that these programs were being used as a model for indigenous documentary efforts by broadcasters overseas. CBS made similar claims, and one of the key reasons ABC expanded its news operation was to service its foreign affiliates with information and interpretation.[6]

However, 1962 is also remarkable for other, seemingly contradictory milestones in television history. One of the most popular entertainment programs of all time premiered that autumn and quickly scrambled to the top of the ratings. *The Beverly Hillbillies* consistently attracted more than a third of all television viewers on Wednesday evenings, packaged between *The Many Loves of Dobie Gillis* and *The Dick Van Dyke Show*. The ways in which all three programs poked fun at the peccadilloes of suburban living apparently tapped into a popular preoccupation with modern family life. In fact, opinion polls from the period showed that most Americans were primarily concerned with their immediate domestic surroundings. Yet at this very moment when Americans were looking inward, television began to expand its field of vision as never before.

Documentaries about compelling national issues such as poverty, automation, and civil rights received prominent airplay. But the single issue that commanded the most attention on the network airwaves was the struggle to defend the "Free World" against the international challenge posed by Communism. Consequently, the networks churned out dozens of prime-time documentaries such as "Showdown in the Congo," "Remarkable Comrades," and "The Rise of Khrushchev."

This book is therefore about a distinctive and complicated moment when political and corporate leaders as well as network officials embraced the television documentary in an explicit attempt to mobilize public opinion behind a more activist foreign policy. No television stations were commandeered by government officials, however, nor was war officially declared. Nevertheless, like earlier mass media campaigns that accompanied the two world wars, this flourishing of documentary activity was part of an ambitious effort to awaken the public to its "global responsibilities" and thereby consolidate popular support for decisive action overseas under the aegis of the New Frontier.

My research did not begin with this analysis in mind. Rather, my original interest in this period was stimulated by the folklore of broadcast journalism. Having worked in both radio and television news, I, like many of my colleagues, harbored an abiding respect for that moment of broadcast history when documentary flourished on network television. I imagined, perhaps naively, that these highly visual and thoroughly analytical television programs must have played an important role in sparking the social activism of the 1960s. The documentarists of this period seemed to have had what every broadcast journalist covets: extensive resources, plenty of airtime, and access to a wide audience. This nostalgia was not mine alone; many journalists and media critics remember the early 1960s as the "golden age" of television documentary.[7]

Yet as I burrowed deeper into the subject, I found that the mythology of this golden age involves forgetfulness as well as remembrance. Most forget, for example, that the pressures of prime-time scheduling played a significant role in shaping the form and content of these programs. They also forget that the golden age of documentary was fostered by close government scrutiny of the broadcasting industry. And they forget that documentary programs, far from being objective, played an important role in the production and circulation of an expansionist Cold War ideology.

As for scholarly analysis, most research regarding this golden age has been devoted to causal explanations as to why the networks committed such extensive resources to what would prove to be a commercially unprofitable genre.[8] Some suggest that the documentary boom emerged as a form of network atonement for the excesses of the quiz show era.[9] Others argue that the industry bolstered its public service programming in response to government antitrust investigations of the networks.[10] And still others credit Federal Communications Commission (FCC) chairman Newton Minow with realigning the public service priorities of network programmers through "regulation by raised eyebrow."[11] Although each of these arguments has some merit, they largely rely on a model of linear causality, suggesting that a particular factor (usually economic or political) sparked this exceptional moment of television history. Furthermore, few researchers have actually analyzed the programs themselves or the social context in which they were viewed. A. William Bluem provides the most comprehensive examination of the texts, but his attention is largely focused on the formal characteristics of the television documentary and its historical antecedents in other media such as radio, film, and photography. Moreover, Bluem's book, which was published in 1965, lacks the critical distance that only time can provide. His enthusiasm for the growing influence of the television documentary does not anticipate the decline of the genre, which began soon after his manuscript went to press. Nor does he sense the tension between documentary claims to journalistic objectivity and the Cold War ideology that shapes these programs.[12]

The literature of film studies also fails to deal with these programs in a comprehensive fashion. The television documentary is orphaned from the mainstream of film scholarship and treated as exceptional. Part of this may be due to the influence of auteurist criticism. That is, the film documentarists who receive the most attention—such as Vertov, Flaherty, and Ivens—are known for their contentious relations with the institutions of mass culture. Preferring to pursue a distinctive vision, each played a role in cultivating the documentary's reputation as an oppositional film practice.[13] Television documentarists, on the other hand, receive only passing mention possibly because of their status as career employees working within the news departments of large corporations. They are, moreover, positioned in relation to a journalistic community that measures its worth through access to the powerful. Their concerns often appear less aesthetic than institutional, and their oppositional status has regularly been called into question. It is therefore not surprising that, even though all but a few network documentaries of the early sixties were produced on film, they receive only cursory mention (usually a reference to "Harvest of Shame") in the history and criticism of the documentary film genre.

What is given far more attention in film scholarship about the 1960s is the work of independent, cinema verité producers. Documentaries by Robert Drew and Frederick Wiseman are analyzed in much greater detail, although their audiences were far smaller than the millions who regularly viewed programs such as *NBC White Paper*.[14] Perhaps these verité filmmakers appeal to our fascination with seemingly autonomous innovators. By contrast, Erik Barnouw, in his seminal history of the documentary genre, refers only briefly to network efforts and dismisses them as a manifestation of superpower antagonisms. "Closely watched by top executives," he writes, "documentaries became institutional, depersonalized. In dealing with remote eruptions—Cuba, Congo, Indonesia, Indochina—they tended to rely heavily on official statements. . . . On both sides of the cold war, television schedules showed the military-industrial stamp."[15] Barnouw concludes that the programs were little more than a reflection of government policies, here again implying a relatively direct, causal relationship.

Barnouw's assessment is not unique, of course. Other forms of historical scholarship often view television programs as a reflection or expression of larger political, economic, and social forces. Moreover, this tendency to treat popular culture as epiphenomenal leads many historians to ignore mass media entirely. Yet even the most innovative historical work often leaves a vague impression of the connections between popular culture and other social forces. So, for example, William Chafe's influential history of the post–World War II period portrays television programming as reflecting suburbanization, reinforcing dominant values, and shaping the daily experiences of viewers on behalf of a growing consumer goods industry.[16] In each case, television is either an instrument or a barometer of forces outside. Similarly, Elaine Tyler May's ingenious examination of the postwar ideology of domesticity tends to link changes in economic and social relations to changes in popular culture in a rather uncontentious fashion. We are told, for example, that, as soldiers returned from World War II, popular culture responded with a new set of images that encouraged women to leave their wartime occupations and return to the home. Suburbanization was likewise bolstered by a pervasive set of popular texts that celebrated home ownership and nuclear families. May does an impressive job of identifying the many distinctive cultural artifacts of the period, but one still wonders how these *changes* in cultural forms actually took place. Were these shifts in representation driven by powerful social forces that allowed the imagery to achieve its authority relatively uncontested? Were the culture industries simply responding to demand? Or were there internal controversies and contradictions within media institutions themselves?[17] These un-answered questions may not be central to May's argument, but they do point toward significant ambiguities that most historical scholarship tends to overlook.

Even research that focuses more directly on media institutions and practices often fails to address the relationship between mass media and social change. This is especially true in the domain of news analysis, in which the emphasis is largely on continuity. Sociologists such as Edward Jay Epstein and Gaye Tuchman have, for example, examined news-gathering procedures and institutional routines, thereby teasing out the daily behavior patterns that regularly structure news content.[18] Herbert J. Gans has directed our attention to the social backgrounds, values, and attitudes that influence journalistic decision making.[19] All have made im-portant contributions. Note, however, that each focuses on systemic ele-ments that lead to patterned behavior. This volume, on the other hand, examines a moment of *transition* when television news organizations de-cisively departed from past practices under specific historical conditions. Moreover, I focus on a form of programming that was produced outside the routines and constraints that are so often the subject of scholarly criticism. Network documentarists during this period were given a broad mandate, plenty of resources, and extensive airtime. They were not pressed by short deadlines, nor were they dependent on a small circle of official government sources. In many ways, these programs were an ex-ception to the practices that have come to dominate television news.

It is precisely because of this distinctive status that documentary is often held up as the best hope for improving the quality of television in the United States. In both trade magazines and the popular press we have been reminded time and again that the problem with television news is its shallowness. By implication, the solution would be the restora-tion of documentary's prominence in commercial television, a reversal of the trend that has dominated TV news for almost three decades. As a result, the genre has been invoked as the celebrated counterexample. Its diminishing presence is considered indicative of network television's continuing failure to live up to its social responsibility, a fact that no doubt helps to nurture the mythology of documentary's golden age.

Yet such yearnings for a return to the mythical past do not belong to the popular press alone. Mary Ann Watson's book *The Expanding Vista: American Television in the Kennedy Years* suggests that television had one brief shining moment when New Frontier reformers prodded the me-dium toward more enlightened forms of programming. Drawing extensively on taped interviews with participants from the period, she constructs a largely uncritical narrative of one of the most "telegenic" administrations in American history.[20] For example, she works hard to describe the broad popular support enjoyed by Newton Minow, the FCC chairman who publicly disparaged television as a "vast wasteland," and she pits this heroic character against the vested interests of the broadcasting industry. Although it makes for good narrative, Watson's account fails to describe the areas of ongoing collaboration between the FCC and the industry. Nor does she wrestle with the fact that, despite Minow's highly visible criticisms of television, the medium remained overwhelmingly popular with audiences throughout this period.[21] Watson's history pays little attention to such contradictions and tensions. Her preference for narrative technique requires heroes, and her protagonists in almost all cases prove to be the white hats of the New Frontier as well as those who joined the posse of sympathizers. According to Watson, their sagacious sense of the new medium not only won Kennedy the presidency, but it also transformed the nature of television. Such narrative requirements not only skew her analysis, but they also narrow her perspective to the view from Camelot.

In this book, I examine the golden age of the television documentary as a phenomenon that can be best understood as the product of converging social, economic, political, institutional, and discursive forces. My analysis points to a dynamic and interactive relationship between these forces. And instead of constructing a historical narrative with inevitable outcomes, I explore the tensions, ambivalences, and contradictions that accompany any such era.[22] Moreover, I analyze this golden age not as a singular moment but as a culmination of an ongoing critique of television that became linked to the politics of the Cold War.

As we shall see, this articulation of culture and geopolitics began in the wake of the 1957 *Sputnik* launch when opinion leaders who decried the supposed missile gap also expressed concerns about the educational system, public morals, and the television industry. Such concerns were an important component in John F. Kennedy's political rhetoric. When he beckoned America to "get moving again," Kennedy envisioned a transformation of the nation's military and foreign policy as well as its most popular medium of mass communication. Consequently, the documentary boom of the early sixties should be understood within the larger agenda of the New Frontier, which sought to forge an alliance of reform factions behind a reinvigorated and interventionist U.S. foreign policy.[23]

Yet this is not the first time that mass media have played an important role in reshaping global geography. Political scientist Benedict Anderson has shown how the emergence of print capitalism was linked to the development of the modern nation-state. He argues that during the nineteenth century the mass-circulation newspaper and the popular novel helped to create the conditions whereby millions of people who were otherwise unknown to one another might "imagine" their national affinity.[24] These imaginings across vast expanses of space played a crucial role in the evolution of the modern nation-state as we know it, a role of equal importance to those played by state institutions, currencies, and legal systems. Of course, such moments of national consciousness are not solitary events. National identities must constantly be nurtured and reinforced. Furthermore, as we shall see, certain moments arise when the nation must be "reimagined" and when those imaginings transcend national borders and take on an international significance. The early 1960s was one such moment, and television was the site where various groups struggled to transform popular images of the United States and to position it as an active leader of the Free World. Their ultimate aspirations for television reached far beyond the borders of the United States. It was hoped that the medium would become an important site for the production and circulation of images that would win the allegiances of viewers around the globe to the community of the Free World.

What follows is therefore more than a book about television news. It is also about a particular moment of transition, the post-Sputnik era—a moment when major corporations sensed an urgent need to transform foreign policy and to escalate U.S. involvement throughout the globe. It was also an era when three major television networks dominated the nation's most popular pastime and reaped some of the most fantastic profits in the history of the American economy. And it was a time of pervasive anxieties about social relations, popular morals, and the nation's sense of purpose. These anxieties manifested themselves in a number of scandals during the late fifties that subjected the broadcasting and advertising industries to widespread criticism. Consequently, prominent social critics such as Newton Minow, Edward R. Murrow, and Arthur Schlesinger Jr.—all of whom would become key figures in the New Frontier—argued for the reform of television. These criticisms, when articulated with debates over citizenship and the "national interest," led in turn to the suggestion that television, with its privileged access to the suburban family home, had an important role to play in the global struggle against Communism.

Yet these changes were not simply imposed on the television industry. News workers had their own reasons to support this agenda and therefore seized this moment as an opportunity to enhance their own status and influence within network broadcast organizations. They pressed for the expansion of documentary as a corrective measure to balance the medium's focus on commercial entertainment. Thus, agitation from within combined with pressures from without to prompt all three networks to shift their attention to the rapid expansion of informational programs. Touting the objectivity of their news-gathering procedures, these organizations dispatched camera crews to the far reaches of the globe to ferret out and document Communist infiltration along the frontiers of the Free World.

Interestingly, the outcomes of these ventures proved to be far more contradictory than one might expect. The same discourse that valorized journalistic professionalism also demanded a form of empirical investigation that led news workers to seek out groups and cultures with ideas that were at odds with the assumptions of the New Frontier. Indeed, many news workers, when pressed to gather documentation of Communist infiltration in foreign lands, returned with film footage and interviews that suggested substantial local resistance to "leadership" or domination by either superpower. The resulting documentaries often strained to contain these discontinuities within a Cold War narrative that divided the world into two opposing camps.

Audience responses to these programs were also far more ambivalent than promoters of the genre had anticipated. Many viewers identified network documentary with the reform agenda of a political and cultural elite. Some candidly expressed their opposition to the programs, and many simply avoided them. This ambivalence among viewers caused internal struggles within the networks, where news executives were pressed to justify these shows according to the commercial logic of television. The programs consistently underperformed when compared with the audience ratings for other prime-time genres. Although pressure from government, corporate, and public opinion leaders spurred the evolution of the genre, it was difficult for news executives to sustain the programs within the context of a commercial entertainment medium. Attempts were made to tinker with the production values and stylistic qualities of network documentaries in order to broaden their appeal. But one of the fundamental problems with the programs was that they almost exclusively addressed themselves to a white, male, middle-class viewer and therefore tended to marginalize large segments of the audience, especially women and African Americans.

In sum, the golden age of documentary resulted from the successful alignment of opinion leaders and national institutions behind a Cold

War public education effort. Yet this moment proved to be rife with contradiction, and by 1963 the documentary began a slow, steady slide from its prominent position in prime-time commercial television. Thus, this book not only details the ways in which the production and reception of television news are woven into a complex web of social relations but also demonstrates how shifting power relations in society are registered in the symbolic forms of a popular medium. It furthermore suggests that, rather than seeing television primarily as a technology or commercial industry, it is most fruitful to examine the medium as a site of contest where various groups attempt to fashion a vision of society that is consonant with their particular political agendas. Finally, my work attempts to explain why the "powerful effects" that are commonly attributed to television often fail to materialize in concrete historical situations. Television may be an important site of public discourse and social struggle, but it is far from being an unmediated reflection of dominant interests or a simple instrument of social control. Although powerful elites may at times be able to shape the terms of public discourse, their ability to control program content and manage the attitudes of viewers has proven far more uncertain.

As this framework suggests, my research has benefited from a number of analytical insights derived from the field of cultural studies. Primary among these is the understanding that the imagery that permeates our daily lives is an outcome of a *circle of production* in which people play an active role. Elites do not simply impose their will, nor do economic imperatives always prevail. Rather, as Antonio Gramsci argued, powerful factions within society must constantly reinvent their authority and vie for the support of subordinate groups as economic and political conditions change. Consequently, symbolic activity is central to the production of political affinities in modern society, and television is one of the most important domains in which these efforts take place. Furthermore, cultural studies has shown us that audiences are neither homogeneous nor passive. The more we study the ways in which people actually use television, the more we find that viewers interpret TV programs in relation to their distinctive social positions and everyday experiences. Media histories must therefore pay attention to the contexts of both production and reception.

Such an approach to the study of television seeks to account for the interactions between multiple levels of social practice at any given moment. Each of these forces is determinate—setting limits and conditions for other forces—but not determining. We rarely find one-to-one relationships when we study historical phenomena; rather, as Louis Althusser suggested, social practices and cultural products are *overdetermined.*[25] For example, institutions such as network news organizations operate in a somewhat autonomous fashion while also responding to outside political and economic forces. News organizations have their own internal logics and rhythms, but these unfold in relation to external trends and tendencies that set boundaries for the relatively autonomous behaviors of these institutions. Consequently, the significance of any moment in television history cannot be understood by simply analyzing a news organization, a technology, or an industry. Instead these phenomena must be examined in relation to a complex field of social forces.

Yet this framework should not be mistaken for a happy pluralism of competing societal tendencies. Rather, the relative weight of the forces in balance at any historical moment must be carefully assessed, and, for example, the powerful logic of capitalism in the modern world must be given its due. Consequently, one can hardly doubt that superpower struggle and the commercial interests of the networks had a profound influence on these documentaries. But this structuring influence should not be emphasized at the expense of a thorough investigation of journalistic practices, documentary texts, and audience behaviors. As we shall see, this golden age, although a product of the Cold War, also became a site for the interrogation of dominant assumptions. This moment of television history opened a space, however modest and tentative, for public discussion and even contestation regarding the messages and the medium. The golden age of documentary is therefore an opportunity to examine a number of important relationships within a historically specific context: relationships between mass media and the national imaginary, between government institutions and corporate broadcasters, between journalistic practices and ideals of objectivity, between highbrow criticism and popular discourse, and between media texts and the interpretive practices of television audiences.

In keeping with this framework, the following chapters are not organized in a chronological or narrative fashion. Instead, I have interwoven textual criticism with contextual analysis throughout the book. Chapter 1 describes the social environment of the fifties and the ways in which criticisms of television and popular culture were articulated with the emerging politics of the New Frontier. These critics hoped to use the medium to alert the public to its responsibilities in the global struggle with monolithic Communism. The second chapter then turns to one of the key outcomes of television reform and analyzes documentaries from the early 1960s that specifically focused on the Communist other. These programs portray life in the totalitarian societies of Eastern Europe, the

Soviet Union, and the People's Republic of China. Not only do they depict a threatening opponent, but they also establish a set of oppositions against which American society is measured.

Chapter 3 then describes the political economy of this period and outlines the increasing global activity of American corporations after World War II. It explains how, during the 1950s, overseas economic expansion generated a conflict between corporate ambitions and the foreign policy of the Eisenhower administration. By the end of the decade, many business leaders worried that America's leadership role was being threatened around the globe, and they called for renewed activism in government policy. Furthermore, chapter 3 shows that during the late fifties television executives began to share this concern about foreign policy and the global economy. This was motivated in large part by the changing economics of the media marketplace. By 1960, 87 percent of American households owned television sets, and broadcasters worried that the domestic television market was reaching a saturation point. Increasingly, they looked overseas for investment opportunities, hardware sales, and new syndication markets. As a result, network executives began to see television as an important medium for raising public awareness of foreign policy concerns.

Those parts of the globe that generated the greatest amount of concern among corporate leaders were countries that were considered vulnerable to Communist influence or infiltration, such as Brazil, Cambodia, and Italy. Consequently, chapter 4 examines documentaries of the middle ground, programs that portray so-called hot spots of political "unrest." Although the Cold War provides a master narrative that structures many of these texts, the documentaries of the middle ground often feature complex and contradictory evidence regarding the role these societies play in superpower struggle. Rarely do these countries fit comfortably into Cold War dichotomies, and therefore the texts must work hard to reconcile incongruities.

Chapter 5 explores the explosive growth of network news operations during the late 1950s and early 1960s. Specifically, it shows that the expanding network investment in international news was justified for a number of internal, institutional reasons. Furthermore, this chapter suggests that prime-time documentary became the locus of fierce competition between the networks as they tested the profit potential of various television news formats. Chapter 5 also explores the ways in which network news employees discussed the relationship between institutional forces and the conventions of journalistic practice, especially the concept of objectivity, for not only did these programs produce interpretations that fit within the ideological parameters of New Frontier internationalism, but they also presented themselves as objective renditions of social reality. My analysis examines this contradiction and describes the boundaries within which these news workers operated. As we shall see, even though the documentaries of this period were organized around the master narrative of the Cold War, the professional practices of documentary producers engendered texts that often invited alternative interpretations by audiences. Consequently, I argue that many of these programs can be read both as endorsements of New Frontier internationalism and as interrogations of American policy that produce contradictory meanings.

Although this assessment helps us further understand the multiple meanings embedded in documentaries of the middle ground, the analysis also can be extended to documentaries that primarily focus on domestic topics. Chapter 6 shows how the framework of superpower struggle structures documentary analysis of issues ranging from civil rights to automation to aerospace development. These documentaries repeatedly interrogate the meaning of life in a "free" society and by implication help to define the boundaries of the Free World. Interestingly, by pursuing the logic of journalistic objectivity as well as the New Frontier reform agenda, these programs also raise questions about gaps and discontinuities within the American system. They question, for example, how racism in the United States affects the nation's pretensions to global leadership.

Chapter 7 adds another layer of complexity to our understanding of these programs by suggesting that the representational strategies of network documentary were also influenced by the fictional conventions of Hollywood film. This chapter traces the discussion among documentary producers regarding tactics for representing complicated social concerns within the context of network television. It shows how narrative and filmmaking strategies adapted from Hollywood displaced earlier didactic styles of representation. It also suggests that these storytelling strategies created boundaries within which social concerns could be examined. Thus the Communist other was not only an ideological category but a narrative one as well. It activated a recurring narrative tension that structured many of these "objective" documentaries. On the other hand, we shall also see how the principle of character identification often encouraged viewers to sympathize with victims of exploitation, many of whom were Communist.

These first seven chapters are organized so as to create a recurring movement back and forth between text and context. This organization aims to portray the overdetermined nature of these texts and this historical moment. Chapter 8 focuses on a detailed analysis of a single documentary, "Panama: Danger Zone," in order to demonstrate more fully the multiple determinations at work in the network documentaries of this period. This chapter also shows how these intersecting forces engender a complicated set of meanings that leave open the possibility of alternative interpretations.

This last point concerning the polysemic nature of network documentary necessarily directs our attention to the audiences of this era. Although it is impossible to know what sense they made of these programs, it is possible to chart some of the contours of popular reception, for just as economic, political, and institutional forces set boundaries for the production of these texts, so too did the social experience of viewers. Chapter 8 therefore describes the social positions of three reading communities and speculates as to how they might have interpreted network documentaries. Despite the powerful master narrative of the Cold War and the compelling discourse of journalistic objectivity, many viewers apparently remained skeptical about these programs as well as the reform agenda of the New Frontier.

Finally, the conclusion looks at the forces that fueled documentary's disappearance from prime-time television. Although these programs regularly produced audiences that were comparable to national newsmagazines such as *Time* and *Newsweek,* they failed to compete with the ratings of TV entertainment programs. Therefore, after a period of initial enthusiasm, corporate advertisers became increasingly reluctant to sponsor documentaries. They expressed concern about relatively small audiences and the negative feedback associated with controversial programs. This dwindling interest in documentary sponsorship along with a shift in presidential politics, in the wake of the Cuban missile crisis, spelled trouble for the genre. Although attempts were made to "soften" the programs and further enhance their entertainment value, the golden age was drawing to a close by the middle of the decade.

In all, this book describes the ways in which documentary programs of this period explored and explained the world. It details the boundaries of documentary discourse regarding matters of important societal concern, and it shows how a spectrum of intelligibility was established by a master narrative of the Cold War. My analysis shows how some political alternatives seemed possible within documentary discourse while others were marginalized or unspoken. It further demonstrates the complex and contested process by which powerful factions attempt to shape the terms of public debate according to their changing material interests.

Finally, this book shows how such ambitious attempts to transform public attitudes and cultural processes are mediated and even resisted by groups, institutions, and viewers.

The concerns raised in this book are not simply historical or academic, however. Television remains a central component of daily life both in the United States and in societies around the globe. Moreover, the challenge of providing meaningful information is as great as ever. We are still pressed to cope with highly complex and increasingly global social relations. Nevertheless, our major commercial television networks—still the most ubiquitous and arguably influential media—continue to be criticized for their shallowness. They have, for example, been chastised for their deferential coverage of the Reagan White House, for their salacious reporting on issues such as domestic abuse, and for their refusal to address many of the most urgent and complicated problems of our time—poverty, racism, sexism, and the unrelenting destruction of our physical environment. Certainly, we, like many of those who sought to reform television during the early sixties, yearn for more active and enlightened public debate about the issues that confront us. And just as certainly, many of us assume that mass media hold the keys to such a forum. Yet this book provides little comfort and no simple tonic for the problems we face in the realm of communication. It does have lessons to offer, however, perched as we are on the eve of significant changes in our media environment.

First of all, this volume explores an early moment in television's expansion beyond national borders, a matter that should be of keen interest to those involved in current debates over globalization, nationalism, and cultural identity. Researchers have become increasingly aware that our sense of self is in many ways affected by our perceptions of others not simply in our neighborhoods but in distant parts of the world. These images of the other are not simply neutral pictures transmitted from afar. They are instead intimately connected to changing economic, social, and political relations. The collapse of the Soviet Union made only too apparent how dramatically our images of Russians changed within a few short years. On television, the "evil empire" suddenly became a nation populated by anxious individuals who invited our sympathy and concern. Conversely, in the months leading up to the Gulf War, Saddam Hussein was transformed from a key U.S. ally to a threatening incarnation of Arab legerdemain. This book explores one similarly important moment of shifting representation and the complex set of forces that fueled the change.

Another contribution this volume makes is to remind us that professionalism, objectivity, and filmic realism are not inherent conventions of television news. Rather, they are social constructs that have a specific history and a particular logic. To privilege these qualities in the realm of public debate is to accord authoritative status to certain speakers and institutions at the expense of others. The present volume shows how, at a particular moment, corporate news organizations used these seemingly neutral conventions in an attempt to control the representation of public issues. It demonstrates why we must be wary of those who try to speak *for* society or the "global community" as a whole. As we shall see, one of the most questionable attributes of the sixties documentary was its pretension to represent all points of view in an equitable and engaging manner.

Finally, the golden age of television documentary has much to teach us as we envision the potential of new media technologies. The early sixties were likewise an era of innovation, and many argued that society was on the verge of a major breakthrough. Color television, the radio transistor, and the launch of the Telstar satellite augured great changes for human communication. Marshall McLuhan, Newton Minow, and David Sarnoff all expounded lavishly about the prospects of a global village. Many opinion leaders also imagined that documentary would be a unique teaching tool that would help to bring that village together. Today, similarly auspicious possibilities are envisioned. Internet, multimedia, and virtual reality all offer prospects for more enlightened and democratic forms of communication. Well-meaning activists labor diligently today to bring about such possibilities just as many camera-wielding documentarists of the early sixties sought to promote positive social change.

Not to diminish their efforts, we must nevertheless draw on the lessons of this earlier era in order to remind ourselves that the agenda of global communication is central to the aspirations of huge corporations that seek control over the flow of imagery and information just as they seek to control market behaviors and competition. Although this study of sixties documentary is heartening because it describes the difficulties of achieving such control, it nevertheless reminds us that the struggle for democratic forms of communication will continue to take place on a terrain that is powerfully influenced by the logic of corporate capitalism. Yet this corporate logic is riddled with gaps and contradictions, creating possibilities as well as constraints. Our awareness of such possibilities can be enhanced by carefully examining the terrain of past struggles over communication and the public interest. By reflecting on the uses of television during the New Frontier, we may be better prepared to cope with future technologies and with what many refer to as the "new world order."

Chapter One
Opportunities Lost and Found

On the second Tuesday of November 1960, more Americans went to the polls than ever before, and the proportional voter turnout increased dramatically as well. The percentage of eligible voters casting ballots in the presidential race rose to 64.5 percent, a jump of four percentage points over the previous election. Many attributed this increase to the enthusiasm generated by the Kennedy-Nixon television debates. After the election, CBS president Frank Stanton wrote in a letter to the chairman of the Democratic National Committee, "[W]hile only 45 per cent of Americans, according to a Roper poll, experienced 'very much interest' in the campaign before the debates, 57% did after them."[1] He contrasted this with 1956, when voter interest hovered around 46 percent throughout the fall. Stanton concluded that television was the key variable, an opinion that many others shared. It was suggested that television, for the first time, had emerged as a major mobilizing force in American politics, and over the next few years there were many who tried to put this potential to work, especially the new administration.

Shortly after President John F. Kennedy took office, the White House was literally inundated by project proposals from the media community. One New York producer wrote the president proposing a series of "television spectaculars" to promote the ideals and policies of the U.S. government.[2] Another recommended a series of progress reports to the nation, called "New Frontiers for Living."[3] Meanwhile, a pair of West Coast producers suggested that a politically-inspired variation of *American Bandstand* be produced and distributed around the globe in order to solicit the allegiance of young people to the agenda of the New Frontier.[4]

Even within the White House, staffers bandied about ideas for harnessing the potential power of television. Frederick G. Dutton, special assistant to the president, pitched a seven-week television series called *Men and Women of the New Frontier,* a program intended "to bring directly into American homes a first hand acquaintance and personal association with the new Administration." Dutton speculated that the programs would generate enough public support "so that Congress [would] more readily follow Executive Leadership . . . even beyond (and sometimes in spite of) the merits of particular legislation."[5] Production assistance from the major television networks would be crucial, according to Dutton. And the newly-appointed director of the U.S. Information Agency, Edward R. Murrow, recommended that the White House tap documentarist Fred Friendly as the series producer.[6]

One would imagine that Friendly, then executive producer of *CBS Reports,* might express some reluctance to compromise his status as an independent journalist in order to serve the government. Yet when the White House later appealed for Friendly's assistance, he too seemed caught up in the enthusiasm over television's political potential. Friendly said he would gladly come to Washington in order to serve the president and closed his letter by declaring, "I am constantly available to Mrs. Lincoln [JFK's secretary Evelyn Lincoln], or a member of your staff, at CBS or, at night, at my home in Riverdale, New York."[7]

Within the White House, discussion of television's motivational role in politics almost invariably drifted to the domain of foreign policy, an area of keen interest to the president but a subject that generated little enthusiasm among voters.[8] In fact, many Americans were explicitly *opposed* to a more activist U.S. role in international affairs. In the summer following Kennedy's rousing inaugural declaration to secure the blessings of liberty to nations throughout the Free World, one Kennedy aide noted, "A reputable recent opinion survey in California, a relatively 'progressive' state, shows, for example, that the foreign aid issue now develops a greater public response than any other single specific issue—and 40% of those polled reacted 'strongly' against it, with 3% for it."[9] Thus the White House faced a formidable task if it was to shift public attitudes regarding foreign policy, and the solution put forward time and again was that television must educate the American public as to its responsibilities in the global struggle against monolithic Communism.

In this effort, the favored category of programming was network documentary.[10] The first four years of the 1960s saw more documentaries produced and broadcast in network prime time than any other comparable period. During the peak season of 1962 the three major networks produced 387 documentaries.[11] Moreover, that same season featured *six* weekly prime-time documentary series as well as frequent specials such as the *NBC White Paper* programs.[12]

The dramatic expansion of network documentary culminated more than a decade of discussion regarding the appropriate uses of television. At the beginning of the 1950s, the new medium promised to offer exciting opportunities for enlightenment as well as entertainment. But as the decade wore on, the industry failed to deliver on such promises, and television became the subject of intense public debate and criticism. What elevated this debate to a position of prominence was the way in which key critics suggested a link between television, middle-class consumer lifestyles, and political apathy. At a time of rapidly growing U.S. corporate involvement overseas, American leaders positioned the debate over television within the context of superpower struggle. They urged the expansion of public affairs programming in order to mobilize popular support for a more activist foreign policy to meet the Communist challenge. By the end of the fifties, television documentary therefore became a prime focus of efforts to reform the medium. Such programming not only promised to reconnect the suburban middle class with public life, but it also offered a form of expert, "value-free" information that would make it possible for a reinvigorated American public to make crucial decisions about global issues. Thus the documentary ideal was based on the hope that television could make explicit connections between the realm of everyday life and the increasingly global interests of U.S. corporations and government.

The Debate over National Television

President Kennedy's appointee to head the Federal Communications Commission, Newton Minow, was the first chairman pointedly to express concern about television *content* and to wage a protracted campaign to alter the nature of prime time. Until 1961, FCC regulation of television largely had focused on technical and economic issues such as equipment standards, station allocations, and frequency interference. Minow's first major address after his appointment as chairman marked a significant departure from past practices. In a speech to industry leaders, Minow disparaged "the vast wasteland" of Hollywood telefilm and called on broadcasters to restore balance and diversity to their prime-time schedules. The chairman's critique of television was not novel but grew out of an ongoing public discussion of the medium throughout the 1950s.

Historian William Boddy has described many of these debates and explains that in the early years of television cultural critics and broadcast executives shared similar assessments of the medium's potential. During this period of experimentation, the networks generated a diversity of programming that ranged from anthology dramas to entertainment spectaculars, from televised symphonies to vaudeville-inspired variety shows. Critics celebrated this broad spectrum of programming because it seemed to exemplify American cultural pluralism. Moreover, it promised that television, unlike radio, might develop distinctive new forms of entertainment and cultural enlightenment. For their part, network executives welcomed this critique because it lent legitimacy to their efforts and distinguished the new medium from other forms of mass entertainment. Therefore, during the early fifties when government regulators were still determining who should be granted new station licenses, applicants who claimed affiliation with a network seemed destined to fulfill their public service responsibility to provide programming for all tastes. Boddy suggests that this strategy served NBC and CBS so well that by the middle of the decade, they had amassed enough affiliation contracts to secure a duopoly position in the industry.[13]

Yet the alliance between the networks and the critics did not last long. As the industry matured and as the networks grew more assured of their control over the medium, the commitment to diversity began to diminish. Increasingly, the networks began to collaborate with Hollywood studios, searching for entertainment formulas that could produce consistently large audiences at lower cost.[14] As a result, live programming began to fall by the wayside, and program diversity diminished as well. By the end of the decade the production of entertainment television was concentrated in Los Angeles and largely controlled by a small number of studios and producers. The networks abandoned not only the creative communities in New York and Chicago but also the television critics. Broadcast executives no longer seemed worried about the approval of newspaper columnists such as Jack Gould or Harriet Van Horne. Even more, they began to attack those who challenged their new programming strategies. The critics responded by pitching barbs at what they described as homogeneous Hollywood telefilm and even began to call into question the basic objectives of the medium. The networks were accused of abandoning the concept of program diversity for a cold, commercial logic. Television, according to the critics, had become a medium of manipulation rather than enlightenment.[15] Instead of a "window onto the world" that the early television industry had promised, the medium had become a display window for a national consumer culture.

Elite television critics were not the only ones to articulate such concerns. Lynn Spigel's history of the popular debates that accompanied the introduction of television suggests widespread public anxiety about the medium's ability to manipulate viewers in their homes. Some worried that television would turn the viewer into a passive automaton. Writes Spigel, "The threat of the 'machine man,' couched in the rhetoric of behavioralism, gave rise to a host of statements on the relationship between television and the family. Would the television set become the master and the family its willing subject? The adage of the day became, 'Don't let the television set dominate you!'"[16] Spigel shows how such concerns were manifested in many forms of popular media.

Nor was this the first time that Americans expressed widespread apprehension over the intrusion of broadcasting into the private space of the home. During the early years of radio, many critics claimed that the new medium would foster mindless audience behaviors, and others worried that it would detract from the vitality of public life. Many alleged that radio would change the individual from an active member of the community into a passive homebody. Just as important, it would allow the listener to participate privately in public events without the mediating influence of community leaders, educators, or clergy. As Heywood Broun put it, one could listen to a sermon on the radio, throw in a few cuss words, and smoke a cigar all at the same time.[17] Even more serious was the prospect that many listeners would opt for an evening of commercial entertainment over more public-spirited forms of programming.

Similar concerns were raised throughout the 1950s by social critics who claimed that the increasingly commercial logic of the television industry had diminished the public service mission of the medium.[18] As historian James L. Baughman has shown, many of these "elite" critics worried that the quality of American culture and of public life was threatened by the manipulative programming strategies of network executives. They watched with consternation as the networks canceled anthology dramas, symphonies, and public affairs programming in favor of game shows and westerns. Rather than blame audience preferences for these programming shifts, critics charged that television executives had failed to fulfill their role as guardians of the public sphere.[19] In 1959 Arthur Schlesinger Jr. wrote, "Even if one dissents (as I do) from alarmist predictions about television producing a nation of imbeciles, one must still wonder about the social wisdom of letting so miraculous and compelling a medium degenerate into electronic vaudeville."[20]

One of the most insidious forces behind this transformation of television was, according to critics, the advertising industry. Not only was Madison Avenue obsessed with high ratings and mass appeal, but it was also accused of cynically trying to manage the values and behaviors of entertainment audiences. In *The Hidden Persuaders,* Vance Packard contended that advertising specialists were able to manipulate consumers by using social scientific techniques, such as subliminal communication.[21] Although Packard offered little documentation to support his claims, the book was a best-seller and generated comparisons between the brainwashing techniques of totalitarian regimes and the advertising strategies of Madison Avenue. Nor was Packard alone in his assessment of mass media. Mica Nava contends that the writings of cultural critics from this period generally portray audiences as "easily duped by advertisers and politically pacified by the buying of useless objects. Their pursuit of commodities and their enjoyment of disdained cultural forms is cited as evidence of their irrationality and gullibility. The idea that certain sectors of the population are particularly vulnerable to the deleterious effects of cultural forms, namely women, children and the less educated, is an assumption running through Packard's book and repeated elsewhere."[22]

The quiz show scandals at the end of the fifties seemed to substantiate many of these concerns. Wildly popular, the TV game shows became the subject of intensive investigation and public debate when it was revealed that the contests were rigged. Perhaps the most respected television critic of the era, Jack Gould of the *New York Times,* blamed the scandals on the increasing pressures to conform to the commercial imperatives of the medium. He also expressed ominous concern over the "spreading virus of materialism" in American culture.[23]

Thus, by the end of the decade, the networks were criticized not only for their programming and commercialism but also for their failure to act as responsible guardians of the public airwaves. Moreover, the industry had abandoned the principle of programming diversity at the very moment that liberal cultural critics embraced diversity as the distinguishing difference between free societies and totalitarian societies.[24] Instead of the cultural and political forum that the networks had promised at the beginning of the decade, television projected the seamy squalor of the marketplace. Furthermore, the critics of television linked this failure in the domain of mass culture to a set of profound political consequences. In a 1958 speech to broadcast news directors that was later reprinted in

Charles Van Doren (left) assesses his winnings with Jack Barry, host of "Twenty-One," the program that sparked the quiz show scandals. (Courtesy of Photofest)

TV Guide, Edward R. Murrow declared, "This nation is now in competition with malignant forces of evil who are using every instrument at their command to empty the minds of their subjects, and fill those minds with slogans, determination, and faith in the future." Pitted against this threat was the American tradition of free inquiry and open debate, a tradition that Murrow believed television should nurture through an increased commitment to news and public affairs programming. Not only would this counterbalance commercialism and stimulate involvement in pubic life, but it also would help to alert Americans to the global challenge posed by Communism. "If we go on as we are," continued Murrow, "we are protecting the mind of the American public from any real contact with the menacing world that squeezes in upon us."[25] This, concluded Murrow, might be good for business in the short term but ultimately disastrous for the Republic.

Toward the end of 1959, under mounting criticism, the heads of ABC, CBS, and NBC met secretly at New York's St. Regis Hotel in order to discuss ways to deal with this growing public relations crisis.[26] Soon thereafter, in an agreement forged with FCC chairman John Doerfer, the networks promised to increase their commitment to documentary programming.[27] Although the networks followed the specific terms of this agreement for only a short time, it did help to signal the growing importance of network documentary as a symbol of public service programming. As we shall see, the documentary was characterized as the key genre for transcending the superficial and commercial aspects of the medium. Produced by network news professionals, it promised to educate and uplift the audience. Although the specifics of the Doerfer plan soon fell by the wayside, network commitment to documentary over the next few years grew far beyond the agreements formulated at the St. Regis Hotel. Documentary emerged as an important tonic for a troubled medium.

Perhaps the most immediate gesture toward government regulators, however, was not the product of explicit network planning and collaboration. Rather, it was the extensive television news coverage of the 1960 presidential election. The three networks spent between twenty and thirty million dollars for what one trade magazine referred to as "the greatest cash contribution" ever made in American politics.[28] In response, national politicians overwhelmingly expressed satisfaction with the medium's increasing attention to public issues. Few could ignore the seemingly salutary role television played in the presidential campaign, least of all the new administration. If the trade press is any indication, the networks seemed confident that by the spring of 1961 they had weathered the worst of their "image crisis."

Television and Foreign Policy

This complacency was quickly undone, however, by President Kennedy's newly appointed chairman of the Federal Communications Commission, Newton Minow. That same spring, in his first address to the National Association of Broadcasters—a speech that traditionally set the tone for ensuing relations between the chairman and the industry—Minow referred to television programming as a "vast wasteland," a phrase that quickly became ubiquitous in popular discussion of the medium. His analysis of broadcasting resurrected many of the concerns voiced during the late 1950s, but what marked Minow's comments as especially distinctive was the fact that he became the first chairman of the FCC explicitly to link television policy to foreign policy. Said Minow:

> [In] today's world, with chaos in Laos and the Congo aflame, with Communist tyranny on our Caribbean doorstep and relentless pressure on our Atlantic

alliance, with social and economic problems at home of the gravest nature, yes, and with technological knowledge that makes it possible, as our President has said, not only to destroy our world but to destroy poverty around the world—in a time of peril and opportunity, the old complacent, unbalanced fare of action-adventure and situation comedies is simply not good enough.[29]

Like the president, the new chairman spoke of the urgent global struggle for freedom and the need for personal commitment and sacrifice. He argued that the trustees of the public airwaves must be responsible for serving the *needs* of the public as well as catering to its more whimsical desires. He concluded the speech by imploring industry executives, "Ask not what broadcasting can do for you—ask what you can do for broadcasting. I urge you to put the people's airwaves to the service of the people and the cause of freedom."[30]

Minow's speech reflected the new administration's view that television was an important vehicle for reaching middle-class citizens in the privacy of their homes in order to reconnect them with public life. More broadly, the speech also symbolized a growing concern by corporate and political leaders about public attitudes toward U.S. involvement overseas. It sought to marshal the resources of television on behalf of a New Frontier agenda for global activism.

The significance of this agenda can be understood first by turning to Elaine Tyler May's history of domesticity during the postwar era. May contends that a suburban family ideal dominated U.S. culture throughout the 1950s and that this ideal had a notable impact on the behaviors of the middle class. Having grown up in an era that experienced depression, world war, and the emergence of atomic weaponry, many Americans sought a form of domestic security that would allow them to take advantage of the fruits of postwar prosperity in the privacy of their homes.[31] The suburban ideal not only invited Americans to seek security in domestic enclaves, but it also encouraged private, therapeutic approaches to social problems. Teen rebellion against prevailing norms was often characterized as juvenile delinquency, a psychologically based form of antisocial behavior. Similarly, women who complained of isolation in the suburban home were advised to undergo therapy to facilitate their adaptation to "normal" life. The role of the average citizen during this era of domesticity was to lead a prosperous, "well-adjusted" family life, not to engage in public confrontation or political struggle. "Domesticity was not so much a retreat from public affairs as an expression of one's citizenship," writes May. "Postwar men and women were endorsing and affirming, through their families, the goals expressed by major political leaders and experts."[32] These suburban families served as

Newton Minow was the first FCC chairman to link television policy explicitly to foreign policy. (Courtesy of Photofest)

examples of social and political progress: they were living representations of the American dream. Furthermore, May points out that this domestic ideal served government economic policy insofar as growth in consumer spending on durable goods and residential construction constituted almost the entire increase in gross national product during the mid-1950s.[33] In such an environment, little dissonance existed between the commercial goals of American industry, the political objectives of the Eisenhower administration, and the ideology of the middle-class family.

Toward the end of the decade, growing criticisms of television achieved a peculiar intensity because they were linked to a reassessment of middle-class lifestyles. Both Murrow and Minow received widespread attention for their commentaries about television, and in both cases their key concern was that material prosperity and mindless entertainment had made Americans lazy and insular. In their eyes, average Americans lacked a sense of purpose and resolve, both of which would be necessary if the United States was to meet the challenge from the East. This was not, however, the first, nor would it be the last, time highbrow critics would express concern about a popular medium and its audiences. Radio, motion pictures, comic books, and dime novels all have been subjected to similar sorts of commentary. What elevated the critique of television to a particularly lofty level of concern among American leaders was that television's shortcomings might be turned into assets. That is, the same medium that was used to mesmerize the masses might transport them to places where they could come to understand pressing social concerns—places dispersed not simply across the continent but also across the globe. And the social concern that was privileged above all others was the question of America's global leadership role.

The growing emphasis on foreign policy stemmed in large part from the dramatic growth of overseas business activities. Throughout the 1950s major manufacturers and advertisers increasingly turned their attention to burgeoning markets in Europe and new markets in what was characterized as the developing world. Resource extraction from the latter also became important as sophisticated manufacturing processes grew dependent on rare minerals that could only be found outside the United States. Furthermore, this expanding web of corporate activity was stitched together by overseas banking operations that began to flourish in the mid-1950s. Thus was constructed a Free World economy anchored by American technology, managerial practices, and investment dollars.[34]

Nevertheless, such an explicit link between American economic prosperity and global hegemony was rarely discussed by mass media throughout the 1950s, and popular commitment to an interventionist foreign policy wavered throughout the decade. There was a strong isolationist sentiment among the public as most Americans saw little reason for maintaining a military presence around the globe. Indeed, the major U.S. military intervention during this era was in Korea, where a muddled policy of containment crumbled when confronted by the prospect of full-scale war.[35] It was in this context that American voters selected a military hero for president in 1952, not because he would lead them to victory, but because he promised to lead them out of Korea. Such a lack of public resolve generated much discussion of a so-called Korean War syndrome.

At the very core of this debate was a great deal of confusion about the nature of the Free World and the U.S. role in defending it against a rising tide of Communist revolution. Was the United States willing to go to war to stop the spread of Communism? The president and much of the populace showed little desire to commit soldiers to combat overseas, especially when American interests had not been clearly spelled out. The Eisenhower administration found itself severely hamstrung by a powerful isolationist element within the Republican Party. Small business entrepreneurs and farmers had little to gain from an active and expensive international campaign to police the frontiers of the Third World. These businesspeople relied little on resources from abroad and were unlikely to market their products overseas. In fact, many of these small entrepreneurs felt that vast pools of cheap labor throughout the Third World were a threat to their operations. American manufacturers in such labor-intensive industries as shoemaking and apparel worried more about cheap imports than they did about Communist aggression in Asia or Latin America. Thus Eisenhower's foreign policy waffled throughout his second term, constrained by public opinion and stiff opposition within the Republican Party.[36]

On the other hand, leaders of capital-intensive corporations in such industries as petroleum, aerospace, and electronics showed growing concern about access to international markets.[37] These executives were in search of solutions to what they perceived as unrest in many parts of the globe. Moreover, many of these leaders realized that this instability raised questions not only of military strategy but of social reform as well. What could be done about conflicts in Vietnam, the Congo, and Cuba? These were the brushfire wars in which Americans were more likely to encounter the specter of famine among the population than the presence of Soviet tanks. What were the politics of the malnourished? In which camp did their sympathies lie? Thus the competition between East and West was not only strategic; increasingly it took on economic and ideological dimensions as well.

By the late 1950s many corporate leaders believed that the Soviets were winning this competition. According to a series of studies published during this period by the Ford Foundation and the Rockefeller Brothers Fund, American leadership of the Free World was in jeopardy.[38] As the Soviet economy was racing ahead, the American economy was still sputtering along in the wake of the 1957 recession. Furthermore, Soviet preeminence in rocketry following the launch of Sputnik in 1957 had diminished American prestige and shifted the nuclear balance of power. The Soviets were suddenly capable of delivering nuclear warheads to North American cities within a matter of minutes. Images of American invulnerability were being challenged, and the elite think tank studies asserted that it was time to "get America moving again."

This agenda was taken quite seriously by key leaders in the corporate community who banded together behind Nelson Rockefeller's 1956 bid for the Republican presidential nomination. But Rockefeller's stinging rebuff by the isolationist faction within the party encouraged many of these corporate leaders to redirect their campaign contributions to Democratic candidates during the next presidential campaign.[39] John F. Kennedy happily appropriated the activist economic and foreign policies advocated by these major think tanks. Indeed, he even borrowed a leaf from Nelson Rockefeller's campaign rhetoric in his declaration of a "New Frontier."[40]

Kennedy's presidential campaign rode a rising tide of crisis rhetoric that began with the *Sputnik* launch in 1957. Kennedy, like Rockefeller, placed a great deal of emphasis on a growing missile gap between the superpowers and warned that space technology was "the shield from behind which [the Soviets would] slowly but surely advance—through *Sputnik* diplomacy, limited brush-fire wars, internal revolution, and blackmail." He argued further, "The periphery of the Free World will slowly be nibbled away."[41] Rather than emphasize conformity and domesticity, the new president encouraged public activism and implied that citizens could make a difference in politics through their personal efforts, even in the domain of international affairs. In fact, Kennedy's inaugural address explicitly summoned public involvement in the global struggle against Communism while ignoring domestic issues entirely.

This shift in leadership rhetoric during the late fifties was not simply the product of high-level debates in foreign policy circles. Rather, scientists, liberal politicians, and social critics—all of whom operated on the margins of power during the Eisenhower era—also invoked Sputnik as

In his inaugural address, President Kennedy focuses on the global struggle against Communism. (Courtesy of the JFK Library)

emblematic of more pervasive symptoms of national decline. Not only were America's economy and space program lagging, but juvenile delinquency, consumerism, and pop culture all were considered indicative of a society gone soft, a nation without a sense of purpose. The Soviet space mission therefore became a key moment of transition in American society not only because it raised the possibility of American nuclear vulnerability but because it enhanced the status of social critics who yoked a whole constellation of social issues to the global struggle against monolithic Communism. America could meet this global challenge only if the public tempered its materialism and rejected complacency in favor of a renewed sense of national purpose. Here it was hoped that television might play an important role.

Furthermore, liberal social critics argued that solutions to most problems confronting the United States would be the product of a more enlightened and more purposeful technocracy. Communist extremism would not be defeated by McCarthyism or right-wing extremism. Rather, Arthur Schlesinger Jr., who would later join Kennedy's White House staff, argued that extremism of both the Left and Right was strikingly similar and was similarly destructive. He contended that the future of the world rested instead at "the vital center," and inextricably linked to this centrism was a celebration of science and expertise as the fundamental material for political progress both at home and abroad. Wrote Schlesinger:

> No people in the world approach the Americans in mastery of the new magic of science and technology. Our engineers can transform arid plains or poverty-stricken river valleys into wonderlands of vegetation and power. Our factories produce astonishing new machines, and the machines turn out a wondrous flow of tools and goods for every aspect of living. The Tennessee Valley Authority is a weapon which, if properly employed, might outbid all the social ruthlessness of the Communists for the support of the people of Asia.[42]

Thus, in the wake of the *Sputnik* launch, the image of the scientist, which had suffered ambivalent representation in mass media throughout much of the 1950s, began to assume a new countenance.[43] By the end of the decade, liberal critics were actively promoting the notion that the only defense against Soviet expansionism was expertise—in rocketry, economic policy, and social planning. No longer the "egghead" derided by Joseph McCarthy and other conservatives, the scientist and the expert began to take the high ground in public policy debates during the latter part of the decade.

The Turn toward Documentary

It is therefore significant that although the golden age of documentary would peak during the Kennedy administration, the networks had already begun to respond to public criticism by expanding their documentary efforts in 1959 and 1960. Of all the programming the networks could have offered to deflect increasing public criticism—symphonies, anthology dramas, live spectaculars, and the like—they chose to commit their resources to the documentary genre, the product of professional expertise. At a time when quiz show producers were under investigation for rigging their programs and advertisers were being criticized for manipulating audiences and television executives were suspected of conspiring with Hollywood moguls, at this precise moment, the networks turned to their professional journalists to render objective analyses of pressing social issues. Thus the network documentary asked viewers to believe what they saw on television once again, for it offered vital information that was presented as the product of untainted expertise. One

CBS press release touted producer Albert Wasserman for having "made it his career to capture on films true stories . . . exactly as they happen."[44]

The network documentarist sought to restore the medium's lost sense of public service and to provide the raw material for enlightened public discussion. Documentary programs therefore were invariably linked to specific notions of political process. NBC producer Fred Freed drew such a connection when discussing a *White Paper* program about mainland China, a country that up to that time had been off-limits to the American broadcast media by order of the U.S. State Department: "We think the more information the public has, the more intelligently they [*sic*] can judge what our China policy should be. We ourselves don't intend to judge, just present as many of the objective facts as we can."[45] Freed argued that information is crucial to the political process and that democratic politics depend on the work of experts to deliver value-free facts so that various options might be weighed.[46]

Newton Minow's "vast wasteland" speech therefore must be understood as an articulation of liberal cultural criticism and New Frontier internationalism. Minow challenged the broadcast industry to provide leadership and inspiration for the viewing public instead of narrowly focusing on marketing studies and ratings reports. He further emphasized television's public responsibility given its privileged access to the privacy of the home. Television must be reformed, argued Minow, not simply to improve its "quality" but to help mobilize a nation locked in superpower struggle. Television must educate and enlighten as well as entertain.

The trade press and subsequent histories of the period have detailed the resistance that greeted Minow's efforts to restore television's diversity and encourage public service. As James Baughman has argued, even though Minow enjoyed strong support from the president and from television critics, he encountered opposition from the television industry and its powerful lobby in Congress. Confronted by these obstacles, Minow quickly retrenched. He shifted his efforts from a broad critique of television to the promotion of particular kinds of programs. And even here he began to pare his list of demands. From a wide-ranging call for the restoration of diversity, Minow more modestly focused on the importance of television as an informational medium. Given that nightly newscasts were then only fifteen minutes long, the chairman stressed the importance of programming that provided interpretation and analysis. "The job of reporting the news is only half done until the pieces are put together," said Minow. "The pattern of news is often obscure, and . . . [the] long reports and news analyses on radio and television are ideally suited to the interpretation of events and the exploration of issues."[47] Baughman claims that Minow, when confronted by stiff opposition, "shifted from seeking, so to speak, both 'CBS Reports' and 'Playhouse 90' to advocating only 'CBS Reports.'"[48]

Even though the industry may have resisted the wide-ranging reform agenda that Minow initially laid out, it did respond to the chairman's more focused initiative regarding informational programming. Minow's "vast wasteland" speech clearly signaled a resurgence of the public scrutiny that preceded the election year. Although no secret meetings were called at the St. Regis Hotel, Jack Gould of the *New York Times* noted a "new receptiveness" to public service programming among network affiliates. This, said Gould, was the greatest significance of the Minow speech. Or as one public affairs producer put it, "All I can say is my phone started to ring right after May 9 and it hadn't rung on May 8."[49] Similarly, syndicators reported a dramatically increasing demand from stations for more public affairs programming, and several independent producers and syndicators set up businesses exclusively to handle this burgeoning demand. David Wolper, the biggest independent producer in the documentary field, said Newton Minow was worth more to him than a high-powered press agent. Indeed, the chairman made it clear that he was most interested in "informational programs which exemplify public service."[50] More specifically he was referring to "more backgrounders, documentaries, commentaries."[51]

Increasing contacts between network news executives and the chairman also reflected this new receptiveness. Throughout Minow's tenure he received a steady stream of letters and promotional materials from ABC that cited the network's advances in news and public affairs. News chief James Hagerty exchanged informal notes with Minow ("Dear Newt," "Dear Jim"), and the two men scheduled informal "chats" to discuss the development of ABC News.[52] Similarly, the head of NBC News, William McAndrew, forwarded a packet of promotional materials about a special series of *White Paper* documentaries on Communism. One ad refers to an episode entitled "Death of Stalin," a program that, said the ad, "supported the NBC thesis that television documentaries needn't be dull."[53] Apparently Minow agreed, for he dashed off a note to producer Irving Gitlin saying, "[Y]ou should be very proud of the series you are doing on Communism. It's an extraordinary achievement. As a citizen I wish everybody could see it and that it would be rerun often."[54] Minow's enthusiasm was later reciprocated by Gitlin, who wrote the chairman to express personal appreciation for the FCC's backing: "Just let me say, as a program producer, that your support and pressure have been tangible assets in the pursuit of my work, and that in a field where standards are very hard to come by, your public support and official statements and actions have in fact made for improvement."[55]

In such environs, network news and information programming flourished, especially those shows with a topical emphasis on the international threat of Communist takeover.[56] At the same time, syndicators of overseas programming beefed up their program catalogs with substantial additions of informational and educational fare.[57] NBC even went so far as to offer 125 hours of free public affairs programming to countries in the early stages of developing a television broadcasting system. "Operation: Documentaries," as it was called, had the dual advantage of assisting new stations for which "programming pose[d] economic problems," while at the same time tying these stations into the interests of NBC and the U.S. government.[58] Thus despite the taboo on government censorship, Minow was able to define areas of mutual concern to leaders of the television industry. He did so by articulating linkages between informational programming and the national interest, between free markets and the Free World.

Of all the concerns raised by the liberal critique of television around the turn of the decade, information programming received the highest priority, and television documentary became an important site of collaboration between the government and the networks. Yet this was a collaboration that had been shaped by years of discussion and debate over the newest medium of mass communication. At the beginning of the 1950s the networks understood public service to mean a diverse menu of programming; one decade later they had come to associate it with expanded news coverage that most prominently featured documentary analysis of international issues, specifically the global threat of monolithic Communism.

Chapter Two

Documentaries of the Communist Other

In 1960 Irving Gitlin, the executive producer of *NBC White Paper*, reflected on the importance of television documentary in an article he wrote for the industry trade paper *Variety*. Addressing a readership of station managers, owners, and NBC affiliates, Gitlin made the case for urgently increasing television's commitment to public affairs programming.

> Since Sputnik we have had U-2, the folding of the [Eisenhower-Khrushchev] Summit, Cuba, the Japanese riots (and these are only the beginning), yet we go on our way as usual. I deeply believe that this country is at a juncture in history more dangerous, more critical than ever before. If this country does not address itself to the business at hand of effective national and international policy, I believe we will see in our time the end of this nation as we know it.[1]

What is striking about this passage is the way in which it closely conformed to the crisis rhetoric then popular among internationalist factions in American politics. Here Gitlin characterized the fundamental challenge facing the United States as one of superpower struggle. Although he argued that the primary role of the documentarist was to educate audiences through objective investigation of social issues, Gitlin's rhetoric reflected the priorities of a George Kennan, a Nelson Rockefeller, or a John Kennedy.

CBS Reports executive producer Fred Friendly struck a similar chord only a few months later in an article written for *TV Guide*. According to Friendly, political indifference was an important part of the challenge facing the United States.

World War II ended one kind of isolationism, the old-fashioned, pre-airplane, far-away-from-it-all view of the Midwest. There is now another kind of isolationism, one more dangerous because it is not generally recognized as such. We have stuck our ostrich heads into the sand of entertainment and creature comforts. Day in and day out for decades we have been living in a world of fiction.[2]

Like Gitlin, Friendly argued that danger loomed on two fronts. Internationally, the United States must be willing to confront the Communist challenge wherever it might threaten to roll back the frontiers of American influence. Domestically, the battle must be joined on the ideological front, where complacency and prosperity had bred ignorance and apathy among the American people. "Are we going to give [the viewers] what they want," asked Gitlin, "or are we going to tell them what they have to know: that we face a world in revolution, that we are in a terrible fix, that we need new ideas, new approaches, and sacrifice if we are to make it."[3]

Giving "them" what they need to know was the network documentarist's primary responsibility. Furthermore, in a world in which the reach of the American media was becoming increasingly international, the responsibilities of the professional broadcaster were becoming more global as well. United States broadcasters operating abroad must be willing to take the message of freedom to the rapidly growing audiences of television viewers around the world, for, as Friendly put it, the United States was lagging in the competition to capture the allegiances of citizens along the frontiers of the Free World. The *Sputnik* launch in 1957 was a critical blow to American prestige, cautioned Friendly, and recent events in the Third World had shown that the United States "also lagged in the ideological struggle to win uncommitted people to the ways of freedom, sometimes because others could not be sure from [the United States'] performance whether [it was] idealistic or self-seeking."[4] The United States must make its intentions and aspirations known to all if it is to exercise global leadership, declared Friendly, and documentary television must play a central role in this effort.

Recent scholarship has suggested that one of the fundamental missions of mass media during the modern era is to construct and maintain popular images of the nation: its identity, its history, its mission. One way broadcasting does this is by providing regular coverage of national events, thus helping to organize the nation's collective sense of temporal order. This encourages citizens to take up a synchronous relationship with their compatriots by consuming news of the nation at a clocked regularity and by partaking in mass-mediated public rituals.[5] During the

Fred Friendly (left), *executive producer of* CBS Reports, *with correspondent Edward R. Murrow, who would soon leave the network to become director of the USIA. (Courtesy of Photofest)*

Kennedy years, television increasingly played such a role by rapidly expanding its live coverage of national events—providing broadcasts of presidential addresses, press conferences, rocking chair chats, and NASA space missions.

Yet mass media help to organize not only temporal relations but spatial ones as well. Daniel C. Hallin contends, for example, that news workers "communicate to us images of our neighborhoods and cities, of the

Irving Gitlin, executive producer of NBC White Paper. *(Courtesy of Photofest)*

nation and the world around it, and even of the universe, images which for many of us may constitute most of what we know about the world beyond our immediate circle of experience."[6] Consequently, it could be argued that, just as Gitlin and Friendly intended, the documentary boom of the early 1960s played an important role by defining the boundaries of the Free World and by identifying the external threat to this community, the Communist other. These programs helped to locate the nation in space and to map the terrain of struggle between East and

West. As James Carey might suggest, network documentaries constructed maps of meaning that operated as representations of and for reality.[7] In the first sense, they "referred to" reality by identifying and organizing landmarks that described that reality. In the second sense, they "stood for" reality and as such influenced the ways in which audiences, after viewing the programs, would perceive and engage the world. Therefore, the "effects" of these programs were not limited to what they had to say about particular places or events but included how they positioned these elements in relation to other elements, drawing attention to some things while obscuring others. Network documentaries created maps of meaning about an increasingly complex and interconnected global environment, one in which the Free World seemed threatened by instability and menaced by Communist infiltration. Major television archives are well stocked with documentaries from this period that support such a claim. In program after program, the viewer confronts the challenge of Communism on the battlefield, in the political arena, and in the classroom. The broadcasting trade press at the time also noted this tendency, arguing that the struggle to defend the "Free World" was the most pervasive single topic in documentary television.[8]

This trend is apparent in the three documentary series that represented the most extensive commitment of network resources during the early sixties: ABC's *Bell and Howell Close-Up!*, *NBC White Paper*, and *CBS Reports*. These "flagship" series were, at the time, considered the definitive expression of network commitment to the documentary form. They were pacesetters in style and content, and as a result they attracted the greatest amount of public attention on the air, in the industry, and in the press. They were exemplars of the genre and merit closer examination. Consequently, this chapter and chapters 4 and 6 explore the textual characteristics of documentaries from these three series. The purpose of this analysis is not to generate a representative sample but to uncover the rules of discourse that structure these programs. How do they construct problems and pose questions? What kinds of concerns receive attention? What others do not? Who is interviewed, and which voices are privileged? What is the narrative logic at work in each program? How might the stories, images, and characters within these documentaries be related to the social context of this era? Finally, how do tensions and contradictions within the programs portray conflicting forces at work in society at the time? Thus, my purpose is not to argue that these texts are somehow representative of the more than fifteen hundred network documentaries from this period. Rather, these programs offer a range of topics and treatments that make it possible to chart a discursive hierarchy that privileges superpower struggle as the central dynamic in these texts. Furthermore, having viewed a wide range of documentaries from this period, I would argue that the addition or subtraction of any combination of programs from this period would be unlikely to alter my analysis in any significant way.

To begin, a thematic survey of these texts shows that during the first season of the *Bell and Howell Close-Up!* series, ABC produced eighteen programs, of which six were explicitly about the Communist threat. These were primarily foreign policy programs such as "Ninety Miles to Communism," a program about Cuba; "The Red and the Black," an investigation of the Red threat in Africa; and "Troubled Land," a profile of peasant revolts in northeastern Brazil.[9] In each of these programs the central narrative conflict revolves around the Communist challenge to the Free World. Another six programs during this premiere season of *Close-Up!* employed the Red threat as a significant subtext. For instance, "The Flabby American" is a report on the physical fitness of the nation that is cast in the context of East-West relations. At a marine boot camp, the opening scene of the program shows young recruits struggling their way through physical fitness exams while the voice-over narrator comments on the high incidence of fatigue among U.S. soldiers during the Korean War. The key question raised at the outset is whether leisure-happy, middle-class Americans could answer the challenge posed by a dedicated Communist foe.[10] Similarly, a documentary about racism, "Walk in My Shoes," argues that any systematically oppressed minority represents an inherent threat to the stability of the American political system.[11] The program further suggests that racism generates complications for U.S. foreign policy, since it specifically threatens relations with newly independent African states. So even though a majority of these ABC documentaries do not specifically focus on foreign policy issues, the Cold War discourse of the New Frontier era structures the treatment of most issues, both foreign and domestic. Consequently, twelve of the eighteen programs during this first season ground the rationale of their arguments in the terrain of superpower struggle.

A similar thematic pattern can be found in the *NBC White Paper* series. Half of the twenty programs broadcast during its first four seasons explicitly revolve around the Communist challenge to the Free World, and three other programs draw on this theme as an important subtext. Therefore, the Cold War is a subject that activates an important narrative tension in most of these NBC documentaries. With *CBS Reports* this tendency can also be observed: all foreign policy programs are explicitly focused on superpower struggle, and domestic issues are often linked indirectly to the same concerns. Thus tropes of "freedom" are woven throughout these texts, and freedom is cast in relation to its other: the often unspoken threat of Communist takeover.[12]

One can roughly visualize the preoccupation with superpower struggle by categorizing the documentaries in these three series according to topic. In the table on flagship documentaries and in the appendix, note that foreign policy concerns are the central focus of more programs than any other category. Each season superpower struggle dwarfs all other policy issues, including civil rights, poverty, and space exploration. American politics draw a great deal of attention in the 1960 election year, and legal issues come to the fore in the 1962 season when CBS does a three-part examination of the Supreme Court. Yet throughout this period global issues enjoy a strong and continuing presence in these flagship series. Furthermore, superpower struggle also crops up in other programs. As noted above, it may provide the rationale for addressing domestic issues such as racial strife or physical fitness. It may also be a central concern in documentary interviews of "great leaders," such as the series of documentary interviews CBS produced with Dwight Eisenhower and Walter Lippmann. In fact, these edited interviews devote a tremendous amount of time to discussing the foreign policy dimension of presidential leadership. Therefore, in four of the five seasons depicted below, superpower struggle is either the main topic or a central subtext in more than half of the flagship documentaries produced each season.

Nevertheless, one needs to analyze these texts more closely in order to appreciate fully the pervasiveness of such concerns. For purposes of

Flagship Documentaries Categorized by Topic

	1959–1960	1960–1961	1961–1962	1962–1963	1963–1964
Season total	11	42	46	44	24
Foreign policy	6	15	22	11	8
FP subtext	3	8	12	6	7
Am. politics	0	7	2	2	3
Law/crime	0	2	3	7	2
Civil rights	1	4	1	2	3
Environment	2	0	2	4	0
Poverty	0	1	2	2	0
Space race	2	3	0	1	0
Health	1	3	2	3	1
Labor	0	3	1	2	0
Interview	1	2	7	5	5

more detailed analysis, I have grouped these network documentaries into three major categories according to the geography they attempt to represent: Communist countries, the middle ground, and the home front. The latter two groups are taken up in chapters 4 and 6 respectively; this chapter focuses on programs that portray Communist core countries.

To begin, numerous scholars have shown that one of the most fundamental ways in which a nation defines its identity and its sense of purpose is by describing the "other."[13] That which lies outside is usually characterized as posing a challenge to the fundamental values of the nation. This opposition between us and them not only alerts the citizenry to a potential threat; it consolidates and solidifies the bonds that hold together an often diverse and physically dispersed population. Such discursive strategies are at work in television documentaries from the early 1960s. The following section pays particular attention to a set of documentaries that portray the origins of Communism and the internal power struggles of the Kremlin leadership during the postwar era. These programs imply a set of radical oppositions between charismatic, coercive dictatorships and rational, modern democracies. They further suggest distinctions between revolution and programmatic reform as well as between ideology and objectivity. In short, they explore the differences between Soviet and American politics.

The other group of programs analyzed in this chapter address concerns about modernity and mass society behind the Iron Curtain. The technologies of surveillance and control are presented as the key to Communist power over vast expanses of the globe. These technologies threaten individual autonomy and impose a mind-numbing equality on subjects within their reach. Like the documentaries in the first section, these programs are products of a liberal imagination that promotes an affinity among American viewers by constructing abstract and loathsome images of the Communist other. Finally, both groups of programs promote an urgent awareness of superpower struggle. Just as Fred Friendly and Irving Gitlin suggested at the beginning of this chapter, these programs are a wake-up call for a prosperous, self-satisfied, and inward-looking nation.

Communism and the Kremlin

The oppositions between East and West become most apparent in programs that deal with prototypal Communist states, such as the Soviet

Union and China. Despite canons of journalistic objectivity, these documentaries proceed from a set of a priori assumptions that reveal a vision shared at the time by broadcasters and government officials regarding television's educational mission. In a letter to presidential press secretary Pierre Salinger, NBC's Lucy Jarvis captured much of this vision when outlining one of her assignments, a forthcoming program with the working title "Blueprint for Red Conquest." Wrote Jarvis:

> It will attempt to explain to the American public in compelling terms the nature of the Communist offensive against the free world. Ranging across many nations, this program will show how the Communists are waging war against freedom on every front—economic, military, political, psychological, cultural. We plan to demonstrate that the Communist offensive is an integrated, carefully planned, relentless assault designed by a whole variety of methods to confuse and destroy freedom.[14]

Jarvis's project, which developed into several *NBC White Paper* documentaries, charts the historical development of Marxism and situates the Communist threat as centered at the Kremlin and spreading out to encompass vast expanses of the globe.

One of the programs, "Who Goes There? A Primer on Communism," offers a historical critique that traces the roots of Communism back to nineteenth-century Europe and the writings of Karl Marx.[15] At the outset, host Robert Abernethy walks on stage from behind a set of larger-than-life portraits of Marx, Lenin, Stalin, Mao, and other Communist leaders. As the program unfolds, it becomes apparent that the posters represent a gallery of rogues united by an ideology of violent revolution. Moreover, throughout the program Abernethy's explanations of the growing influence of monolithic Communism are punctuated by ominous drumrolls and crashing cymbals. While this operatic staging lends a dramatic tone to the presentation, Abernethy presents himself as the quintessential modern technocrat, restrained in manner and dressed in a conventional business suit. In essence, the documentary is an illustrated lecture that traces the historical development of Communism. But at the same time the program strives to conform to the conventions of narrative television by generating characters, conflict, and a unified plotline. It draws together a story of global Communist revolution, outside of which stands the narrator, an omniscient and rational voice.

Using a series of historical illustrations, Abernethy begins the narrative with the ravages of early industrialization, noting the arduous working conditions that ultimately gave rise to widespread protest and labor organizing throughout Europe. According to the documentary, the

Robert Abernethy surrounded by a gallery of rogues in "Who Goes There?"

democratic socialists were able to respond to these changes by promoting peaceful reform through trade unions and political parties. But others, Abernethy announces as the drums begin to roll, "in their search for salvation, they lost democracy. We call these people Communists." The cymbals crash as he enunciates the word *Communist,* and Abernethy then turns from the camera and walks over to the poster of Marx, continuing, "Their great prophet was Karl Marx. An angry, outraged, brilliant outcast who's probably had more influence on more men than any human being since Mohammed." Abernethy continues by noting, "Marx gave to the world ideas that millions of people have made their religion. Yet Marx himself was an atheist." Accompanied by a crescendo of rolling drums and a climactic crash of cymbals, the narrator concludes, "There was something about him that reminded his friends of the devil." As Abernethy speaks these lines, the camera scrutinizes the visage of Marx by reframing a series of portraits with close-up and extreme close-up images of this nineteenth-century Lucifer. Within the conventions of television entertainment, such tight framings are commonly associated with intense emotion or villainy. Therefore, the spoken text, the visual imagery, and the dramatic percussion suggest a man driven by delusions of grandeur and prophecy.[16]

Searching for a psychological motivation, Abernethy then provides a brief biography of Marx. He recounts the economic and medical problems that dogged the prophet of Communism and notes that three of Marx's children died as a result of inadequate medical care. Thus Marx's narrative motivation is explained by the very privation that modern societies of the Free World seek to overcome through prosperity, nutrition, and medical science. This analysis is reinforced by Abernethy's observation that the first Communist revolution did not take place in a capitalist society, which Marx had predicted, but in a premodern agrarian society. "How did it happen?" asks Abernethy. "The fact is that the threat of Communist revolution then and now is greatest not where capitalism is strongest, but wherever men's demands for reforms are denied. The Communist revolution in Russia was far more the product of repression than capitalism." By implication, the modern-day threat to the Free World is strongest where systematic, liberal reform is absent.

The program then moves on to brief biographies of Lenin and Stalin detailing a history of terror and conspiracy at the highest levels of Soviet government. Through it all, Abernethy argues, the doctrine of Marx was a seminal influence, a master plan for totalitarian takeover. The documentary further contends that the histories of Russian and Chinese expansionism have now been yoked to the ideology of global Communism. Thus the program attempts to contain very complicated historical forces within a single narrative structure. While gesturing toward the importance of specific national contexts, the program implies that Mao and Khrushchev are, in essence, the Janus-faced visage of a monolithic Communist threat that originates with Marx. Gesturing toward the gallery of rogues, Abernethy concludes by saying:

> These are some of the faces of Communism, and each face is molded by the special interests in the nation in which you find it. These are the people who go there. And how far they go depends on who goes here.
>
> Can our power and our will check their imperialism? Can our self-discipline match their totalitarianism? Can we help wipe out the conditions that invite revolution? Above all, can our freedom and our faith deny their ideology? We think they can. Thank you for watching and listening.

The binary oppositions set up in this closing are typical of many network documentaries during this period. The oppositions not only propose a characterization of the Communist world, but they also define a set of assumptions about the Free World. In Abernethy's concluding remarks we can see that the West exercises its power as a check against the excesses of a new brand of Eastern imperialism. America is portrayed as a land of democratic individualism where power emerges only through a form of collective self-discipline. On the other hand, subjects behind the Iron Curtain have discipline imposed from above; they are manipulated by ruling cliques who seize power through revolution and subversion. This tide of revolution will continue to rise unless it is neutralized by expanding prosperity throughout the Free World. Educated and well-fed citizens are less likely to be duped by Communist ideology. Finally, and "above all," the West is cast as God fearing and righteous even though liberal pluralism of this era relegated religion to an ambiguous role in modern society. Perhaps more to the point, faith is positioned here in relation to freedom. The scientist, the technocrat, the documentarist all employ open, rational methods of inquiry and political choice. Westerners have faith that their approach to the world is true and objectively verifiable. Communists, on the other hand, are driven by the ideology of their misguided, demonic prophet, Karl Marx. In the Communist world, ideology obscures the true nature of relationships in the objective world, and therefore Communist leaders fear scrutiny and exposure by Western news media.

A similar set of explanatory strategies are at work in one of the advertisements by the program's sponsor, Upjohn. Like much of the documentary, the commercial is a series of photographic stills and illustrations. It opens with the sound of dramatic beats from a kettledrum and pictures of Hitler framed in close-up and extreme close-up. As we hear the sound of passionate German oratory in the background, a calm, authoritative voice-over narrates a series of stills:

> While this man was shouting [Hitler], this man marching [Mussolini], this man bowing [Tojo], this man watching [Stalin reviewing troops], these men were working quietly in a laboratory at Upjohn. [Stills of lab scientists. Music shifts to orchestral strings and soaring flutes.]
>
> They too were hoping to change the world—the year, 1938. [Depression era shots, melancholic music.] They were part of a nationwide movement toward ending malnutrition. Their contribution was Unicap. A capsule containing the essential vitamins in easy-to-take form. [Slides of product. Music more upbeat, but unobtrusive.]
>
> Today, the picture of America has changed. [Good life shots.] With improved diets and better understanding of nutrition, America's health is second to none in the world. Thanks in part to the men who weren't shouting or marching, but just working quietly at Upjohn, hoping in their way to change things.

Note once again the oppositions between science and ideology, between the rational and the irrational. The commercial also directs our attention to the fundamental importance of programmatic liberal reform versus violent revolution. Finally, the ad dramatically distinguishes between rational public policy and charismatic dictatorship. Likening the leadership of Stalin to the leadership of the Axis powers, the commercial invites the viewer to compare the Communist world to the legacy of fascism. This final comparison recalls Arthur Schlesinger Jr.'s assertion that extremism on both the left and the right of the political spectrum ultimately meets in the form of totalitarianism and that the opposite of such extremes is in fact the "vital center," an enlightened, democratic pragmatism.[17]

Two other programs in this NBC series are case studies of the Soviet Union that further explore the relationship between charismatic leadership and monolithic Communism. Both were heavily promoted by the network and garnered ratings in the high teens, comparable to entertainment programs in the same time slot. Moreover, these programs drew explicit kudos from FCC chairman Newton Minow as mentioned in chapter 1.[18] The first program examines the power struggle that ensued after the "Death of Stalin."[19] It opens with newsreel footage of the 1952 party congress, which narrator Chet Huntley refers to as a "love fest" for the Soviet dictator. Thus, from the outset, the nature of totalitarian leadership is distinguished by the absence of free inquiry and open criticism. We also are told that while Stalin is being worshiped, the economy is failing and the Soviet leader has mounted a series of vicious purges to deal with mounting unrest. As if to emphasize the totalitarian nature of the Soviet regime, the viewer is shown newsreel film of the dictator arriving at the Bolshoi Ballet. In the midst of economic calamity and violent repression, Stalin fritters away the evening at the theater. Greeted by a standing ovation, he basks in the adoration and then gestures for the applause to cease. Immediately, the documentary cuts from Stalin's gesture to a shot of the audience sitting down as if on cue. Through the tempo of the editing, the viewer experiences the awesome power of Communist dictatorship.

This sequence prefigures the program's analysis of Soviet leadership. Here charisma and ideology mask the true material relations in society, a contradiction that must be negotiated through repression and terror. Therefore, when the program turns to the issue of leadership succession in the wake of Stalin's death, it is characterized as a grab for dictatorial power. As the viewer observes top Soviet officials standing around the body of Stalin at the funeral, we are told power is divided among them, but the narrator cautions the viewer that only one will end up with it all. The unspoken comparison is that unlike democratic regimes, Soviet leadership must be absolute, and those who bid for power must quash

The awesome power of dictatorship on display at the Bolshoi Ballet in "The Death of Stalin."

opposition. Out of this struggle for power emerges the little-known figure of Nikita Khrushchev, who rises to the top through a shrewd, systematic campaign to eliminate his rivals.

Like the Axis leaders of World War II and like Stalin, Khrushchev
must rely on ideology, repression, and charisma if he is to lead a Communist nation. Interestingly, one cannot help but notice a gangster motif
as well. Although the film does not explicitly refer to gangland politics in
its description of the Soviet power elite, it should be noted that, like the
Mafia, Communists are characterized in this program as hierarchical,
violent, and well organized. Also like the Mafia, leadership is exercised
through authoritarian uses of power that inevitably result in bloodletting
and intrigue during transitions of leadership.

"The Rise of Khrushchev" picks up this narrative thread with the May
Day parade in Red Square.[20] We are told that for the first time in years
the parade lacks a military presence. Instead, there is talk of coexistence
and peace coming from the Soviet leadership, but we soon learn there
also is a power struggle going on within the Kremlim between Khrushchev,
Molitov, and Malenkov. Khrushchev is characterized as a ward-heeling,
glad-handing politician whose power base exists at the grassroots level of
the Communist Party. Pitted against him are young, high-level techno-

Portrayals of Soviet leaders invoke the gangster motif in "The Death of Stalin."

crats. As a result, the Soviet peace initiative, the withdrawal of troops from Austria, and the superpower summit are explained as mere posturing that grows out of an internal power struggle. Similarly, Khrushchev's attack on the "cult" of Stalin at the party congress in 1956 is portrayed as just one more attempt by Khrushchev to solidify his position within the party.

Although an alternative reading of this period might emphasize the range of possibilities that this power vacuum engendered, the focus instead is on the evil machinations of Soviet power brokers. Khrushchev's renunciation of Stalinism is but one more gambit in a high-stakes contest. Thus, the "real" Khrushchev is revealed when his policy of liberalization leads to unrest in Eastern Europe and in turn to the 1956 Soviet crackdown in Hungary. As archival news film conveys the resulting carnage and rubble, narrator Chet Huntley comments on the cynical nature of Soviet policy: "The Soviet Union has made it clear to what lengths it will go when its empire is threatened. A kind of peace has been restored. Nikita Khrushchev has survived. This is the price of his survival."

After the Hungarian uprising Khrushchev faces another attempt to oust him, but we are told that he shrewdly outmaneuvers his opposition by packing the Communist Party Central Committee with his supporters. Invoking the committee's authority, he forces his opponents into exile. The narrator points out that finally, after four years of struggle, Khrushchev has consolidated his power. This moment of closure is then linked to the recent history of U.S.-Soviet diplomacy. Huntley suggests that the many twists and turns in superpower relations over the course of the 1950s are to be understood as the product of Soviet duplicity and intrigue. Thus changes in Soviet diplomacy are not the product of a rational policy process but of internal power struggles. The documentary warns of the dangers of accommodation by emphasizing the radical otherness of the Soviet system.

Yet the meanings of the text are much richer and more complex than this single narrative of leadership struggle in a foreign land. The association of Khrushchev with ward-style politics at the beginning of the program sets up another level of meanings that permeate the documentary as well. It is Khrushchev's ability as a political infighter—stacking the membership on the Central Committee—that ultimately saves him in his greatest moment of trial. Structured into the text is not only a tale of Khrushchev and his cynical approach to foreign policy but also a story about styles of power. While Khrushchev's ward-heeling style is distinguished from the gangsterism of the Stalinist period, the constellation of

"The Rise of Khrushchev" is explained by the glad-handing tactics of a ward-style politician.

meanings associated with both of these forms of power is intriguing when compared with the political ideology of corporate liberalism.

If, like Robert H. Wiebe, we trace the roots of corporate liberalism in the United States to the Progressive Era, it reminds us of the opposition between Progressive politics and ward politics during that period.[21] Progressivism promoted notions of continuity, planning, and process. It was cool, professional, and self-effacing. By comparison, ward politics were seen by the Progressives as emerging from the chaos of the ethnic ghetto. This brand of politics was personalized, charismatic, and fraught with corruption and intrigue. The dominant personalities associated with ward politics were flamboyant and passionate to a fault. Indeed, the liberal imagination constructed images of ward politicians and Mafia crime families out of a similar set of attributes. Not surprisingly, these images of the other have resonance with the narrative construction of Soviet leaders and Soviet society in the documentaries of the early 1960s. Accordingly, the program about Khrushchev conveys as much about the American system as it does about the Soviet Union. Its construction of Communism is the mirror opposite of modern, corporate liberalism.

Sociologists Philip Elliot and Philip Schlesinger have argued that such oppositions are also consonant with "master patterns" in Western media portrayals throughout the Cold War era. Some of the polarities they point to in representations of West and East are reason/violence, rational/irrational, objective/emotional.[22] Although these oppositions are certainly at work here, it is also important to note the ways in which the programs are specifically connected to an American context in the post-*Sputnik* period, an era that was characterized by a resurging faith in government activism and expertise. The urgent cry to get America moving again focused on the need for a mobilization of technical know-how in order to meet the challenges posed by Soviet strategic capabilities. Such a mobilization required widespread public concern over the Soviet threat, and therefore the threat had to be made explicit. It had to be described. But it also had to be portrayed as an opposition that could be *managed* by the distinctive attributes that characterized the *American* system. Such a mobilization therefore required that the nation be "reimagined," to borrow from Benedict Anderson's notion. It could no longer survive as an isolationist, consumer society led by an avuncular war hero. Rather, it had to be reimagined as an aggressive leader of the Free World—a prosperous, modern, and liberal alternative to the Soviet system. Therefore, in describing the Soviet other, these programs also suggest a style of politics that traces its heritage back through the New Deal to the emergence of Progressivism at the turn of the century. The documentaries therefore imply a mode of politics that has a long heritage but is tied to the particular history of the post-Sputnik era.

Surveillance and Control

Interestingly, the event that was the touchstone for this resurgence of corporate liberalism was the 1957 launch of a satellite that signaled a triumph of Soviet technocracy. The apparent contradiction between these documentary portrayals of Kremlin politics and Russian scientific accomplishments is manifest throughout this period and is a subject that receives a more detailed treatment in chapter 6. For now, it bears mentioning that these documentaries portray Soviet leaders as threatening not simply because they were domineering and charismatic but also because they adopted modern technologies of surveillance and mind control. Programs from this period seemed to argue that because the politics of Communist leadership were fraught with chaos and intrigue, the only way to hold on to power was to monitor constantly for signs of opposition and unrest. There was no more prominent symbol of such surveillance than the Berlin Wall, and indeed each network produced several documentaries on the topic during the early 1960s.[23]

ABC *Close-Up*'s "Behind the Wall" opens with a montage of images along the Berlin frontier. We see guard dogs, barbed wire, loudspeakers, and East German soldiers in watchtowers using mirrors to reflect sunlight into the lens of the documentary camera.[24] Their attempt to blind the inquiring gaze of the Western news media appears to be aimed at blocking even the slightest flow of information across the wall. After the opening narration and a commercial break, the documentary returns with the same view along the wall, and we hear martial music blasting across the divide from loudspeakers in what the narrator refers to as "Soviet Germany." As the music concludes, we hear an East German official explaining the rationale for the wall. As the same official continues to speak and the camera cuts to his office, we notice only then that his voice had been manipulated to sound as if his initial comments were broadcast over the loudspeaker system itself. This technique is used after all three commercial breaks and serves to emphasize the prison camp mentality that the program constructs. The East German official is positioned within the text as if he has the power of centralized surveillance and thought control. It is suggested that his presence is ubiquitous, like the presence of Big Brother in George Orwell's novel *1984*.

Indeed, the program itself details the surveillance apparatus in redundant detail. We hear one East German émigré tell of being pressured to spy on her comrades, and others recount the many limitations on free expression. We hear complaints that there are no labor unions, and a West German labor leader who has visited the East concludes that life on the other side is simply dismal: "They have no hope, they have no interest. It appears that people over there just do their work and go on just existing. They don't really live. You haven't got the feeling of being among people who are alive. And I think the reason for this is that everything appears to be so very hopeless and so very senseless." The documentary attributes this largely to the fact that East Germany is a satellite of the Soviet Union. Its government is controlled by Kremlin insiders, leaving little power in the hands of German citizens. One exile recalls, "Ulbricht once said [the government] must look democratic, but we must have everything in our hands."

Thus the images of life on the other side of the Iron Curtain stress the concentrated nature of Communist power, and, by implication, it also produces meanings about the Free World. As with the NBC "Primer on Communism," this program on Berlin suggests that labor unions in the West are a restraint against centralized power. They also are a legitimate form of incremental, progressive change.[25] Communist societies, on the other hand, are distinguished by an absence of checks and balances. There are no countervailing forces. Moreover, the individual under Communism has no rights and no hope and therefore takes little initiative. Control is in the hands of a centralized clique that uses the technologies of surveillance and propaganda to sustain its power over vast expanses of the globe.

Clearly, this portrayal of life in the East sets up a radical opposition with life in the West. But also notice the ways in which it suggests anxieties about mind control that are consonant with criticisms of advertising and mass media in the United States during the late 1950s. Indeed, the opposition between East and West is consistent with the master patterns of the Cold War described earlier by Elliot and Schlesinger, but this program is furthermore tied to a specific historical moment in which it was suggested that the true opposite to life behind the Iron Curtain was not self-satisfied Eisenhower conservatism but the cosmopolitan activism of the Kennedys. This documentary suggests, like U.S. opinion leaders of the period, that the influences of Madison Avenue and the encomiums of mass marketing had to be declined in favor of a more vigorous involvement in public life.

NBC's documentary "Red China" also conveys apprehensions about centralized power, surveillance, and propaganda but further articulates them with a set of fears regarding the nature of mass society itself.[26] The program begins with film footage of a road crew hauling construction materials without the benefit of trucks or heavy equipment. The workers sing as they toil in the hot sun. Their labor is low-tech, manual, and governed by the rhythms of the work group. Moreover, their individuality is submerged by the framing of the image as the camera cuts from a long shot to an extreme long shot of antlike workers sprawling across a vast expanse of mountain terrain. As an opening metonymy, the scene reduces the individual in Chinese society to an inconsequential status, and this effect is heightened by an edit from the road crew to a mass rally in Red Square, where political activity is framed in a similar fashion. Mass labor, mass politics—individuality in China has been superseded by a social organism that is policed by a powerful state apparatus. The next image is of a border guard maintaining surveillance at the frontier of this intensely communal society. Individual choice to enter or to exit, even at the far outreaches of the country, is subject to control by the state.

This documentary analysis of China is structured as a historical narrative. It traces the country's economic development after the Communists took charge under a leadership with close ties to the Kremlin. Mao Tsetung is referred to as "a classic Marxist" who zealously adopts centralized planning and absolute state control. He mobilizes peasants, crushes his opponents, and attempts to expand Chinese influence by going to war in Korea. A description of the first five-year plan is accompanied by various shots of manual, mass-labor operations. "Workers swarm over the countryside like ants," remarks narrator Chet Huntley. "They build irrigation ditches, canals, dams." By 1955 the country's steel production has doubled, coal is up 50 percent, iron 100 percent. "Almost no underdeveloped nation in history has industrialized at such a pace," says Huntley. "At a price, the price is what can be squeezed out of the people, especially peasants." As he speaks of this human toll, the camera cuts to shots of peasants peddling irrigation waterwheels. Rather than wonder at the ingenuity and commitment that bred such rapid economic expansion, the image invites us to pity the peasant whose status has been reduced to little more than a cog in a machine—a machine that regulates not only human labor but human emotions as well.

We are told that by the end of the fifties, China has developed the "emotional fervor of a country at war." The people live in communes, march to work with their labor brigades, and at night engage in orchestrated self-criticism. The narrator remarks: "True Communism, Peking says, is now close at hand. The peasants work for the government. They

Manual mass labor used to build a mountain road in "Red China."

Chinese workers "swarm over the countryside like ants."

are told their loyalty is owed to the government. They are told the old biological family is obsolete. They own nothing. They are paid by the commune, mostly in food. What they produce belongs to the commune." China therefore represents the most extreme form of Communism, the total sublimation of personal thoughts and feelings to the state. Private property rights and family relations have been eliminated in order to produce the most monotonous and threatening form of equality. Individuality has been rendered obsolete by the new social order.

Clearly this portrayal suggests deep-seated American anxieties about an alien and potentially threatening way of life. It also implies that the bonds that hold the U.S. populace together are structured by their opposition to Communist societies. "We" Americans enjoy individual choice, material prosperity, and an intimate, private family life. In large part what defines *us* is our opposition to *them*. Regardless of the personal differences and factional rivalries that pervade our society, Americans share a fundamental set of assumptions that make life worth living. The program suggests that "our people" share a deep bond of comradeship, despite the fact that most have never met. It further implies our profound difference from hundreds of millions of people we probably will never directly encounter. Here again, however, these oppositions are operating at a level of abstraction that is common throughout the Cold War period.

What makes these programs even more specific to the New Frontier era are the ways in which the criticisms of mass society behind the Iron Curtain resonate with anxieties about mass society and consumer culture in postwar America, for the images of monotonous equality and the manipulation of everyday life within China are not so different from the characterizations of average Americans as mindlessly enamored by a bland, middlebrow culture of consumption. Getting America moving again meant not only rising to the Communist challenge but also rising above the easy indulgences of a lifestyle that reduces everything—music, television, food—to a banal and undifferentiated level of mediocrity. Soon after the Kennedy administration took office, it became clear that criticisms of television and advertising would be juxtaposed to New Frontier pretensions to high culture and great ideas. The opposite of mass society behind the Iron Curtain was not mass society throughout the Free World but a more "enlightened" form of public culture and politics. The documentaries of this era shared this agenda and therefore suggest that their mission of enlightenment in the vast wasteland of television is linked to a significant shift in the culture and politics of the United States.

In sum, documentaries from this period that focus on "pure" Communist states not only emphasize the effects of political extremism, but they also suggest a set of oppositions against which the community of the Free World is constructed. That the two sides are such polar opposites suggests that, like earlier characterizations of the Mafia and of urban political machines, Communism's radical otherness is largely a construction of the corporate liberal imagination. What is missing from the texts is a sense of the complex internal dynamics and historical forces that shaped Communist societies. Furthermore, the programs feature few, if any, encounters with the everyday lives of people in these countries. Their world is an abstract category rather than a collection of personal histories and lived experiences. The function of this category is to help consolidate and unify citizens of the United States behind a more activist foreign policy.

Furthermore, the otherness of Communist societies is so profound that the programs are pessimistic regarding possibilities for accommodation between East and West. They tend to obscure or overlook the ways in which past U.S. leaders had found grounds for cooperation with the governments of Joseph Stalin, Chou En-lai, and Ho Chi Minh. Nor is there any suggestion that Nikita Khrushchev's many conciliatory gestures toward the United States were anything more than isolated acts of diplomatic legerdemain. Conflict between the superpowers appears inevitable in these documentaries, suggesting that spheres of influence must be sharply defined. The United States must take vigorous action to defend the boundaries of the Free World rather than risk another Munich. Indeed, comparisons to the British experience with Adolf Hitler before World War II are not uncommon in these programs. The programs posit an essential nature to "pure" Communism, one very much like George Kennan's famous Moscow cable that was appropriated as the basis for U.S. postwar containment policy.[27] Accordingly, Communism is, by its very nature, bellicose, expansionist, and undifferentiated.

The radical oppositions between East and West that these programs suggest fit comfortably into the aggressive foreign policy agenda of the New Frontier. They construct a clearly defined opponent with threatening characteristics, yet they also profile an opponent that is vulnerable because of weaknesses in its very nature. Not unlike the propaganda films of World War II, these documentaries seem to aim at inspiring a mixture of alarm and self-assurance. That is, they construct an opponent that is threatening but not too threatening, an opponent that can be subdued by a resolute Western alliance. It is not surprising that such a pattern should reemerge in American media given that many of the producers and correspondents at the television networks entered the fields of journalism and filmmaking during the Second World War.[28] Veterans also occupied key positions in the Kennedy White House and at the State Department.

As we shall see, however, such reductive and dichotomous oppositions have limited application in the network documentaries of this period. Although they explain the source of expansionist Communism as emanating from the core countries, these oppositions fail to describe adequately the focal terrain of struggle during this era, the vast and variegated expanse of the Free World. Chapter 4 addresses what I refer to as documentaries of the middle ground. But for now, suffice it to say that one of the key differences between these two sets of programs is the fact that the clear oppositions that operate in the documentaries of the Communist other begin to break down when attention shifts to the middle ground. In other words, the stereotypes of life behind the Iron Curtain were functional largely because the flow of information was limited and little filmed documentation existed to contradict the facile stereotypes of Communist society. On the other hand, the trouble spots of the Free World were open to the investigative ventures of the American networks, and this fostered far more complex and even contradictory representations of the issues at stake in the Cold War. But before turning to those programs, we should examine the political and economic climate that encouraged all three major television networks to invest in the global expansion of their television news-gathering operations.

Chapter Three

Going Global

In the summer of 1960, Sig Mickelson, the head of CBS News, met with board chairman William Paley to discuss, among other things, the network news budget. In personal notes drafted from that conversation, Mickelson wrote, "[Paley] wondered whether Fred Friendly was overspending and I pointed out that generally the Friendly shows' cost runs somewhat below costs for a comparable Gitlin [NBC] program. . . . He pointed out that 25 million dollars was a lot of money and hoped it was being effectively spent."[1] Indeed, twenty-five million dollars was a great deal of money for a network to spend on news and public affairs in 1960, and soon those expenditures would grow even larger as CBS and its network competitors all expanded their "actuality programming" over the next few years. It is furthermore remarkable that resources for documentary production were offered to people such as Fred Friendly and Irving Gitlin with very few strings attached, for not only were *CBS Reports* and *NBC White Paper* expensive, but at the time they returned little in advertising revenues.

Why would the networks indulge their documentarists? As discussed in chapter 1, prime-time documentary emerged as a major television genre in response to an industry image crisis that grew out of public debate over commercial television during late 1950s. This shared sense of crisis among television executives was further exacerbated by the threat of federal antitrust action against the networks. Documentary therefore emerged as a prominent foil against charges of rampant commercialism and oligopoly within the industry.[2]

Nevertheless, such an analysis fails to explain why documentary was selected as *the* form of public service offered by the networks in their hour of atonement. Why not an expansion of children's programming, educational fare, or high cultural performance? Why not a reprise for the anthology drama or the network symphony? Why not an expansion of television's potential to offer a national forum for public debate and discussion? Or better yet, why not return a portion of network option time to local broadcasters to be used for community programming? In short, why network documentary? And more specifically, why documentary about the struggle to secure the Free World from Communism?

Prime-time documentary became an important television genre at the very moment that major U.S. corporations were rapidly expanding their operations overseas. Television networks were no exception to this trend. In response to the anticipated saturation of the domestic television market, all three networks stepped up their involvement in foreign markets. The networks therefore began to take exceptional interest in global issues, and each network's growing commitment to documentary television must be considered in this light. Documentary not only pleased government regulators and public officials, but it also helped to make the case for U.S. action to defend these expanding operations. Given such a context, network expenditures on documentary production appear less as an extravagant form of atonement than as a sound investment for media corporations that anticipated dramatic future growth in markets throughout the Free World.

American Corporations Move Overseas

The most important change in the U.S. economy after World War II was the internationalization of American corporate enterprise.[3] Between 1951 and 1961, United Nations statistics show that the United States accounted for 80 percent of all private foreign investment. In fact, capital exports grew twice as fast as exports of American merchandise, and by the early 1960s the United States had outstripped its European rivals in the total amount of investment abroad.[4] The following list illustrates the growth of U.S. direct private investment abroad from 1945 to 1965 (figures are in millions):[5]

1945	$8,369
1950	11,788
1955	19,395
1960	32,778
1965	49,217

Pierre Jalee contends there were two distinct periods during this postwar economic expansion. The first was an era of moderate growth in the export of U.S. capital with much of it targeted for the European continent. The second period began in 1955 after the completion of Europe's economic recovery. At this point the expansion of capital exports became more vigorous and was accompanied by an increasing emphasis on the Third World. By the early 1960s, U.S. investors who already had achieved dominant positions in the European and Latin American economies were rapidly expanding their influence in other parts of the world as well. Between 1960 and 1965, U.S. private investment shot up 57 percent in Asia and 106 percent in Africa.[6] Furthermore, this growing investment in overseas operations was accompanied by the internationalization of American banks, which established branch operations in every major world market.[7] During the early sixties, the foreign assets of these banks rocketed from $3.5 billion to $52.6 billion.[8] As Harry Magdoff argues, "the business economics behind the upsurge of foreign banking [was] similar to the motives behind the movement of industry abroad: a relative shrinkage of business opportunities on the domestic front and attractive profit opportunities overseas."[9] Indeed, overseas investment looked increasingly attractive to business executives who voiced concern about saturated domestic markets. For them, global business opportunities offered the prospect of expansion as well as a hedge against reversals in the domestic economy.

Overseas markets also provided important resources for domestic operations. As early as 1954 the Commission on Foreign Economic Policy noted that new and sophisticated manufacturing processes enhanced U.S. demand for raw materials such as tin, platinum, asbestos, chromite, mica, manganese, and dozens of other metals and minerals. These resources were particularly important to the defense industries, and one presidential advisory board warned, "The loss of any of these materials, through aggression, would be the equivalent of a grave military setback."[10] Such developments had implications for the civilian economy as well. A mineral such as mica—listed by the government as a strategic material—was also used in a wide range of industrial and consumer goods such as condensers, telephones, dynamos, and toasters.[11] Thus, during the postwar period, U.S. leaders realized that their country's military and economic power was becoming more and more dependent on open access to other countries.

Accompanying this shift in the economy was a shift in American foreign policy. Prior to World War II, global relations had been organized into an imperial system that delineated exclusive spheres of economic and political control. Beginning with Roosevelt's World War II diplomacy, U.S. policy makers persistently pressed for an orderly transition from a regime of colonial empires to a free market *global* economy.[12] Yet at the same time the United States sought to control the course of events in the postcolonial world through foreign aid, the International Monetary Fund, and the United Nations. These mechanisms, along with substantial amounts of private overseas investment, fostered a dominant position for the United States. In essence, there was a transformation to what Kwame Nkrumah described as neocolonialism, whereby the former colonies continued to serve the economic needs of the developed world despite their hard-won political independence.[13] "When the African and Asian states achieved their independence," notes historian Stephen Ambrose, "they found themselves in the same position as the Latin American countries. Their economy remained extractive, their principal sources of income were owned or controlled by the West, and their masses continued to live in poverty."[14]

By the end of the 1950s these conditions generated both resentment and political turmoil in many parts of the so-called Free World. In an effort to address these problems, President Kennedy contended that he needed two things. First of all, he wanted to build up American nuclear and conventional forces so as to enhance the U.S. government's ability to intervene in "trouble spots" around the globe. Accordingly, he sought congressional approval to increase defense spending by more than 25 percent during his first two years in office.[15] Secondly, JFK wanted to "lift the masses" of the Third World out of poverty so that they would no longer be ripe for Communist insurgency. He wanted to encourage political reform and economic development at the local level in order to undermine the appeal of more radical solutions. United States policy makers therefore sought out indigenous liberals for leadership positions in client states of the Free World and supported their governments with American resources and expertise. The goal was to foster government reforms and economic modernization without opening the door to Communist insurgents.

In many ways, Vietnam was to be the working prototype for this blueprint. Yet, according to historian Frederick Siegel, European allies were shocked that the Kennedy administration chose Vietnam in view of the fact that U.S. officials knew so little about the country. Siegel explains, however:

> The lawyer/social engineers of the Administration saw this lack of specific knowledge about Vietnamese culture and history as an asset of sorts. Armed

JFK wanted to lift up the masses of the Third World. These Colombian children apparently shared the same aspiration as they greet the visiting president. (Courtesy of the JFK Library)

with abstract social science models about how economic and social development takes place, they were anxious to impose their hothouse ideas on an unwilling Vietnam. There was even an ironically idealist cast to this ignorance. Americans, free of the caste snobbery which had hindered European attempts to remake the lesser peoples of the world, were convinced that in their ideas about the inevitable stages of economic growth, stages modeled on the American experience, they had the keys to producing a prosperous commercial world free of Communist oppression.[16]

In sum, it was the convergence of material, political, and strategic interests that sponsored the application of a universal and supposedly neutral social scientific method in South Vietnam and other "developing countries." It was this same convergence of interests that fostered an expansionist foreign policy and promoted the concept of a Free World as central to the national purpose. Television executives were not isolated from these developments. They too were concerned about the saturation of domestic markets and the uneven performance of the domestic economy under the Eisenhower administration. They too sought to diversify their operations and tap the growth potential of overseas markets. As we shall see, television executives had good reason to promote public concern about the future of the Free World.

The 1950s Television Economy

During the 1950s broadcasting experienced the same heady growth as other segments of the national economy. The size of the audience continuously expanded throughout the decade, as did the expenditures of television advertisers. Therefore the heavy initial investments in fixed capital made by the networks during the early development of television began to pay off by the mid-1950s as equipment costs began to level off and advertising revenues continued to surge upward. By the end of the decade, the industry's revenue from advertising surpassed $1.5 billion annually, nine times the figure for 1950.[17] A booming national economy certainly contributed to this trend, but television also drew advertisers away from other media, and by the middle of the decade television assumed undisputed leadership as the most powerful national advertising medium. Even the recession of 1957–1958 failed to stem the increasing amounts that advertisers were spending on television, and a 1960 FCC report showed that the average *after-tax profit* for the industry as a whole stood at a robust 9 percent—considerably higher than autos, chemicals, or textiles. In fact, broadcasting's profits were higher than those of almost any other industry group.[18]

Nevertheless, these impressive commercial gains concealed a growing sense of uncertainty among broadcasters during the latter part of the decade. In January 1958, NBC fired three top-level vice presidents, saying it was looking to trim costs in the face of declining profits. CBS was suffering a similar fate and reported a flock of sponsor cancellation notices as advertisers complained about slack ratings.[19] CBS president Frank Stanton told affiliate executives, "The year 1957 has reminded us that the maintenance of the level of [network] profits is not automatic." He further pointed out, "It would take only a relatively small amount of sponsorship loss to wipe out network profits entirely."[20]

With viewing at its peak and advertising revenues on the rise despite a national recession, what could be the basis for such a gloomy prognosis? Stanton cited rising programming costs and potential antitrust action from the Justice Department as the most pressing problems facing the industry. Left unsaid, however, was an even greater concern, the emergence of another powerful competitor. The trade newspaper *Variety* commented, "The revolution, for that's exactly what it amounts to, took place in '57 when the food spenders, the tobacco spenders, and the soap spenders (the big three) took official cognizance of ABC as a network to be treated on equal footing with the others."[21] Thus 1957 marked the demise of the two-network economy that had dominated television since its earliest days. Within that world CBS and NBC had thrived as two great leviathans that generated ever increasing profits and could afford to indulge in drama, symphony, and television spectaculars in addition to cop shows, game shows, and westerns. There was room on the schedule for marginally profitable yet "important" programming. There was room for what industry leaders and government policy makers liked to call "balance." Yet there was little room for competitors within the context of this television duopoly. Other media firms had tried to establish national television networks during the early fifties but had failed largely because they could not acquire affiliation contracts with viable local stations in key markets. It was primarily for this reason that the DuMont network folded its operations in 1955.[22] And American Broadcasting Company, which was spun out of NBC in the wake of a 1943 antitrust ruling, showed little promise of challenging its much more powerful competitors during the early years of television.

The reason for ABC's disadvantaged status was simple. The FCC television licensing procedures of the 1940s and early 1950s heavily favored NBC and CBS in small markets. Thus, in many big cities, where the FCC granted three or four VHF allocations, ABC and DuMont were able to achieve parity with their larger rivals. In locales with only one or two VHF allocations, however, the weaker networks were effectively squeezed out of the market. Their only alternative was to seek affiliation with UHF stations. But this was an unsatisfying solution given the fact that during the 1950s most television households did not own UHF receivers. As a result, ratings for UHF stations were usually dismal, and this dragged down the national ratings figures for the smaller networks. This in turn limited their attractiveness to major advertisers, who were looking for national exposure for their products. Furthermore, it discouraged program producers from pitching new projects to executives at DuMont and ABC.

Curiously, it was an antitrust ruling in the *film* industry that ultimately helped to pry open the television duopoly. In the late 1940s, when the Supreme Court ordered Paramount Pictures to divest itself of its theater chain, the newly organized Paramount Theatres corporation began searching for a merger partner. Under the leadership of Leonard Goldenson, Paramount Theatres finally joined forces with ABC in 1953 and set out to revitalize the network's operations. Over the next five years American Broadcasting–Paramount Theaters poured more than twenty million dollars into program development, three times more than it spent to upgrade facilities.[23] Moreover, the shows it developed heralded a new approach to network programming. "We believe television is a habit medium," said network president Oliver Treyz, and ABC therefore focused its attention on the habits of those who were most likely to purchase the products advertised on television, young suburban families.[24] Live variety, drama, and orchestral music programs—shows that earned kudos from critics—all were expensive to produce and appealed to older audiences. Instead, ABC zeroed in on the baby-boom families with programs such as *Maverick, The Rifleman,* and *Disneyland.*[25] "People like what we're giving them," said Leonard Goldenson, chairman of AB-PT. "First we build a habit factor, get them used to watching us, then we can do something about upgrading the programming. We're not interested in the critics."[26]

Since it could not generate a genuinely national audience, ABC aimed for the demographic group with the greatest appeal to advertisers. Moreover, these families primarily lived in the major metropolitan areas where the network was likely to have a VHF affiliate. Not only did ABC now have distinctive appeal with advertisers, but its strong ratings in large cities helped overcome its weakness in smaller markets. By 1958 this commercial strategy was clearly working. ABC's billings climbed 24 percent that year, compared with 11.3 percent for NBC and only 3.6 percent for CBS.[27] Executives at the two major networks began to voice concerns about a saturated marketplace as they cast a wary eye on their new competitor. Television had entered 85.9 percent of all households by 1959, and these executives worried that the number of viewers could be expected to level off in the near future.[28] With audience growth slowing, television's total advertising revenues were expected to follow suit. Thus ABC's rise to prominence came at a difficult time. A third national network would foster a surplus of available advertising spots. With more ad time chasing fewer dollars, network rates were expected to tumble as a result of competitive bidding. There was concern that television's era of rapid growth had reached its culmination, that the industry had reached "maturity."[29]

In the face of this challenge, the two major networks paid greater attention to the same sort of Hollywood telefilm projects that had proven so successful at ABC. Moreover, they tapped some of the talent that brought ABC such success. Robert Kintner, after being ousted as president of ABC in 1956, took over at NBC television and responded to the new competitive environment with programs such as *Wagon Train* and the detective thriller *Peter Gunn.* James Aubrey, former ABC vice president in charge of telefilm projects, moved to the top slot at CBS television, and with him the network began to drift away from its previous commitment to serving all segments of the viewing audience with a "balanced schedule." Instead, CBS placed greater emphasis on ratings as a barometer of network achievement. By the end of the decade, all three networks were being programmed by men who had worked under Leonard Goldenson during the formative years at ABC, and evening prime time began to reflect the intense competition for ratings and advertising.[30]

Government Regulation

In the midst of this transition to a three-network economy, the television industry came under increasing pressure from government regulators. Dean Roscoe Barrow of the University of Cincinnati Law School fired the opening volley in 1957 with an FCC report that recommended certain network practices be prohibited on the grounds that they restrained competition.[31] Specifically, Barrow zeroed in on the "option time" clauses in network affiliation contracts that required local broadcasters to carry as much as twelve hours of network programming during specific parts of the day. In recommending that the practice be prohibited, the Barrow Report struck at the very heart of network power and profitability. Without option time, the networks argued, they could not guarantee national exposure to their clients. Barrow's recommendations therefore were received by industry executives as an assault on the very foundations of network broadcasting.[32] Although these recommendations were not immediately implemented, the industry was clearly shaken, and option time remained a controversial policy issue into the next decade. In 1959 the Justice Department filed a formal opinion that concurred with Barrow, finding option time to be a flat violation of antitrust laws, and rumors persisted throughout the late fifties and early sixties that the government would soon file suit against the networks.[33]

At the same time, federal legislators began to express concern about the networks' increasing emphasis on ratings and revenues to the exclusion of other responsibilities inherent in broadcast trusteeship. In early 1959 Warren Magnuson, chairman of the Senate Commerce Committee, called hearings to look into the influence of ratings on programming decisions. Of particular concern to Magnuson were indications that the networks were eliminating public service programming in order to reduce costs. Although network heads assured the senator it was not true, Magnuson pointed out that he was not only concerned about cuts in the production budgets of public service programs but also dismayed by the tendency to place such programs in marginal time periods.[34] According to Magnuson, commercial considerations seemed to be obstructing the discussion of significant public issues.

This pressure to produce high ratings at most any cost reached its peak during the quiz show scandals of the late 1950s. Producers of the quiz programs, anxious to maximize audience draw, not only fed the answers to selected contestants but provided acting lessons to participants in order to heighten the air of drama and suspense during the broadcasts. When one of the top money winners, Charles Van Doren, confessed before the House Legislative Oversight Committee on November 2, 1959, he drew more sympathy than scorn from the public, however; it was widely assumed that he had been little more than a pawn in the high-stakes struggle for ratings.[35]

Still, the scandal was seen as indicative of larger problems in the industry and in society. In fact, the House subcommittee that heard Van Doren's testimony also probed graft and corruption charges lodged against President Eisenhower's chief assistant, Sherman Adams.[36] Later, this same subcommittee probed charges regarding ex parte contacts between FCC chairman John Doerfer and influential broadcasting executives. This web of immorality and deceit received lavish attention in the press, and concern began to mount that government officials, particularly those at regulatory agencies, were not doing their jobs. United States attorney general William P. Rogers publicly prodded the FCC to be more vigilant in policing the broadcast industry. Furthermore, Oren Harris, chairman of the House Legislative Oversight Committee, argued that a lax regulatory atmosphere enhanced the influence of advertisers at the expense of responsible broadcasters.[37]

It was at this point that the networks, under the guidance of FCC chairman John Doerfer, first agreed to increase their commitment to public service programming.[38] Yet the networks also sought to use this as an opportunity to enhance their control of programming at the expense of advertising agencies and sponsors that historically enjoyed significant influence over program content. When the top network brass met secretly at the St. Regis Hotel in December 1959, one of the major topics of discussion was "ways in which to keep program responsibility entirely within the networks and out of the hands of advertisers and busybodies."[39] In what broadcasters then perceived as an era of market maturity and intensifying competition, the network heads were becoming ever more sensitive to the issue of product control. Leonard Goldenson had built his broadcasting empire by seizing complete control of ABC's schedule and fashioning it for the youthful, middle-class family. Other network executives were not unaware of the advantages of such a strategy.

Therefore, behind the smokescreen of scandal reforms, Frank Stanton sought to follow the lead of his competitor and turn the situation to CBS's advantage. In addition to endorsing the Doerfer plan to increase network documentary production, CBS set up an internal standards and practices unit to study network operations and to safeguard against programming abuses.[40] While all of this projected an air of good citizenship, it also positioned CBS executives as the ultimate arbiters of all issues related to programming.[41] Stanton's actions set in place mechanisms designed to head off another quiz scandal, but also, most pointedly, they had the effect of trimming the influence of sponsors and advertising agencies. The latter had been the primary producers of quiz show programs, and the network exploited this weakness. Testifying before the FCC in February 1960, Stanton, with Goldenson's support, pressed his advantage. Both network chiefs advocated a "magazine concept" that would give the networks absolute control over programming, restricting client influence solely to the confines of the advertisements themselves.[42] In response to an increasingly volatile television economy, the networks were consolidating their grip on the evening schedule.

At the same time, the major networks sought to extend their financial investment in the programs they broadcast. The growing market for daytime syndication of off-network reruns dramatically enhanced the profitability of programs produced on film, and therefore the networks began to press for production partnerships with the studios that supplied their prime-time fare.[43] What is more, the networks expanded their own production facilities in Los Angeles in order to produce a greater share of prime-time telefilm.[44] The networks did not want to eliminate independent producers for fear they would be accused of violating antitrust laws; however, they clearly understood the growing returns that might be reaped from the syndication of network reruns.[45]

Another reason networks grew more interested in controlling program production was that the cost of acquiring television shows was rapidly rising. In 1956 one hour of prime time cost the networks an average of $70,000. By 1962 the figure had jumped to $110,000 per hour. When combined with growing expenditures on news, this meant that between 1956 and 1961 overall production costs at NBC rose some 70 percent. What was perhaps even more disconcerting was the fact that the networks' share of industry profits during the same period had declined from 23 to 14 percent.[46]

In 1961, despite the healthy overall state of the advertising economy, television insiders were deeply concerned about the future prospects of network television. "The old days of automatic expansion are over," declared *Variety* in a front-page article.[47] In the spring of the same year, both CBS and NBC announced major cutbacks in their administrative and operations staffs. CBS eliminated more than one hundred jobs, attributing most of the cutbacks to the declining amount of live television production in New York. NBC made substantial cuts as well in what was pegged as a major efficiency drive.[48] Although the drop in live production certainly contributed to these economy measures, it should also be pointed out that both networks were fully aware of the fact that ABC had enjoyed tremendous success over the past few years with an administrative and sales staff that was half the size of its larger rivals.[49] As a result, the pressures to streamline operations may have been heightened by concerns about the new competitor in a nearly saturated television advertising market.[50]

In short, even though the television industry proved to be immensely profitable during the late fifties and early sixties, network executives had a number of reasons to feel uncertain about future performance. As a result, all three networks sought to maintain a competitive position in the Nielsen ratings, limit the effects of government regulation, and reverse their declining share of industry profits. Toward these ends they sought tighter control over the prime-time schedule and pursued a financial interest in the programs they broadcast. They also set up their own telefilm production and syndication operations, as well as expanding their news divisions. When taken together, these actions had the effect of vertically integrating the operations of each network in a maturing and increasingly competitive industry. They also increased the scope of network influence over the cultural and informational spheres.[51] Therefore, in 1963, when the national economy took off under the stimulative economic policies of the Democratic administration, television was well positioned for a period of continued profitability and expansion. But during the six years prior to that time, network executives consistently expressed uncertainty about the future prospects of domestic television. It was this sense of uncertainty that drove the networks to vertically integrate their operations and to seek diversified business opportunities. This same impetus was also behind the rapid expansion of U.S. television interests overseas.

The Attraction of Foreign Television Markets

The rapidly increasing size of overseas television markets certainly made them attractive to American networks in search of new business opportunities. In 1961 the United States Information Agency (USIA) estimated there were more than fifty-five million television sets in foreign countries, an increase of 20 percent in the preceding year alone.[52] Not only was the worldwide audience for television growing, but many stations abroad were hungry for programming to fill their expanding broadcast schedules. The same year the Television Program Export Association estimated thirty million dollars in overseas program sales by American syndicators, and by 1964 the figure had more than doubled to sixty-eight million dollars, with telefilm sales in eighty countries.[53] By the middle of the decade, foreign markets accounted for 60 percent of total syndication sales.[54] By that point industry analysts would point to overseas operations as "the difference between profit and loss for the entire [syndication] industry."[55] Furthermore, they projected that this revenue stream would keep growing as television receiver sales continued to expand overseas and as developing countries grew more prosperous.

Foreign markets therefore appeared as an attractive complement to the growing involvement of American television networks in the financing, production, and rerun syndication of prime-time programming.

Television executives reasoned that the only costs associated with these new overseas markets would be the costs of language translation and distribution. Thus foreign sales seemed to provide a ready opportunity to extend the profit margins on already existing telefilm programming. By 1963 overseas syndication was so important to the industry that three out of four prime-time programs were being syndicated abroad.[56] Consequently, all three networks showed growing interest in international markets during the early 1960s.

ABC moved most aggressively overseas largely because of its disadvantaged status in the United States. Burdened with UHF affiliates in many markets, ABC could do little more to improve its ratings without federal action to enhance the status of these affiliates.[57] In the international field, ABC was also operating at a disadvantage owing to the fact that it was the last network to move off American soil. It found that many lucrative markets, such as Europe, Canada, Australia, and Japan, had already been commandeered by its network rivals. Although ABC did not shrink from the competition in these countries, it did look to newer, more speculative markets as offering greater growth potential. ABC was therefore very active in Asia and the Middle East, but the terrain where the network made its most ambitious effort was Latin America.

When the USIA made its 1961 study of television around the world, it estimated that Latin Americans owned 10 percent of the television sets in the "non-Communist world."[58] Not only was the use of television increasing rapidly in the region, but so was foreign investment. Between 1950 and the mid-1960s, U.S. private investment in Latin America almost tripled to 11.5 billion dollars.[59] American corporations were showing confidence in the growth potential of the region, and television executives were clearly caught up in the enthusiasm arguing that Latin America would reward farsighted investors. At the time, USIA officer Wilson Dizard wrote, "Almost every major U.S. distributor is selling telefilms at cut-rate prices in such countries against the day when these markets will become stronger."[60]

One of the further attractions of this region was that, as opposed to Asia or Africa, Latin America seemed more culturally homogeneous. Therefore many syndicators reasoned that the greatest cost of foreign syndication, language dubbing, could be spread across program sales throughout the region and the multicountry market could be viewed as a whole.[61] Richard Dinsmore, vice president and sales manager of Desilu Sales, Inc., one of the largest syndicators, explained: "Were I asked to rank the foreign markets in order of dollar importance to U.S. distributors, I would rate them more or less as follows: 1. England; 2. Canada; 3. Japan; 4. Australia; 5. Italy. Latin America, as a unit, would rate second or third, although individual country sales may not be as large as they are in some of the other countries I have just listed."[62]

Latin America therefore offered ABC a large and supposedly unified market. In an effort to guarantee its competitive position and expand its influence south of the border, ABC began to invest in television stations and line up local affiliation contracts. By the end of 1962 the network had invested more than ten million dollars in minority interests in twenty television stations abroad, representing close to 4 percent of total corporate assets.[63] By 1968 this would grow to more than sixty-four stations in twenty-seven countries, with over half of them in Latin America.[64]

Apparently, this strategy paid off. In 1963 ABC marketed its first multinational program package with the sale of more than five hundred thousand dollars in Desilu programs to nine countries. It was the largest single sale in Latin America to date. Donald Hine, programming manager in charge of the sale, connected this success to ABC's broader strategy. Hine remarked, "This kind of centralized [sales] activity results in greater efficiency for the producer, the distributor, and the stations."[65]

ABC's emphasis on efficiency and centralization also led the corporation to establish an integrated operation for the sale of transnational advertising. Its first major overseas venture led to the formation of the Central American Television Network (CATVN) in 1960 with affiliates in El Salvador, Nicaragua, Honduras, Guatemala, and Costa Rica. Shortly thereafter it formed a companion network of South American affiliates. Through these networks, ABC hoped to offer one-stop shopping for American advertisers who wished to market their products throughout the Western Hemisphere.

One of the most interesting aspects of ABC's strategy is how closely it conforms to the larger contours of American corporate expansion during the late 1950s and early 1960s. When announcing the formation of CATVN, Donald Coyle, vice president of ABC's international division, justified the initiative by proclaiming that the most profitable U.S. business ventures in the future lay in overseas markets. Coyle based his assessment on a number of factors. First of all, he pointed to "the competitive squeeze on the domestic front brought about by high market penetration which in some cases approach[ed] the saturation point." A second factor was the growing amount of international competition, especially from rebounding European and Japanese manufacturers. And the third, but most important, consideration was "overseas market growth, expanding industrial power, rising standards of living and increased economic stability."[66]

In this spiral of economic and social development, television clearly had a role to play. Coyle argued, "It is highly desirable from the standpoint of the economies of these countries themselves that television be brought in—so it can fulfill its natural function as a giant pump fueling the machine of consumer demand, stepping up the flow of goods and services to keep living standards high and the economy expanding." Perhaps not surprisingly, Coyle's analysis reads as if it were drafted by the Ford Foundation or the Rockefeller Brothers' Fund, and indeed it is important to note that, like these major foundations, the boards of directors at all three networks were endowed with top executives from transnational banks, law firms, and corporations.[67] Coyle's argument, like the think tank reports published in the late 1950s, rests on the assumption that the U.S. corporations must aggressively pursue business opportunities around the globe both for the good of the American economy and for the ultimate prosperity of peoples in less industrialized parts of the globe. Wrote Coyle:

> In El Salvador alone over 100 new industrial plants have been constructed in the past five years. The untapped oil, lumber, iron and coal resources of Guatemala, Nicaragua, and Honduras are coming to life. New jobs are being created, purchasing power is growing, the standard of living is rising. The five Central American countries imported 125% more in 1957 than they did in 1950, and the volume is still increasing. In addition, population is growing at a faster rate than any place else on earth. The demand for goods and services in future years will be huge.
>
> U.S. industry will be competing with the rest of the world in attempting to fill that demand. To compete successfully it must use the most potent selling force known—television, the medium for personal selling and personal communication.[68]

Coyle therefore suggested that overseas markets offered a "win-win" proposition. The introduction of American technology, business techniques, and popular culture would spur development and earn the allegiance of new trading partners. Furthermore, the introduction of television would help to break down local and regional differences. ABC chief Leonard Goldenson called CATVN "the first major move toward the establishment of a common market of Central American countries."[69] Yet Goldenson was not alone in wishing this Latino common market into existence. Such ambitions were an important part of American foreign policy during the postwar era. Unlike the earlier colonial period when the relationship with distant territories was primarily extractive,

U.S. policy now sought to erase trade barriers and colonial ties in order to enhance local living standards and open new markets for international commerce.

According to ABC, television had the potential to play a decisive role in all this. Since early radio days broadcast networking in the United States was based on the notion of overcoming geographical and cultural differences in an effort to forge national audiences and national consumer markets. ABC's Central American Television Network similarly promised to transcend geographical and cultural barriers in an effort to create regional audiences on a scale that would be attractive to multinational corporate advertisers. In fact, with the prospect of satellite television on the near horizon, Leonard Goldenson's ambitions were more than regional. "We're getting ready for world-wide tv," said the ABC chief in defense of his aggressive overseas expansion campaign.[70] ABC was clearly caught up in the project of constructing a culturally and economically integrated Free World.

The importance of global markets was similarly emphasized at CBS in a 1960 message to stockholders from Chairman William Paley and President Frank Stanton, who noted, "Of the eight CBS Divisions seven operate internationally, and prospects for increased earning from these overseas operations, particularly in television programming and phonograph records, are most promising." The report further explained that CBS telefilms were being distributed in forty countries and already represented close to 15 percent of total syndication revenues.[71] And three years later international sales in seventy countries generated revenues that exceeded domestic sales for the first time.[72] Because of its early involvement in the international marketing of telefilm, CBS was a prominent figure in each of the major overseas markets, including Europe, Japan, and Australia. CBS also demonstrated thoroughgoing interest in markets throughout the developing world, especially Latin America. In Argentina a joint venture with producer Goar Mestre and a group of local investors led to the establishment of a television station and production facility on the outskirts of Buenos Aires, then the second largest city in the Western Hemisphere. Within a year, PROARTEL was producing twenty of the top thirty programs in the four-station market and was announcing plans to move on to the second largest market in Argentina, the city of Córdoba.[73] Thus Mestre, with CBS backing, began to set up a national Argentine network with emphasis on live, local programming. Although ABC demanded that its Latin American affiliates broadcast ABC telefilm during prime time, CBS pursued a more decentralized strategy whereby local production was the driving force behind

PROARTEL's success, and CBS telefilm was used to fill gaps in the broadcast day. Media consultant Martin Codel summed up the difference between the two approaches by quoting Fernando Eleta, a Panamanian businessman then in the process of setting up his own station. Wrote Codel:

> Eleta makes no bones about his intense dislike for ABC. Don Coyle pressured him hard, he said, but he doesn't like ABC's business methods or its programs. Its thinking is inflexible, as he put it, entirely in an American groove and altogether wrong for Panama and, for that matter, for Central America.
>
> According to Eleta, ABC proceeds on the assumption that American-type shows are basic to good programming and will always be popular down here. . . . [Eleta] is convinced that Spanish-produced, Spanish-language shows, local and indigenous, especially live musicals which are so popular in Mexico, Brazil and Argentina, are the basic trend in TV in Latin America. He's sure Azcarraga in Mexico and Mestre in Argentina are on the right track in producing such shows live and on tape for syndication to all the Spanish-speaking world.[74]

Eleta's assessment cogently highlights the differences between the two organizations. ABC set out to establish a network that would ensure demand for ABC telefilm and provide one-stop shopping for transnational advertisers. CBS, whose telefilm was already in high demand, showed less interest in extensive station investments. Nor did it attempt to organize an integrated regional network. Nevertheless, it did continue to place a great deal of emphasis on global program syndication, which, after all, was the most profitable component of the global television market at the time.[75] Therefore, even though some researchers have argued that CBS did not expand overseas as aggressively as its smaller rival, international operations at both networks generated a significant and growing share of total revenues throughout the early 1960s.[76]

Yet no television network was more concerned about global markets than NBC and its parent company, the Radio Corporation of America. In 1963 RCA was proud to announce that it had 11,700 products and services for sale or lease in 120 nations and territories. Employing close to ninety thousand people, the communications giant pointed out that more than 10 percent of its workforce was stationed abroad. The corporation's activities ranged from satellite contracts with the Canadian government to picture tube plants in Europe. RCA had its finger in most every pie. For example, in 1963 RCA Italiana doubled its sales of television receivers, and, according to the corporate report, the future looked even brighter. "When Europe adopts color television," it noted, "RCA can expect to be a major beneficiary."[77]

Indeed, the Sarnoff empire manufactured and marketed a full range of color television equipment, from receivers to transmitters to recently introduced videotape recorders. And NBC, RCA's broadcast subsidiary, was most directly involved in the sale of network programming and station management services. These management services were designed to assist foreign governments and investors in establishing new television stations. Such contracts included administrative, technical, and personnel services as well as management of station construction and the installation of equipment. The typical contract ran five years, with NBC showing more interest in equipping and programming the station than owning it. Such contracts could prove extremely lucrative, as became clear in 1964 when NBC signed a contract to set up a thirteen-station network for the Saudi government. It was the biggest single American television contract to date and posed little financial risk for the corporation.[78] By the mid-1960s the "peacock network" was providing programming and management services to three hundred stations in eighty countries.[79] NBC's scope of operations as well as its links to RCA made it the quintessential multinational network.

Overall, the impact of these growing international operations should not be underestimated. Although all three networks would later face reversals abroad, the early part of the 1960s raised hopes for significant future growth overseas. Corporate memoranda and trade publications were almost rhapsodic in their prognoses regarding global television. Indeed, Marshall McLuhan's notion of a "global village" emerges at the very moment that these networks began to expand overseas. Even though the actual development of global television would not prove as smooth and linear as the rhetoric imagined, there can be little doubt that all three networks were positioning themselves to reap a growing bounty in markets throughout the Free World.

Technologies of Global Communion

The commercial advantages of integrated world markets, however, were only part of a larger picture. Because of the increasing popularity of TV around the globe and in anticipation of the impending launch of the first commercial communications satellite, many corporate leaders, such as RCA chairman David Sarnoff, envisioned television as ushering a new epoch in human history as well. In a 1961 speech at the University of Detroit, Sarnoff predicted:

RCA chairman David Sarnoff flourishes a radio made with transistors, the technology that promised to revolutionize modern communications. (Courtesy of Photofest)

Ten years hence—if vigorous foreign growth continues—there will be TV stations in virtually every nation on earth telecasting to some two hundred million receivers. An audience of a billion people might then be watching the same program at the same time, with simultaneous translation techniques making it understandable to all. In a world where nearly half of the population is illiterate, no other means of mass communication could equal television's reach and impact on the human mind.[80]

Many government policy makers apparently agreed with Sarnoff's prognosis. In his first speech to broadcast executives, FCC chairman Newton Minow remarked, "No one knows how long it will be until a broadcast from a studio in New York will be viewed in India as well as in Indiana, will be seen in the Congo as well as Chicago. But surely as we are meeting here today, that day will come—and once again our world will shrink."[81] Thus global television promised not only to speed communication and expand the range of diffusion, but it would also foster the spread of democratic and dialogic politics. Just as regional trading pacts such as the European Common Market enhanced the free flow of goods, television would make possible, according to Minow, an "uncommon market for the free exchange of ideas."[82] Such an exchange was important because of its utopian appeal and because policy makers contended that better communication would lead to better understanding—not simply among nations but among peoples of the world. Discussion, compromise, and democratic process are at the core of this vision.

Yet this rhetoric also was shaped by liberal notions of noblesse oblige. It was not simply a matter of dialogue among equals but also a matter of educating the poor and the ignorant in distant parts of the globe and of opening their eyes to the possibilities of the modern world, for the dawning of the age of global television also was the era of the Peace Corps and of rapidly escalating development aid to Third World countries. Thus the reason to enhance communications was both to deliver information and to alter the worldview of people in premodern societies. According to communications researcher Daniel Lerner, development could only take place if such individuals could envision themselves as part of a larger national and global community.[83] Consequently, television was a crucial medium that would help illiterate populations see beyond the boundaries of tribe, custom, and tradition. Moreover, it was suggested that television could cultivate the aspirations and expectations of modernity.

Richard N. Gardner, deputy assistant secretary of state, who at the time was deeply involved in planning the United Nations satellite pro-

The 1962 launch of the Telstar satellite augured the arrival of global television. (Courtesy of Photofest)

gram, argued that global television could forge "new bonds of mutual knowledge and understanding between nations" because it would foster a shared symbolic system throughout the world.[84] Furthermore, he projected that someday satellite radio and television signals might be broadcast directly into homes around the globe. And when such a day arrived, the boundaries of superstition, ignorance, and nation would be breached. Satellite broadcasting would bring together the "family of man."[85]

Criticism of American Television in Overseas Markets

Despite this enthusiasm, the overseas operations of the three U.S. networks were received with ambivalence in many foreign countries. Although American leadership in programming and technical services was widely acknowledged, it proved to be an unwelcome influence in many locales. Hollywood telefilm represented 80 percent of all global syndication sales in 1962, and many of these deals included action/adventure programming, which, although popular with foreign audiences, also opened the door to criticism by indigenous programming competitors and local social critics.[86] American producers were characterized as having a near monopoly on "blood, murder, mayhem, and sex."[87] As early as 1960 many governments began to consider import quotas, and by the following year restrictive legislation was pending in England, Mexico, Australia, Brazil, and Argentina.[88] In Mexico the government did in fact impose restrictions on certain action formats, using fines and license revocation as punitive measures. At the very moment that American telefilm exports were expanding, the networks were facing stiff criticism abroad as well as at home.[89] Indeed, during the debate over U.S. exports, the Mexican government cited Newton Minow's "vast wasteland" speech to bolster its position.[90]

Reacting to this pressure abroad, the networks pointed with pride to the growing number of documentary offerings in their telefilm catalogs. The genre therefore was not only a foil against domestic criticisms but also proved useful overseas, where it enjoyed a high level of prestige. In countries where television was recently introduced, documentary made it possible for government officials and broadcast executives to tout the wonders of the medium as an educational device. Consequently, many station managers began to shop for a "balanced" package of program imports, especially broadcasters located in countries where it was necessary to justify television as a complement to development.[91]

Network syndicators therefore were well aware of the documentary's allure. Both CBS and NBC boasted in 1960 that their catalogs of public affairs programming distinguished them from other telefilm distributors, and ABC responded that it too would soon be moving in a similar direction. All three pointed proudly to their achievements in documentary in order to deflect criticism of controversial entertainment series.[92] Thus a significant and growing international demand for public affairs programming was emerging, as reflected by the fact that NBC and CBS grossed more than a million dollars in such sales during 1961.[93] And while global sales of documentary would continue to grow throughout the early sixties, sheer dollar volume does not begin to suggest the cultural significance of such programming. These documentaries not only operated as a foil against television critics, but they also offered domestic and international audiences access to a future vision of liberal democracy and economic prosperity throughout the Free World. Time after time the programs made the case for programmatic reform and modernization as opposed to violent and chaotic revolution. This vision, carried via television, was seen as an increasingly fundamental part of the ideological struggle against Communism. Wrote ABC's Leonard Goldenson: "In Cuba we have seen how the battle for democracy can be lost. We are in grave danger of losing it in many countries of Latin America, Asia, and Africa. We must get our message of democracy to the uncommitted countries as soon as possible, then let them see us as we are, not as the Russians paint us to be."[94]

The Imagined Community of the Free World

Goldenson's plan for global TV reminds us that the late 1950s and early 1960s were a time of growing unease among U.S. corporate and political leaders regarding political changes in the Third World. Particularly worrisome was the fact that independence movements in postcolonial locales often coupled nationalist sentiment with socialist reforms and a nonaligned foreign policy. By the end of the fifties a consensus emerged within corporate and foreign policy circles that such movements posed a threat to U.S. interests and therefore necessitated a military buildup and an activist policy of social and economic intervention abroad. It was argued that the United States needed to play a more vigorous role to foster the integration of the Free World behind American leadership. This consensus was embodied in the Kennedy campaign platform and in the policies of the new administration. In fact, the substance of the new president's entire inaugural address was devoted to foreign policy issues and U.S. global leadership.

The cultural dimension of this campaign deserves careful attention, for leaders such as John Kennedy and ABC's Leonard Goldenson believed that television would play a significant role in this global struggle. Yet this notion regarding the powerful effects of television was largely based on hunches and assumptions of the era. Recent scholarship has more systematically begun to analyze the complex relationship between mass media and the construction of political affinities across vast expanses of space. By turning our attention to some of this work we can begin to understand why U.S. leaders felt television would play an important role in securing the boundaries of the Free World.

Our review begins with the literature regarding the role mass media have played in the construction of modern nation-states. Numerous scholars have shown that nation-states are a fairly recent phenomenon designed to integrate economic, political, and cultural activities within clearly defined geographical boundaries. Prior to the late eighteenth century, states were defined by centers; borders were porous and indistinct; and the exercise of power involved a series of alliances between military and aristocratic leaders.[95] This began to change with the American and French revolutions.[96] Not only was divine rule displaced, but these new states were envisioned as voluntary political associations in which sovereignty ultimately resided with the people. Yet these new nations did not emerge from a "natural" association of individuals who shared a single language, culture, or ethnic identity. At the time of the French Revolution, for example, less than half of the new nation's population spoke what would come to be characterized as "proper" French. Thus one of the significant characteristics of these revolutions was that they sought to integrate various cultural and linguistic groups who were geographically dispersed into a voluntary political association. It was argued at the time that nation building was beneficial both politically and economically, thereby linking the processes of industrialization, modernization, and geographical integration.

Benedict Anderson contends that these developments were accompanied by a change in consciousness as well. Previously, the average person's loyalties were mostly local, whereas loyalty to the modern nation-state was not so much a matter of face-to-face affinity as it was an imagined relationship. "It is imagined," writes Anderson, "because the members of even the smallest nation will never know most of their fellow-members, meet them, or even hear of them, yet in the minds of each lives the image of their communion."[97] Such popular imaginings were made possible by the rapid expansion of print capitalism during the eighteenth and nineteenth century and especially by the growth of the newspaper industry. Newspapers were important because they standardized language and implied a community of address among individuals who were otherwise anonymous to one another. Furthermore, with the development of telegraphy and news wire services, information throughout the nation was standardized and prioritized according to what were presumed to be the shared interests of the readers.

On the other hand, some modern nation-states evolved not as the product of popular will but as an elite reaction *against* popular agitation by regional groups within the borders of existing empires. Here, ruling aristocratic or dynastic elements tapped one variant of the many different nationalisms within their realm of influence and promoted it throughout the empire as serving the collective good. Hugh Seton-Watson has characterized this policy as "official nationalism," and nineteenth-century Russia provides one example of this strategy at work. In response to emerging nationalist movements in the Ukraine, Finland, Russia, and the Baltic states, Czar Alexander III took a number of steps to shore up his regime and integrate his empire. First, he enforced Russian as the official language throughout his realm for the purposes of education and administration. Secondly, the czar sought to integrate administrative functions of the government. Thirdly, he nurtured education, modernization, and mass communications. And finally, his regime promoted symbols of Russian nationalism in an attempt to win popular allegiance to a unified nation-state. All this was done as a way to head off regional forms of nationalism within the empire.[98]

During the early 1960s, the foreign policy of the New Frontier can best be understood as somewhat analogous to this policy of Russification. Just as the Russian czar reacted to popular uprisings within his geographical sphere of influence, so did the U.S. foreign policy establishment react to what was referred to as the growing number of "brushfire wars" in the Third World. Of key concern was the prospect that these struggles might ultimately lead to the establishment of governments that might position themselves outside the realm of U.S. leadership, outside the Free World alliance.

Like the nineteenth-century czarist policy of Russification, one of the major objectives of the New Frontier was to contain political unrest across a vast geographical expanse and to project the image of the American nation as serving the collective welfare within the community of the Free World. Just as the Russian leadership sought to coopt local nationalisms that arose in Georgia, the Ukraine, and the Baltic states during the nineteenth century, so too, did U.S. policy makers envision a response to "unrest" in Southeast Asia, Latin America, and the Middle East that would position these emerging nationalisms within the fold of an American-led Free World.

Yet unlike the imperial regime in Russia or the colonial project of Great Britain, the United States needed to promote the image of a popular, nonauthoritarian leadership within its geographical realm of influence. Ever since the administration of Franklin D. Roosevelt, U.S. policy had been explicitly committed to the decolonization of Asia and Africa, and this commitment restrained the U.S. government from pursuing geographical integration through the exercise of raw imperial power. Instead, the postwar empire of the United States had to be predicated on a respect for popular and national sovereignty. Rather than official nationalism, this policy might best be characterized as a form of official internationalism. And unlike earlier empires that had been bound together by strategic forms of point-to-point communications (e.g., telegraphy and wireless) and by the cooperation (or subjugation) of local elites, this American empire would require a form of communication that could win the "hearts and minds" of average citizens throughout the Free World. Just as the newspaper made the modern nation-state a viable unit, television promised to solidify the Free World. It is in this context that we can begin to understand how the utopian discourse of global television articulated the material interests and aspirations of government officials, corporate leaders, and broadcasting executives. And more specifically, it helps us understand why many government and broadcast executives considered documentary to be one of the most promising ways to use television to bring together the community of the Free World.

Technologies of Strategic Advantage

Within the inner circle of the Kennedy White House, this fascination with television's strategic potential stemmed in part from JFK's successful presidential campaign. Once he was in office, it was further stimulated by the surprisingly strong ratings of the president's live press conferences. Indeed, Kennedy himself became fond of referring to television as his favorite propaganda weapon.[99] Moreover, the promise of *international* television further enhanced the stature of the medium in the eyes of the administration. In February 1962 Jacqueline Kennedy's television tour of the White House proved to be the highest-rated program of the season; more important, it was estimated that global syndication of the program—facilitated by the networks and the United States Information Agency—brought the total audience to several hundred million.[100] The president therefore was quite conscious of television's power to project images across national boundaries and of the administration's power to influence those images.[101]

Nor was the president alone in making this assessment. In the spring of 1962, Tedson Meyers, administrative assistant to FCC chairman Newton Minow, penned a report that was the product of consultations with top officials at the White House, State Department, Central Intelligence Agency, U.S. Information Agency, U.S. Aid for International Development, National Association of Broadcasters, Ford Foundation, and European Broadcasting Union. The report introduces itself by noting, "The Kennedy Administration holds office at the precise moment when the United States can begin to exploit the potential power of international television and radio broadcasting in our national interest."[102] It then goes on to advocate a centralized body within the State Department or White House that would coordinate international broadcasting policy in order to (1) assist in the development of foreign broadcast systems so all countries of the Free World could be linked into the U.S. global communications network, (2) encourage American investment in communications projects overseas, (3) ensure access to foreign markets for U.S. programming, (4) stimulate the production of American programming that serves foreign policy objectives, and (5) establish government criteria for the content of programs targeted for international distribution.

Shortly after the report reached the White House, it was leaked to the press. Whether it was leaked as a trial balloon is unclear, but it generated swift and impassioned protest from network executives concerned about government involvement in program production and distribution.[103] Already sensitive to existing pressures for programming reform, broadcasters expressed concern about the possibilities of explicit government censorship. As a result, the White House publicly distanced itself from Meyers's recommendations. Nevertheless, the report seems to provide a summary of the administration's strategic interests in global television.[104] As correspondent Robert Lewis Shayon noted a year before the Meyers report was drafted, "In the global chess game that we and the Russians are playing there are many pieces, and international TV is clearly one of them."[105]

On one level, this chess game involved candid use of global broadcasting for propaganda purposes. This was largely the domain of Radio Free Europe, the Voice of America, and the USIA.[106] Such overseas information activities had increased only incrementally during the Eisenhower years. When JFK took office, however, he not only named a prominent television newscaster to head the USIA—Edward R. Murrow—but he increased the budget dramatically, almost doubling it within two years to $217 million.[107] Despite the increase, USIA resources were still reportedly stretched to the limit given the agency's broad mandate to promote U.S. ideology throughout the globe. Indeed, one high-level analysis of world opinion contended that the Cold War concerns of the administration were not shared by many citizens of the Free World.

"People in developing areas do not express deep concern for democracy and such abstractions as free speech and personal independence. Avoiding Communism usually is considered of little importance in under-developed nations, in comparison with the great importance attributed to it in the United States," concluded the report.[108] Such findings led USIA director Murrow to arrange a meeting between the president and leaders of the three networks, hoping he could encourage closer cooperation between broadcasters and government. Murrow was particularly interested in network documentaries, and in a memo to the president he wrote, "This Agency does not have the capability in terms of money or manpower to produce a significant number of television documentaries. This means we must follow the route of acquisition, adaptation, and distribution, and this, in turn, means we must acquire secondary rights to the maximum number of features and documentaries prepared and produced by the three American television networks."[109] Murrow therefore sought, and received, permission from the networks to distribute documentaries that promoted American interests in countries where the networks were unlikely to sell them in syndication. In this way, network executives explicitly cooperated with government efforts to use television documentary to promote a vision of the Free World that was consonant with U.S. policy.

On another level, however, television's role in the global chess game with the Soviet Union involved the private, commercial activities of broadcasters as they moved into overseas markets. Despite the fact that the administration officially distanced itself from the intrusive recommendations of the Meyers Report, government regulators such as Newton Minow continued to prod industry leaders to be sensitive to the political implications of their television exports. Said Minow:

> Your country will look to you to exercise your trust with responsibility. We will look to you to be concerned not only with commercial check and balance sheets, but also with democratic checks and balances; not only with avoiding red ink, but also with preventing red dictatorship.
>
> Your government will not and cannot monitor or censor your world programs—either the programs you send or the programs you receive and show to America. That's going to be the job of your conscience and your character. The penalty for irresponsibility will be more serious for the nation than the revocation of a station license. If this is too much responsibility for you, you should not be involved in international television.[110]

Besides such explicit public advocacy, Minow also used more informal channels to advocate a linkage between public service broadcasting and the national interest. In correspondence and conversation he emphasized that television's informational capability would play a key role in combating Communist propaganda. Network executives clearly took notice and responded to these cues by touting their growing news and public affairs operations.[111]

In part, Minow suggested that broadcasters should help to project a positive image of the American nation, an image of model democracy that operated through enlightened reflection and debate. He also indicated that broadcasters should take it upon themselves to project the image of the other, the monolithic Communist threat, and finally that broadcasters should pay attention to the important struggles taking place along the boundaries of the Free World.

Without establishing a specific mechanism for government censorship, Minow's rhetoric promoted public service programming that would serve America's foreign policy interests—this despite a period of sluggish advertising sales at all three networks.[112] The chairman therefore did not exercise his authority through explicit rules or economic sanctions. Rather, it was the discourse of global television that suggested the parameters for corporate behavior, parameters that made it difficult for broadcasters to focus on profitability while ignoring the ideological implications of network programming.

This is the context that shaped government oversight of the broadcasting industry during the early 1960s.[113] When Minow criticized the performance of commercial television, he was not simply referring to the medium's failure to deliver high cultural fare. He also was arguing that television did not do enough to keep citizens informed of America's global interests and of the threats posed by monolithic Communism. Moreover, he was concerned that commercial television programming projected the wrong image of the United States in overseas markets. In his renowned "vast wasteland" speech Minow showed an acute awareness of the political implications of global television. He pondered: "What will the people of other countries think of us when they see our Western badmen and good men punching each other in the jaw in between the shooting? What will the Latin American or African child learn of America from our great communications industry? We cannot permit television in its present form to be our voice overseas."[114]

Therefore, the New Frontier vision of broadcast reform was not simply one of Camelot, quality television, and democratic process; it was also a vision of global struggle against a Communist threat, for the discourse of international television embodied strategic considerations as much as democratic idealism. Changes in the U.S. economy and in foreign policy during the 1950s, along with the continuing decolonization of the Third

World, generated a crisis for American leaders. By the end of the decade, the United States was at the zenith of its postwar power, but it was also struggling to integrate and defend a vast geographical area of influence. Moreover, it was struggling for the allegiance of diverse peoples within the Free World. This attempt to integrate, defend, and mobilize popular support across international boundaries can best be understood by placing it in a wider historical context that pays attention to the relationship between mass communications and the construction of "imagined communities." The Kennedy administration therefore confronted a challenge that was very much like the one that confronted leaders of imperial regimes during the nation-building era of the nineteenth century. And like the leaders of that earlier time, the administration sought to use new communication technologies to integrate its sphere of strategic influence. Yet the circumstances that confronted the U.S. government during the postcolonial era were very different from those that confronted earlier empires. The discourse of global television reflects this, and it suggests that the new medium had a distinctive role to play. There are four reasons why the technology of global television may have appeared so promising to American policy makers and network executives.

First of all, television—as a means of visual communication—promised to mobilize popular allegiance to the Free World among both literate and nonliterate citizens. Such popular allegiance seemed important in the postcolonial world because alliances with local elites no longer were sufficient owing to the fact that most nationalist movements in the Third World had been predicated on the concept of popular sovereignty.

Secondly, global television fostered the image of democratic dialogue, and this was an important feature of U.S. efforts to distinguish the Free World from the Communist world. That is, the supposed *difference* between East and West rested on the free flow of information and ideas. Therefore, it was not appropriate for the United States simply to exercise raw imperial power as the European states had done during the colonial era; rather, it had to promote images of democratic choice and popular U.S. leadership.

Thirdly, global television, like the newspaper of the nineteenth century, implied a community of address and a clocked consumption of information and images. It would foster both temporal and spatial integration of populations throughout the Free World. Yet unlike the newspaper, television promised to bring people together across boundaries of the modern nation-state on a regular basis.

Finally, international television promised to bring a regular flow of information about the outside world into the United States. The medium might help American citizens to see themselves as part of a global community and as playing a leadership role in the Free World. Such a sense of community was essential if the U.S. government was going to undertake a massive increase in military and foreign aid programs.

Documentary therefore was considered an especially important television genre because of its ability to enlighten and inform. It would not only counter Soviet propaganda but would foster an imagined comradeship among citizens of the Free World. Its detailed examinations of social and political issues would offer an explicit vision of the values, attitudes, and ideals that motivated the New Frontier. As the executive producers of *NBC White Paper* and *CBS Reports* explained at the beginning of chapter 2, documentary promised to portray both the problems and possibilities that confronted citizens throughout the Free World at the dawn of a new decade.

Chapter Four

Documentaries of the Middle Ground

Although the documentaries discussed in chapter 2 might have encouraged viewers to support a more aggressive U.S. military posture, the point of these documentaries was not to mobilize Americans for an all-out war with the Soviet Union. Nor were they designed to foster a frantic search for Communist infiltration of the American homeland. Unlike Frank Capra's *Why We Fight* series during World War II or the paranoid feature films of the McCarthy era, the documentaries of the New Frontier were primarily an effort to focus attention on the middle ground between the two superpowers, for there lay the great amorphous frontier of the so-called Free World. Although the boundaries of the Communist sphere were conspicuously marked by the Iron Curtain, the allegiances of countries such as India, Panama, and even France were much more uncertain and therefore the object of intense concern for U.S. corporations, network broadcasters, and the Kennedy administration. This vast terrain was also incredibly diverse in its many languages, cultures, and politics. Consequently, documentaries from this era seemed to ask: How would one recognize the boundaries of the Free World? What holds it together? And why is it worth defending? Such questions needed to be answered in order to legitimize the administration's proposed expansion of military and foreign aid programs. Furthermore, as mentioned in chapter 3, these are the same sorts of fundamental questions that mass media have historically addressed in their attempts to construct and sustain modern political affinities among large, diverse populations. Benedict Anderson has pointed out, for example, that during the nation-building era of the nineteenth century, newspapers played a vital role in constructing popular images of the nation and of national empire.[1] Now, in the age of television, the major

U.S. networks invested a tremendous amount of effort to foster an imagined community of the Free World.

This, of course, was a complicated task. Unlike the programs discussed in chapter 2, the documentaries of the middle ground had to negotiate ideas and images that did not fall into the easy categories of East and West. For example, the programs had to explain the relationship between the purported equality of Free World member states and U.S. pretensions to global leadership, for American postwar policy explicitly advocated the elimination of colonialism, the promotion of free trade, and the installation of democratic governments throughout the globe. The programs therefore had to distinguish leadership from imperial dominance. Moreover, given the presumption of equality and community, they had to explain economic, political, and cultural differences as significant but not so significant as to threaten the coherence of the Free World. Accordingly, programs such as *CBS Reports* profiled "The Freedom Explosion" in Africa as Nigerians voted in their first popular elections.[2] Meanwhile, on ABC, John Masters traveled "Back to Bhowani" to explore the changes in Pakistan since independence and to reflect on the mixed legacy of imperial British rule.[3] Thus one of the key missions of documentary was to consider the tumultuous and distinctive changes occurring in countries throughout the globe but then to recuperate these differences within the framework of community. How well was each nation progressing toward the collective vision of modern democracy and free trade? What dangers and obstacles stood in the way? What could the United States do to encourage stable, systematic progress?

Another way in which documentaries managed diversity was to suggest that one of the fundamental bonds that linked the nations of the Free World was the external threat posed by monolithic Communism. In this respect unity was constituted by a common enemy, and therefore the programs repeatedly foregrounded the prospects of Communist influence or infiltration. Each documentary took the issues confronting a specific nation and raised them to a level of abstraction that positioned the country within the context of superpower struggle. The country either fell in one camp or the other. It was either a member of our community or a pawn of monolithic Communism.

Historian William Chafe offers a useful way of understanding this process of abstraction by suggesting that it has always been difficult for American presidents to rally public support for foreign policy initiatives that are candidly self-serving. As a result, presidential administrations have repeatedly elevated specific economic and strategic concerns to a moral plane by suggesting that the issue at hand has universal implications.[4] Thus Woodrow Wilson sought to make the world safe for democracy; Franklin Delano Roosevelt drafted the Atlantic Charter; and of course the early trajectory of America's Cold War policy coalesced around the Truman Doctrine. In each case the argument for a more aggressive foreign policy was constructed as a moral struggle between forces of good and evil rather than as a self-interested struggle for geopolitical power. This phenomenon certainly permeates the documentaries of the New Frontier, which repeatedly characterize political contestation in other countries as a form of instability or "unrest" that inevitably opens the door to infiltration from the malignant forces of Communist expansionism. One of the primary missions of the documentarist, then, was to mark the boundaries of the Free World by probing for traces of Communist influence.

This chapter begins by examining documentaries that portray countries suffering from underdevelopment and political unrest. In these programs we shall see how the nations of the Free World are characterized as sharing certain aspirations. It is suggested, for example, that all countries, despite their cultural differences, go through similar stages of economic and social development. Ultimately, the nations of the Free World will grow closer as programmatic social and economic reforms make underdeveloped states more like their modern industrial counterparts. At the early stages, however, this progress is threatened by outside agitators, and these documentaries carefully probe for indications that the natural process of development is being disrupted by Communist infiltrators.

The second set of programs analyzed in this chapter focuses on societies in which infiltration has led to insurrection. Here the Communist challenge is made explicit as documentarists probe for signs of outside influence. The programs assume the peremptory right of network news organizations to investigate local revolutions for signs of Communist involvement and to advocate U.S. intervention should such indications appear. Moreover, they suggest that the nature of conflict on these battlegrounds between East and West requires new strategies, specifically the application of social scientific expertise.

In sum, both sets of documentaries deal with two key concerns: What makes *them* like *us*? And what factors might make them susceptible to Communist influence? The programs suggest that all citizens of the Free World share aspirations for modernity and democracy. What threatens these goals are traditional vested interests that resist needed reforms and thereby open the door to infiltration by Communist subversives. Why then do our fellow citizens of the Free World fall prey to the deceptive appeals of such subversive forces? Because they are either untutored or too poor to recognize their long-term interests. As in the first two chapters, we shall see the liberal imagination at work as these programs convey a profound distrust of the gullible masses and suggest that their salvation ultimately rests with education, reform, and expert leadership.

Reform and Development

The dynamics of social change and superpower struggle play a formative role in the *CBS Reports* documentary "Brazil: The Rude Awakening."[5] By way of introduction, correspondent Eric Severeid narrates a montage of newsreel footage with the following commentary: "The United States became conscious of Cuba when a man with a beard seized power three years ago. We became conscious of Brazil when a man with a mustache quit power two months ago. Cuba is gone. As Brazil goes, so goes South America." This opening formulation is accompanied by emblematic shots of Castro passionately delivering a speech to adoring crowds, and by comparison we then are shown shots of the Brazilian leader, dressed in a business suit, speaking to the media in an executive office setting, the radical versus the moderate. Cuba is gone. Brazil may go. Quadros is like a leader of the Free World, and yet his country is teetering "on the verge."

We are accordingly informed that Brazil is about to "explode" unless reforms are instituted and the Communists kept at bay. Daniel Quadros, "the white knight of honest government," shocked his constituency when he resigned after only seven months in office. He had been an active reformer domestically and a nonaligned figure in international circles. "They called Quadros the only alternative to Communism," notes Severeid, and yet he resigned from office citing frustration with the forces of reaction—foreign and domestic—that continued to oppose reform.

Upon resigning, Quadros did not elaborate specifically on these forces of reaction. Therefore the documentary sets out to explore the problems that drove him from office. It explains first that Quadros's predecessors had saddled him with high government debt and an inflationary economy. But even worse, Quadros confronted a country divided between north and south.

In the south of Brazil, says Severeid, is São Paulo, the "engine" of the Brazilian economy. "The real importance of São Paulo," he notes, "is its

Rebel leader Fidel Castro contrasted with Brazilian "white knight" reformer Daniel Quadros.

huge middle class. . . the backbone of a modern consumer economy." To
the north is rural Brazil, which is exploited by the south. It "stokes the
engine" of this modern economy with raw materials and mineral resources, yet it receives little in return. As we watch black folk dancers,
Severeid informs us that the contrast is dramatic: "In the northeast the
poor seek food and some surcease from this life's misery in their ancient
African religious rites. In the south [cut to televised classical dance per-
formance], the rich seek distractions. Debutantes perform classic Portuguese dances as a highly skilled hobby." The gulf between north and
south is the gulf between black and white, between primitive and modern, between tribal and classical. Severeid comments on this division
when he rhapsodizes, "São Paulo, pride of Brazil, envy of Brazil, and
stranger to Brazil; closer in spirit to New York or Paris or Rome than to
Recife, Bahia, or Fortaleza."

In comparison with São Paulo, the north is a land of poverty, feudalism, and sugar plantations. We are told that 2 percent of the people own
50 percent of the land and that human hands are cheaper than tractors.
Slavery was abolished in Brazil long ago, but workers remain on the land
as little more than serfs. The labor is hard; the diets are poor; and the
life span is a little more than thirty years. Severeid profiles a family, and
we learn that their daily earnings are thirty cents. Three days' pay will
buy two pounds of meat. In an interview with the plantation owner, he
tells us his employees are poor because they do not work hard and they
do not save their money. If he paid them more, they would work even
less.

Commenting on this state of affairs, Severeid concludes, "In today's world, Brazil cannot endure half modern and half feudal." This
apparent appropriation of Abraham Lincoln's aphorism regarding the
antebellum United States is not unintentional. The documentary has
constructed the plantation economy of northeastern Brazil as a sort of
modern-day version of the Confederacy. And perhaps no less intention-
ally, the documentary then turns to the urban plight of those who have
left the plantations; many poor blacks have flocked to the cities of Brazil
in search of a better life, and their plight may serve as a cautionary alle-
gory for the United States, which has experienced a similar migration.
Rising expectations and urban poverty make for an explosive mix, we
are told. In Brazil, as in the United States at this time, black urban communities are often described in documentaries as pockets of potential
unrest. Also as in the United States, the documentary tells us that liberal pressures for reform in Brazil are being resisted by the forces of
reaction.

Cutting cane at an early age in "Brazil: The Rude Awakening."

"It is written on the walls," says Eric Severeid, " 'Long live Cuba! Long live Fidel!' "

In Brazil, says Severeid, the question is whether these developments will lead to civil war. Says the governor of one Brazilian state, "It's very hard to speak about freedom and choice, of Christian civilization, to people who do not have water in their homes and schools for their children and hospitals for their sick people." As we survey the miserable conditions of a Brazilian slum, Severeid adds, "It is also very hard to speak to people in such condition about democracy, individual rights, and the dangers of Communism. Where poverty grows, the influence of Castro and Communism grows in proportion. [Cut to shot of urban graffiti.] It is written on the walls, 'Long live Cuba! Long live Fidel!'" Thus feudalism, underdevelopment, exploitation, tribalism, and urban migration have generated a boiling cauldron of popular unrest. This dark side of Brazil is a land of mystery, violence, and passion. Christianity and democracy have no meaning here. What does have meaning is the passionate politics of Fidel. Standing in front of a map of Brazil, Severeid directly addresses the viewer with the crux of the issue: "Brazil has become a propaganda battleground. Castro's Cuba has polarized the struggle for the soul of Brazil. Should Brazil go his way with the promise, or illusion, of quick results, or continue the slow way of democratic reform while life for a good many millions gets worse? How we handle Cuba itself will have a good deal to do with the outcome."

Severeid comes down squarely on the side of progressive, incremental reform as the only means of meeting the Communist challenge. Yet he is cautious regarding the role that the United States should play. He notes Brazilian resistance to America's involvement in its economy and its politics. There have been criticisms in the past, says Severeid. Furthermore, in a series of interviews, Brazilian politicians assure us that their country wishes to pursue an independent course, outside the camps of the major superpowers. Nevertheless, in the last interview of the program, a former American ambassador to Brazil says the United States should go ahead with a major aid package for Brazil, but it also should be made clear that the United States will only give aid to those political leaders who "stick with us." In closing, Severeid comments: "We can help Brazil, but we have neither the power nor the right to make it over. Nor has Russia the power to make it over her way. Brazil is for Brazilians. God, and under her new policies, the U.S. government, helps those who help themselves."

Thus the program presents a confusing set of propositions. The viewer is asked to care about Brazil because it is a potential member of the Free World. Moreover, it shares certain features that make it similar to the United States: a capitalist economy, an elected form of govern-

In summation, Eric Severeid directly addresses the audience regarding the future of a key ally.

ment, a split between north and south, a legacy of slavery, and the migration of African Americans from the countryside to the cities. But its differences are just as prominent. Poverty seems more widespread in Brazil and more intense. The country's reform-minded young leader faces such strong opposition that he quits within a matter of weeks. Brazil seems to *need* assistance from the outside world, yet it resists the external influence that goes with it. The country teeters on the brink of economic collapse and political unrest. Its urban slums are seething with the same passionate resentments that brought Fidel Castro to power. Brazil is therefore part of the Free World, and yet it is other. It is worthy of U.S. concern, and yet there are constraints on American intervention. The tensions that structure this program are the very tensions that marked U.S. policy throughout this period. How was the Kennedy government to exercise its leadership given the contradictory pressures at work? Should Brazil be allowed to pursue the "natural" course of development? How might the United States render assistance? And under what conditions should it intervene? The choices are not easy, and the documentary urges restraint. Yet it also characterizes Brazilian unrest as a breeding ground for monolithic Communism, thereby suggesting that, should the crisis worsen, local sovereignty might have to be subordinated to the larger interests of the Free World.

Similar tensions are at work in Robert Drew's "Yanki No!" which was produced for ABC's *Bell and Howell Close-Up!*[6] The documentary begins at a meeting of the Organization of American States (OAS) in Costa Rica, where, amid heated debate, the United States is insisting on the passage of a resolution condemning China and Cuba. As the Venezuelan delegate, Foreign Minister Arcaya, walks out in protest, the camera follows him on his return trip to Caracas to find out why the Venezuelans would resist American leadership on this issue. Shot in cinema verité style, the program pursues grassroots documentation of the Communist appeal in Latin America. At breakfast the morning after his return, Arcaya tells the documentary crew that if they wish to understand why the U.S. position in Latin America is being undermined, they must visit the slums of Caracas.

On the ensuing tour of the city, the camera tilts down from the modern high-rises of Caracas to a street-level view of the slums. A hand-held camera trudges through back alleys of a shantytown while the narrator comments on the plight of local inhabitants in a neighborhood with "no streets, no addresses, no mailboxes. . . . No letter could reach them; they don't exist." The documentary then brings some of the nameless faces of poverty to life by telling the story of the Manzanilla family. In a shanty constructed of scavenged materials, the husband, Gabriel, tells of his fruitless search for work over the past five months. He also tells of a former employer who refuses to make good on the back pay that is still owed to Gabriel. As we watch the family members going about their household chores, we sense their feelings of entrapment and hopelessness. These sentiments are further accentuated by a rainstorm that comes dripping through their roof and sends a torrent of floodwater down the streets of their neighborhood. From these scenes of urban despair we cut back to Arcaya's apartment, where his son, de Gracio, is animatedly debating the problems of Latin America with his college friends. They conclude that such conditions will change only if there is a revolution.

Yet revolutionary politics has been staunchly resisted by American foreign policy, and the documentary offers a short historical recitation of U.S. support for military dictatorships throughout Latin America. It concludes that the failure of past U.S. policy has been made only too clear by the Cuban revolution. Thus the first part of the documentary's analysis centers not on a knee-jerk hostility toward Communism but on a cool critique of the poverty that robs individuals of their identities and the military dictatorships that resist needed reforms. By comparison, Cuba has offered these people hope, but now the program turns to expose this hope as ideologically based, as false consciousness. The viewer is taken on a tour of Cuba in order to understand the attractions and deceptions of life under Fidel Castro's regime.

We travel first to a small fishing village where Jesus Morero, his wife, seven children, and his mother-in-law are moving from a grass shack to a modern house. As we follow the family's progress on moving day, the narrator tells us that "Jesus is being collectivized. He is losing his freedom." However, we also are informed that Jesus sees things differently. He says his life is improving and he does not see the need for democratic elections in light of the popular actions being taken by Fidel. In fact, one might observe that Jesus is voluntarily relinquishing the political freedom he never had in exchange for the basic material necessities the revolution is providing. We watch as his children joyously explore their first encounter with indoor, running tap water. In tight close-up we see their hands at play under the running faucet. Moreover, their enthusiasm for the new home is emphasized as the camera follows them marching from room to room rhythmically clapping their hands and chanting, "Cuba sí, Yanki no."

Here the ideological mission of the network documentary confronts a serious challenge, for the photographic images of Cuba refuse to slip politely into the clearly defined oppositions outlined in chapter 2. In fact, the intimate portrayal of Jesus, shot according to the conventions of Hollywood narrative, invites the viewer to *identify* with a Cuban family that has declared its loyalty to Castro. In its effort to investigate the source of Castro's support, this scene paints a sympathetic picture of Jesus and makes one wonder if his allegiance to Fidel is perhaps the best and most logical choice he has. On the other hand, the voice-over narration, written under the personal direction of ABC chairman Leonard Goldenson, attempts to contain this revolutionary enthusiasm by arguing that Jesus has been tricked into giving up his freedom. Like his children, he has fallen prey to the charisma of Fidel and the ideological agenda of monolithic Communism.

This moment of narrative rupture is emblematic of one of the fundamental tensions at work in all the documentaries of the middle ground. Here the spoken narration and the visual documentation, the abstract and the specific, the global and the local all collide in a telling manner. This is a documentary that was personally commissioned by ABC chief Leonard Goldenson and that was intended to document the growing threat of Communism in the very countries where ABC was rapidly increasing its financial investment. As we have seen in chapter 3, Goldenson's ambitions were similar to those of other network broadcasters as well as many other U.S. firms. Moreover, his ambitions for global television were consonant with the interests of an incoming presidential administration that was wrestling with the defense of its far-flung interests. Thus it is not surprising that Goldenson should become personally involved in the subject. Nor is it surprising that he took a business trip to Latin America in 1960 in order to survey investment options and that while touring the area, he cabled the documentary producers with specific suggestions for the program.[7] What is surprising, however, is the deeply contradictory nature of the outcome. The first half of the documentary not only paints sympathetic portraits of the dispossessed, but it also questions the wisdom of previous U.S. foreign policy. It shows the misery that has been fostered by a system of exploitation and military dictatorship that had been propped up by Yanki sponsorship. On what grounds, then, should the United States legitimately intervene at this current moment of crisis?

The answer becomes apparent as the latter part of the program turns away from this grassroots documentation of Castro's support and focuses instead on a climactic rally in Havana, featuring Fidel "at his messianic best." Here we observe Castro's manipulative, charismatic powers at work; we encounter the face of Communist manipulation and the resulting gullibility of the untutored masses. For example, we see rally organizers aboard a parked truck handing out signs printed with political slogans to enthusiastic participants. The camera singles out a young woman in the crowd. And when she spots the camera, she smiles broadly and crows in English, "This is a Cuban girl speaking that represents the feelings of the people of Cuba that we love Fidel because he's our leader for always. Please tell this to the United States, please, please." Yet this seemingly spontaneous affirmation is positioned in the context of a highly organized rally in which even the slogans on the signs have been prefabricated by the Communist leadership. Therefore her affirmation cannot be read as sincere. Rather, it must be seen as part of the orchestrated delirium that is characteristic of Communist politics.

As the camera moves freely about the rally, it offers sweeping vistas of the gigantic assembly as well as tight close-ups of participants with their eyes riveted on Fidel. We are told that Castro turns to this popular assembly for his political legitimacy. Rather than practicing the art of electoral politics, he practices the politics of popular unrest. He is a "messiah" promising to raise the poor and the oppressed from obscurity by giving them what those in the shanties of Caracas can only dream of:

he offers them hope; he offers them a home; he offers them an identity. But the documentary prefers that we see these as false promises, for the politics of the mob are the politics of the anonymous, irrational masses. Castro's political style is robbing them of their individual integrity.

As we watch Fidel passionately speak of empowering blacks, Indians, women, the aged, and the poor, the crowd goes wild. This frenzy of popular politics is repeatedly punctuated by close-up and extreme close-up shots of Castro as he denounces the OAS meeting in Costa Rica and the declaration of San José. He calls the document a pretense for further Yanki imperialism in the Western Hemisphere and counters that Cuba is charting an independent course. Castro proclaims, "We have done away with the yes men and learned to say *no!*" The crowd's thunderous response—"Cuba sí, Yanki no!"—marks the rally as both threatening to the United States and antithetical to modern democratic practices. Here the delirious crowd sharply contrasts with the image of individual citizens making reflective political choices in the privacy of the voting booth. Castro's power is therefore positioned as illegitimate, and the crowd appears deluded. As with the documentaries discussed in chapter 2, the crowd is portrayed as an excessive incarnation of mass society: faceless, passionate, and protean. Castro's Communism, like all Communism, is threatening because it poses a challenge to the delicate system of checks and balances inherent in Western politics and replaces representative government with charismatic leadership.

These are the stakes in countries along the frontiers of the Free World. Although the local, historical context may render social unrest intelligible, the politics of revolution are characterized as a breeding ground for Communism. The local and the specific are thereby elevated to a level of abstraction that positions them within the context of super-power struggle. The legitimacy of U.S. intervention overseas therefore turns on the presence of Communist subversives and the resulting manipulation of those whose fundamental aspirations for prosperity and freedom are no different than those of other citizens of the Free World. The documentary, then, acknowledges the importance of local contexts and of specific national interests, but it also repositions them within the geopolitical ambitions of the United States. Like the nineteenth-century imperial strategies discussed in chapter 3, these documentaries propose that local nationalisms should be subsumed within the American project of the Free World. And this proposition hinges in large part on the documented presence of the Communist threat.

Consequently, one of the key concerns of these programs is to understand the techniques by which Communists infiltrate societies along the frontiers of the Free World. Where are the first inroads made? How do Communists sidetrack the "normal" course of economic and social development? One of the few documentaries from this period that actually portray a Communist organization in action is an ABC *Close-Up!* episode called "Remarkable Comrades." At the time of its 1961 broadcast, American foreign policy makers were deeply concerned about Italy because it then had one of the largest Communist parties in the Free World and because one in four Italians cast their ballots for "the hammer and sickle."[8] In a letter to McGeorge Bundy, President Kennedy's adviser for national security affairs, ABC producer John Secondari explained why he recommended the program: "We believe this [documentary offers] the most complete look inside a Communist Party ever presented on American television. As such, we think this program can make a significant contribution to public awareness of Communist strategy in the non-Communist world and ways to combat it."[9]

The documentary opens with conventional political speeches at a massive Communist Party rally, but it also surveys the carnivalesque atmosphere surrounding the rally, complete with food, song, and celebration. These contrasting images set up the "contradiction" around which the program revolves, that is, the popular appeal of the Communist Party among diverse segments of the Italian population, the party within the party. The opening scene concludes with the singing of the Internationale during which the camera cuts between panoramic crowd shots of the flag-waving masses and more intimate portrait shots of individual participants. Meanwhile, the narrator comments: "One wonders how many of these sturdy comrades at other times sang other political hymns. How many of them were devoted fascists? In this crowd you can find all sorts of political backgrounds: the innocent, the disillusioned, and the firm believer."

As with the documentaries regarding pure Communist states, an analogy is drawn here between fascism and Communism. Furthermore, the concept of the gullible masses establishes an important explanatory strategy for the rest of the program. Although not physically coerced, the masses appear susceptible to manipulation, and an Italian journalist then informs us that 90 percent of party members know nothing of international Communism. Rather, they are attracted by the everyday power the party wields in Italian government and business.

The camera then travels to the northern part of the country, the "red belt," and profiles a peasant family whose material well-being has improved remarkably under the guardianship of the party. As the camera follows Josira Verabizi riding her bicycle home from a day's labor in the fields, the narrator remarks that, "paradoxically," life has never been better for her. She has a bike, modern conveniences, and she no longer lives in the barracks where she raised six children in a single room. Her modern apartment building was constructed by the government in response to pressure from the Communist Party. As she begins to prepare dinner in her modern kitchen, the narrator comments:

> Josira is full of seeming contradictions. She thinks Mussolini was a great man. She is against religion, but she believes in God. Her family [cut to the dinner table] consists of three generations of Communists. And as they eat, they talk of the class struggle, the need for revolt, the sort of talk one might hear in Moscow or Peiping. Yet their cooking is the best and richest in Italy. Their appetites appear to be satisfied.

The paradox presented by the Italian Communist is that she is materially well off. Josira is not the desperate émigré huddled in the slums of a major urban center, nor is she the starving plantation serf. Rather, she lives a modest but picturesque life in a small town in the Italian countryside. The legacy of servitude she inherited has ended, and yet she wants more.

Therefore, the attraction of the Italian Communist Party is that it can provide more than a modern apartment and a bicycle. Next we visit a Communist clubhouse where "a comrade need hear little doctrine" but may enjoy all the facilities of a neighborhood tavern. Then we are off to a co-op store stocked with goods produced by more than two thousand cooperatives throughout Italy. The narrator informs us that the Communists own some of the biggest businesses in the country, providing everything from olive oil to grave plots.

Still there is more. As we return to the rally, the narrator remarks that the party's most notable asset is that "it has, for a Communist organization, a sense of humor and fun." Here the documentary rapidly intercuts shots of propaganda posters with wine, song, lotteries, fireworks, and even "a merry-go-round with a hammer and a sickle on it." There is something for everyone, even weekly dance parties for the fashionably dressed teenagers. While watching them jitterbug, we are told there is nothing drab about these Communists, for "one thing is clear, the girls would rather look like Jackie Kennedy than Nina Khrushchev. This alone makes them remarkable comrades." These scenes obviously do not project the stereotype of brainwashed automatons or half-starved slum dwellers. Italian Communists appear to share many of the same tastes as citizens of other modern countries. We soon learn, however, that they are susceptible to subversive influences emanating from a highly centralized and purposeful party apparatus. In the city of Bologna, we visit, according to the narrator,

> the most important Communist leadership school this side of the Iron Curtain. School is permanently in session. [The curriculum] is intended to train them in doctrine. It also affords the faculty a chance to determine which ones have outstanding capacities for party work. Discipline is strict. Young men and women are kept apart. Discussion ranges all topics and facets of doctrine. For instance here is young Communist reaction to the question, how can we overcome the prejudices against us? [One student] says, most people are well disposed, but some people just will not see the truth. This other one adds, we must try in every way to involve Catholic organizations in our peace movement.

Two things mark this scene at the leadership school as particularly important. First of all, it is constructed with the same Hollywood editing grammar as the rest of the program; however, the effect here is quite different.[10] We see an establishing shot of the school, a master shot of the classroom, and close-ups of the teacher and students. Yet the film then moves very quickly from close-up to extreme close-up, a framing that is usually associated with moments of passion or villainy in Hollywood style. At the same time, the inflection of the narrator's baritone becomes foreboding and intense. This scene is therefore unlike earlier segments in which party members and activities were framed at a more respectful distance while accompanied by upbeat acoustic guitar and a more sprightly voice-over narration.

As these formal elements change, so too does the content of the narrative. These do not seem to be "remarkable comrades"; instead they appear to be Stalinist infiltrators. They coldly calculate the tactics by which they will dupe the masses, and they strategically assess the merits of penetrating other organizations. They are disciplined, celibate, and, by implication, linked to a global, monolithic conspiracy. They must study the doctrine of Marxism and adhere to the strictures of an inflexible hierarchy. Although the scene is relatively short, it attempts to corral the preceding, largely positive images of Italian Communism within the abstract dichotomies of superpower struggle. This scene crystallizes the nature of the Communist threat in Italy, something that has been ambiguous up to this point. Those party members who joined for mundane and even logical reasons are now repositioned as gullible to subversive influences. The Communist Party "delivers the goods" to its members because the party wants something in return: power and control.

The ideological work done by this scene can be highlighted by considering how the producer might have treated similar footage filmed at a

Catholic seminary instead of the school in Bologna. Since the church is cast as an important alternative to Communism in this documentary, images of Catholic schooling would no doubt be given an entirely different inflection despite a comparable emphasis on celibacy, discipline, doctrine, and hierarchy. In other words, young men studying for the priesthood would be characterized not as infiltrators but as servants of a higher calling who abstain from earthly pleasures in order to bring the truth of Catholic doctrine to other people. The activities of the seminarians therefore would have benign, if not salutary, implications for Italian society, since the church is characterized as the defender of Western, democratic values.

The ideological assumptions in "Remarkable Comrades" are further accentuated by the fact that the program valorizes the Catholic Church as the best hope for stemming the increasing power of the Communist Party. Yet what the documentary ignores is that the history of Italian politics up to that point had not been manipulated by the Communist Party so much as it had been subject to the intrigues of the Catholic Church (an organization that, in fact, had ties to fascist regimes before and during World War II). Thus, in its attempt to position Italian politics within the context of East-West struggle, the program transforms the church into the primary bulwark defending democracy. At the same time, it ironically associates the Communist Party with the fascist legacy in Italy.

As such, the documentary strives to transcend the historically specific in order to describe Italian politics as an abstract moral struggle between democratic government and external forces of subversion. Recalling William Chafe's observation about the American public's reluctance to support self-interested foreign interventions, one can see this documentary elevating the situation in Italy to a Manichaean clash between universal forces of good and evil. Moreover, this attempt to abstract the issue to a higher plane is powerfully enhanced by the program's pretensions to objectivity. The documentary journalist, as a disinterested professional, takes the viewer to Italy to *see* Communist infiltration firsthand. Like a virus that can be observed under a microscope or a recession that can be tracked by economic indicators, Communist infiltration in Italy is characterized as a social fact removed from ideological considerations. Journalistic objectivity and filmic realism are invoked so as to present Communism as a cancerous growth that invariably calls for drastic intervention.

Still, this preferred closure is a tenuous one, for these very same conventions of documentary objectivity and realism also undermine the stability of the text. Journalistic norms required that the ABC crew travel to Italy and gather "actuality" in order to substantiate the program's assertions. Unlike Frank Capra's World War II film propaganda, this footage could not be shot on a studio back lot. Consequently, "Remarkable Comrades" does an extensive empirical profile of the Communist Party, much of which comes across as evenhanded, if not sympathetic. There is a tension structured into the text by the "actualities" that show the party has developed strategies that effectively address social and economic needs among the Italian working class. In fact, the Communists have instituted the very reforms that other documentaries have argued are necessary in order to *prevent* political unrest.

At this point "Remarkable Comrades" turns southward to Sicily, the stronghold of the Christian Democratic Party and the church. Paradoxically, Sicily is the poorest region of Italy, and yet this is where the Communists are weakest and the church strongest. While observing a float of the Virgin Mary portered through the streets of a Sicilian village, the narrator comments, "On shoulders such as these stands the anti-Communist Italian government. It is these people who give most of that 52 percent of the vote that keeps it in power."

Here again the documentary evidence generates contradictory meanings and tensions. The poor of Sicily are characterized as least susceptible to the attractions of Communism; at the same time, their opposition stems from their emotional embrace of the church. Thus "old religious rituals" here become the foundation of "centrist" politics.[11] Here superstition is uncomfortably yoked to the rational project of Free World democracy. The church and the village social structure provide a support system and a surveillance system that defend against the influences of Communism.

Fears that this support system is disintegrating under the pressures of modern life become the concluding theme of this program. The documentary closes by following the progress of a young Sicilian headed to the northern industrial cities of Italy in search of work. As we see him bidding farewell to his family and crowding into a trainload of "others like him," we are told that these transplanted Sicilians are "the chief target of the Communists." We see young men, families, and children racing northward into the embrace of the Communists. Niccolo is met at the station by another Sicilian émigré who whisks him off to the Communist club. Explains the narrator: "These are islands of warmth for the southerner. Here he can talk and hear his own dialect. Here he can find what he badly needs: the lesson of experience in others, advice, even leadership. The sort of help he might have received from his parish priest at home. For the southerner can bring his family with him, but his priest stays at home." Thus in mass society, in which the individual feels increasingly anonymous, the party is providing the cultural and political network that positions him in relation to others. Once again, New Frontier discourse must strain to mediate contradictory documentary evidence, for it is the industrialization of the Free World that is breaking the bonds of identity and tradition in order to produce material prosperity and emotional poverty. Meanwhile it is the Communist Party that offers the individual a sense of identity and participation. In order to manage this seeming paradox, the narrator once again marshals images of subversion and infiltration. Things are not as they appear, the narrator explains. The social embrace of the Communist Party is superficial and insincere. Behind the facade, the party leadership is working to exploit the needs of the individual.

In the program's concluding scene we watch a procession of peace demonstrators marching into the hills outside an Italian city as the narrator informs us that the Communists have infiltrated this peace network and are attempting to turn it to their own advantage. Although we cannot pick out the Communists among the demonstrators and although there seems to be nothing amiss, the scene embodies the clandestine nature of the Communist threat in Italy, for here again, the aspirations for fulfillment of basic human needs are turned to the advantage of the party. The narrator concludes:

> There are lessons to be learned in Italy: that prosperity doesn't necessarily defeat Communism; that an increased standard of living creates demands for still more; and that Communism is prepared to exploit dissatisfaction; that economics are not enough. Yet if the Communists have succeeded in Italy, they have also failed. They have not convinced the majority of Italians. They have not won Italy. They probably never will. For in these hills is the birthplace of Western man. Here were written the first laws. Here man achieved peaks of thought and expression seldom ever equaled. Here was the Renaissance. All these things are in every Italian, even in the Italian Communist. Perhaps it is what makes him so remarkable a comrade.

In essence, if there is hope for the Free World alliance in Italy, it is hope that is based on this legacy of Renaissance rationalism and republican Roman law. The Communists may infiltrate and exploit, but the best hope for freedom is based on liberal principles. Like the countries of the Third World, Italy must hold fast to these if it is to ward off the threat of Communist subversion, for deep within, each individual harbors similar aspirations, and each society will inevitably develop in response to these needs unless that process of change is derailed or skewed by Communist infiltrators.

Armed Conflict

Although popular political unrest, as described in the preceding section, was common throughout the Free World, "brushfire wars" were the exclusive province of the "underdeveloped" nations of the Western alliance. In these countries many years of smoldering unrest finally had exploded into an armed conflagration. Since Communist involvement was always suspected, finding the source of the spark was as important as containing the spread of the flames. Accordingly, the departure point for programs such as NBC's "Angola: Journey to a War" was to inquire first about the prospect of Communist influence.[12]

The program opens with a shot of a missionary sitting on a riverbank talking with a reporter about the system of labor exploitation in Angola. The setting is tranquil and pastoral. Yet this equanimity is disturbed not only by the missionary's graphic description of exploitation but by the quiet intrusion of a black man paddling a white passenger downstream in the background of the frame. As the missionary continues to speak, the camera follows the canoe as it slips off into the distance. Like the documentaries discussed earlier, the image reminds us of the recurring aphorism that Communism is most attractive to those who live in societies that have resisted political reform and economic modernization.

Angola is therefore a logical candidate for political unrest; indeed, the Portuguese colonizers claim that they are battling rebels who are inspired by and equipped by Communist subversives. On the other hand, indigenous rebel leaders claim the issue is not Communism but colonialism. Angola is one of the few remaining colonies in Africa, and many nations, including the United States, have sided against a recalcitrant Portuguese regime that even refuses to allow a United Nations fact-finding mission inside the country. As unrest throughout the country has mounted, the Portuguese have kept strict control over the flow of information. Therefore, the audience "hook" for this program is to offer the viewer a privileged view of a conflict that may have serious repercussions for the Free World. Indeed, NBC touts the value of the documentary at the very outset by showing footage of its reporters testifying before a United Nations tribunal about the conditions they found during their travels on both sides of the battle lines. Their expertise and empirical

Rebel soldiers in "Angola: Journey to a War."

research are positioned as politically neutral, a substitute for a United Nations investigation.

The program turns first to the visually documented findings of reporter Robert Young, who ventured behind rebel lines and traveled from village to village inspecting the traces of warfare. Speaking in the first person, Young takes us along with him on his journey to the interior where we meet with villagers and observe the conditions of their daily existence. We hear first-person accounts of plantation life, labor exploitation, and the indignities of the colonial system. As with their daily toil, we learn that the odds are stacked against these villagers in their struggle for freedom. For example, we witness a motley brigade of guerrillas shouldering antique rifles as they drill for battle. Young finds no signs of Communist infiltration or indications of Soviet weapons. Instead, he describes an arduous struggle against the Portuguese, and we watch as villagers reenact enemy atrocities and escort us to grave sites of fallen comrades.

Young's narration and the visual imagery present a sympathetic portrait of the Angolans. The villagers appear to be gentle, even naive. We learn of their simple subsistence lifestyle and their economic vulnerability. They welcome Young warmly most everywhere he goes. As he enters one village, however, the chief seems guarded and skeptical. "But when he found out we were Americans," says Young, "everything changed." Much cheering, smiling, and hand shaking then ensues. Americans seem to have a special status among the villagers, representing both political freedom and modern prosperity. "Charley and I found ourselves unwillingly becoming doctors," narrates Young. "Although we never had any previous training for the job, people looked to us to perform miracles. Almost everyone seemed to have some kind of illness." Thus the villagers in this documentary seem to share the fundamental aspirations of all citizens of the Free World, and Americans appear to be at the pinnacle of modern development.

From the other side of the battle lines, Robert McCormick reports from Luanda as one of the first foreign correspondents allowed in by the Portuguese. In the capital city, images of war are displaced by signs of economic growth, prosperity, and racial harmony. Broad modern boulevards bustle with auto and bus traffic. The city of Luanda comes across as a familiar, Western landscape in the heart of Africa. This orderly island of progress, according to McCormick, is built on a stable foundation provided by the Portuguese military. He suggests that the presence of the military helps to mediate among contending forces in what could be a volatile situation. Surveying the military presence in some detail, McCormick accompanies Portuguese soldiers into the bush as they attempt to flush out rebel forces. Yet McCormick's sympathetic portrayal of the colonizers is afforded considerably less airtime, and we return behind rebel lines for concluding scenes in the villages of the guerrillas. Here Young observes teenagers drilling for battle and describes the devastation of local agriculture. Escorted back to the border, he bids farewell to a group of rebels only to learn later that their village was destroyed the next day by Portuguese forces. "It's hard to understand," he reflects, "how good can come out of such evil."

Having looked at both sides and established the facts, the documentary comes to the conclusion that this is indeed an internal civil war and not a part of the superpower struggle. Although the program discourages U.S. involvement, it nevertheless legitimizes American inspection of local conflicts throughout the Free World. It further reserves America's right to intervene should Soviet involvement be detected. Thus superpower struggle remains the fundamental framework for documentary investigation despite the fact that this particular program does not promote the notion of American intervention. At the same time, on a less explicit level, the documentary also suggests a number of other conclusions.

First of all, it rejects colonial notions of progress in the Third World. The Portuguese are wrong because they are colonizers who have not

Fighting with antique rifles, the rebel army shows no traces of Communist infiltration.

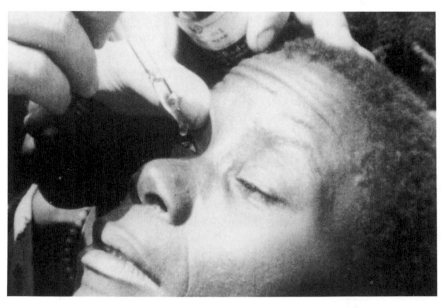

"People looked to us to perform miracles," says NBC correspondent Robert Young.

afforded the Angolans political and economic free choice. They have stifled the natural process of development by frustrating economic and political reforms. Therefore, we should conclude that colonialism is a fundamental violation of the principles of the Free World—despite the fact that Luanda seems more like a modern Western society than the villages of the hinterlands. This apparent contradiction is based on the supposition that, given the chance, the villagers would aspire to the very same goals and lifestyles as other citizens of the Free World.

Second, the documentary suggests the legitimacy of American television networks operating as surveillance or intelligence operations to ferret out the facts about potential Communist infiltration of societies around the globe. In fact, NBC promoted this documentary as a sort of de facto substitute for a United Nations fact-finding mission. Thus it is suggested that journalistic method can uncover objective facts and produce a comparable analysis to that which might have been produced by a multinational panel of United Nations investigators. Cultural and political bias can be contained by scientifically founded procedures.

This faith in economic development and impartial social science also pervades another network documentary of this era, *CBS Reports'* "Vietnam: The Deadly Decision."[13] Produced shortly after the coup that toppled South Vietnamese president Ngo Dingh Diem, the program examines the political instability of a key ally in Southeast Asia. The opening montage features combat footage while voice-over narration talks about an ugly war on the other side of the world. The program then cuts back to the United States, where Senator Wayne Morse declares that Vietnam is not worth the blood of a single American boy. This is juxtaposed with a young woman in Saigon saying she hopes the war gets over as soon as possible, "one way or another." This seeming ambivalence on both sides of the Pacific is then recuperated by the master discourse of the Free World as Madame Nhu, the sister of Vietnam's recently assassinated president, warns that Vietnam will decide the outcome of the third world war. "Tiny little holes can sink a big vessel," she warns. Like the other documentaries of the middle ground, this opening montage suggests that local knowledge is a form of ignorance that may ultimately be fatal, for the destiny of all free citizens is inextricably bound together across vast expanses of the globe. We should care about Vietnam as we should care about Latin America, Italy, or Angola.

Following this opening montage, Charles Collingwood informs us that South Vietnam is now staging its first "free" presidential election in years. On the campaign trail the camera records American secretary of defense Robert McNamara stumping with General Khan, the military leader who seized power in the chaos that followed the assassination of Diem. McNamara, now serving under Lyndon Johnson, pledges military and economic support to Khan should he win the election. Then, in a classic gesture of American politics, he clasps and raises Khan's hand in an exultant victory salute. At the same time, McNamara chants, "Vietnam, mu nam," while the crowd responds with wild enthusiasm.

It would be easy to read this scene as a celebration of democratic process. Here we see Khan engaging in the familiar practices of campaign politics, and we might interpret McNamara's visit as nothing more than a senior political figure campaigning on behalf of a local candidate. Yet this same set of images also raises contradictory questions. Why should an American official campaign in a foreign election as if he were stumping for a local candidate? And why is he clasping hands with a military figure who seized power in a most undemocratic fashion? In fact, what distinguishes Khan from Castro?

Turning to early newsreel footage and historical analysis, the first part of the documentary attempts to negotiate such contradictions. In this footage, Vietnam is represented as a complex environment in which the only constant is the threat of Communist infiltration. The United States inherited the situation from the French, and like the French it now maintains control over much of the country through modern weapons and airpower. But the Vietcong, with backing from Eastern bloc allies, have developed guerrilla warfare techniques that make it difficult to stabilize the country. They have "mastered the art of disappearing," we are told, a reference that resurrects the motif of Communist infiltration. Collingwood explains to the viewer that "the United States got into South Vietnam through the best of motives," but with each crisis it has grown more deeply encumbered. For a while President Diem seemed to provide necessary leadership so that South Vietnam could make it on its own. But Diem's popularity sagged and with it the prospects for holding the line against Communism. In an interview, McNamara says that unlike Diem, Khan has potential as a strong leader who can turn back the tide of Communist infiltration and subversion.

Yet leaders of democratic societies can only be as strong as the support of their followers, so midway through the program we are transported to the countryside, the Mekong Delta, where CBS correspondent Peter Kalisher interviews an American military adviser. While the duo is strolling through a hamlet and mingling with local residents, the adviser explains the strategic importance of winning over the villagers. He says this is largely a matter of appearing as a strongman who is going to provide protection. Furthermore, he claims it is a matter of learning their language, drinking tea with them, and sharing watermelons. "It's gonna be the man who can give them the most, or show them that he can support them better, that will win their confidence and win their support. As you know, it's the man who can get the support of this farmer who will eventually win this war." Thus the villagers appear as friendly but uncertain about their political allegiances. The major question this documentary probes is whether the South Vietnamese people have the will or the desire to fight off the aggression of the Vietcong, for the enemy's ability to disappear hinges on the support or indifference of these very villagers. Speaking in direct address, correspondent Kalisher says the United States has written a blank check for the Vietnamese, but it takes desire to win, and they have yet to demonstrate such desire. "The countryside is out of tune with the cities, the population with the government," he says. Therefore Washington has decided, according to Kalisher, that General Khan "is our only chance."

Returning to Collingwood, the documentary then turns to those modern techniques that might reconfigure the attitudes of Vietnamese citizens. He contends that social scientific expertise is playing a more prominent role in this war than in any other war to date, shaping the psychological, social, and economic forces at work in Vietnam. As in other documentaries discussed in this chapter, the masses are characterized as malleable, ignorant, and in need. It is important to fight not just the Vietcong but also the social conditions and political naiveté that sustain their insurrection. For example, the camera takes us to a prison camp where inmates are being taught new job skills in the hope they will not go back to the Vietcong after they are released. Thus modern rehabilitation programs attempt to remake the individual according to political imperatives.

The documentary also describes how the technologies of surveillance are being applied in a war zone with no recognizable battlefronts and against an enemy who often is not in uniform. On a visit to the Mekong Delta, we learn the government controls only 15 percent of this crucial agricultural region, the "rice bowl" of Vietnam. Here the fear of infiltration is palpable. Enemy explosives can strike anywhere, anytime. As a result, the United States has encouraged the government to relocate villagers to "strategic hamlets" with controllable perimeters, hamlets that look somewhat like prison camps. We are told, however, that this rational solution is being resisted by a people whose backward cultural disposition makes them cling to their traditional family homes. Like other moments of this documentary, the program struggles to reconcile the pragmatic actions of U.S. officials with principles of liberty and human dignity that serve as foundational distinctions between East and West.

Indeed, the program itself comments on these contradictions in a concluding roundtable discussion among CBS correspondents in which Peter Kalisher characterizes American ambitions most bluntly: "Our position here is we don't want South Vietnam. Cold-bloodedly, we don't care what happens here so long as the Communists don't get it and with it Southeast Asia. Now the way to get that is by increasing the living standard of the people. But that I think perhaps is secondary. What we want to do is deny this to the Communists."

In a nation where people are uncertain about their political affinities, U.S. policy makers are employing social scientific expertise in order to remake the popular ambitions of the South Vietnamese. This is done not because of a commitment to the Vietnamese people but because of a U.S. commitment to fight monolithic Communism wherever it threatens to expand its sphere of influence. Unlike Italy, where Western traditions provide a bulwark against Communism, Vietnam must be modernized and Westernized if it is not to fall into the Communist camp. The key obstacle confronting policy makers is that the otherness of the Vietnamese people—their traditions (the women do not dress like Jackie Kennedy), their suspicions (they do not trust social engineers), and their unpredictable political allegiances (all they want is protection by a strongman)—requires that they be remade into modern citizens of the Free World. We are told that Vietnam is the laboratory for developing new techniques for fighting Communist inroads in the Third World. Yet the irony is that "our" noble ends have justified the strategic use of surveillance and control techniques similar to those used behind the Iron Curtain. In South Vietnam, the individual has been rendered the subject of foreign, centralized power. Furthermore, the economy is propped up by subsidies and favoritism. Here, on one of the key battlegrounds of the Free World, the principles of democratic politics and free-market economics have been severely compromised. Although clearly supportive of U.S. global leadership, the program's narrative framework struggles to mediate and contain the contradictions suggested by the documentary evidence.

In sum, documentaries of the middle ground confronted a complex set of tasks. First, they had to examine the conditions that marked a particular country as a society in crisis and therefore worthy of the viewer's attention. Next, these documentaries had to reconcile the "foreignness" of each specific society—its difference—with the similarities among countries within the community of the Free World. Thus the otherness of these societies had to be recognized but distinguished from the radical otherness of countries behind the Iron Curtain. In order to care about foreign allies, the viewer had to feel somehow connected to the fate of citizens throughout the Free World.

This aspect of New Frontier documentaries reminds us of sociologist Philip Schlesinger's contention that national cultures are ongoing sites of contestation over the boundaries that define the nation itself. A process of inclusion/exclusion is therefore constantly at work in modern cultural texts and artifacts.[14] His argument can logically be extended to explain the ways in which network documentaries attempted to define the community of the Free World during the post-Sputnik era. These programs repeatedly move back and forth between concrete particularities and global abstractions in an effort to map the boundaries of community and the geography of superpower struggle. As we have seen, the fit between these various levels of analysis was often unstable, if not contradictory. Consequently, the methodology of empirical documentation often clashed with the interpretive abstractions of New Frontier internationalism. This conflict can be understood as a tension between the real and the ideal as well as between the local and the global. But as we shall observe in succeeding chapters, it was also a product of conflicts between the political agenda of the New Frontier and the institutional practices of television news.

Chapter Five

Television News Comes of Age

In March 1959 a special committee of top CBS executives issued a report to the board of directors regarding the network's public image. In light of numerous federal investigations into broadcast industry practices, the committee concluded, "CBS should undertake a strong and continuing public relations campaign with one general objective: to counteract and, if possible, to overcome the impression that its management does not *care* enough about any of its responsibilities except making a profit."[1] This campaign was designed to influence television critics, regulators, and the general public at a time when the industry was undergoing the image crisis described in chapters 1 and 3.

Chief among the committee's recommendations was a shift to the "magazine" concept of advertising, which would allow the network to assume greater control over program content and scheduling. Such control, it was reasoned, would allow the network to balance its commercial and public service responsibilities more effectively. As part of its public service efforts, the report also recommended a new series of program offerings by "one of CBS's most valuable public relations assets," the news division.[2] Most prominently, it advised the network to develop a flagship news program scheduled for midweek during evening prime time. Initially, the program was to be produced on a monthly basis with the intention that it become a weekly venture as soon as possible. This strategy was designed to counter public criticism that informational programming was relegated to the cultural ghetto of Sunday afternoons, but just as important, it was aimed at restoring "the unchallenged initiative and leadership of CBS News in the television news field."[3]

In the hallways of the network, the committee report marked the first official acknowledgment that a prime-time documentary series bearing the network moniker would become the centerpiece of CBS's renewed commitment to public service.[4] It was hoped that the column inches of newsprint devoted to the new program might serve as an antidote to daily press coverage of everything from radio payola to network antitrust complaints. The report expressed a deep concern about the industry's image crisis coming from the very highest levels of the network hierarchy and made it apparent that *CBS Reports* was the child of corporate planning from its very inception.[5]

Clearly, then, CBS had good reason to turn to its news division at this particular moment both because of the industry image crisis and because of its expanding business interests overseas. Yet we still must consider the intervening institutional forces that mediated the relationship between political economy and cultural artifact. I do not wish to suggest that these programs were merely a reflection of elite interests. Nor do I wish to argue that a conspiratorial cohort of corporate leaders issued marching orders to the news managers of the major networks. Rather, we must understand why broadcast executives *and* news workers saw the escalation of network documentary production as working in their particular interest and therefore sought to articulate their objectives with the project of the New Frontier.

The first part of this chapter therefore examines the forces at work within each network news division. The late 1950s and early 1960s were a period of rapid growth in television news, and we will explore the role that documentary played in this transition. Our analysis will then turn to the peculiar status of the network documentary itself. In an era that valorized science and expertise, documentary was the product of television's professionals. This is what made it so attractive to network executives, government officials, and television critics. But what was the nature of this professionalism? And why did network news workers presume the exclusive right to analyze the great issues confronting the Free World? The latter part of this chapter examines the conventions of documentary journalism as described by those who produced, those who commissioned, and those who criticized the programs. This discourse reveals profound contradictions between the genre's aspiration to be methodologically objective yet thoroughly committed to the Cold War agenda of the New Frontier.

CBS News

Corporate commitment to *CBS Reports* emerged at a moment of crisis for the network. Clearly there were problems with the quiz scandals and government inquiries, but there was also intense conflict between top management and the network's leading reporter, Edward R. Murrow. The cancellation of *See It Now* in 1958, television's most widely respected news program, had generated a wave of criticism in the press and among influential Washingtonians. Even worse, Murrow publicly and pointedly lashed out at network policy in a speech to television executives the following October. Arguing that the medium had sacrificed the public interest for corporate profit, Murrow claimed that the American people were poorly informed and generally unprepared to deal with the challenges confronting the nation. Although it is impossible to gauge the effect of the speech, it was cited often by other critics of television and was reprinted in *TV Guide*.[6] Murrow's accusations angered top network officials, and within a year America's most respected newscaster took a "sabbatical" from CBS while the rumor mill ground away with tales of retaliation and intrigue.

If the Murrow incident is any indication, the general morale of the CBS news division was suffering. The problem was compounded by CBS's noticeable slippage in the field of broadcast news. NBC had capitalized on its strong showing at the 1956 political conventions by fashioning a nightly news program around the anchors of its convention coverage, Chet Huntley and David Brinkley. With press attention and ratings momentum on its side, NBC was methodically chipping away at the Tiffany network's vaunted news leadership.

There were other morale problems as well. CBS unquestionably had the strongest stable of network correspondents in the business, among them Howard K. Smith, Charles Collingwood, Walter Cronkite, Charles Kuralt, David Schoenbrun, and Daniel Schorr. Its production staff was similarly endowed with the talents of Fred Friendly, Irving Gitlin, Al Wasserman, Don Hewitt, Fred Freed, Avram Westin, Robert Northshield, and Perry Wolff. In sum, CBS News harbored a remarkable collection of both talent and ego. Sol Taishoff, owner of *Broadcasting* magazine, privately referred to CBS news workers as "the toughest stable of prima donnas in the business."[7] In a similar vein, management consultants hired by CBS noted the often tense and uncooperative atmosphere among the staff.[8]

Both talented and competitive, these news workers found few outlets for their abilities within the television medium. Most were primarily working in radio, and as the prominence of network radio was eclipsed by television, their status within CBS seemed to decline as well. Years of corporate attentiveness to the commercial development of television had focused on entertainment, and by the late 1950s television news remained little more than a broadcast bulletin service. "Serious news" was to be found only occasionally on network television and then only in the cultural ghetto of Sunday afternoon.

Restless for change, the news department became the source of internal dissension within the network organization. "Unquestionably," wrote the CBS special committee, "the ideas which many of our articulate critics form about CBS and about broadcasting are based in part on conversations with, and statements and speeches by, our newsmen, and to some extent producers and directors."[9] Whenever the network found itself under public attack for its lackluster "public service" performance, it could count on little allegiance from within. Commenting on one case of damaging information leaked to a newspaper reporter, CBS news chief Sig Mickelson wrote in a memo to Frank Stanton that "someone from within the organization [had] been fanning the flames."[10]

Therefore the network's decision to explore new options for news and information programming must be seen as a response to internal as well as external pressures. News workers were taking advantage of the network's vulnerability to advance their own cause. And CBS executives hoped to address this discontent with their plans for expanded documentary programming. Instead of a warmed-over version of Edward R. Murrow's *See It Now,* it is significant that CBS brass envisioned a program that would showcase the abundance of talent within the news division in a national, prime-time format. Both Mickelson and Stanton made it clear that the new series might include the participation of Murrow, but the program was primarily intended to open opportunities for other news workers as well. This was not to be Murrow's program; rather, it was designed as a showcase for the brightest talents within the news division.[11]

Pressure to expand news hours on the television schedule came from other sources as well. CBS originally had built its broadcast news reputation on international coverage, most specifically the war in Europe during the 1930s and 1940s. In the television era, news executives hoped to maintain their reputation for global coverage. In 1959 CBS News followed President Eisenhower to New Delhi for what it claimed was the first American television coverage of breaking news from Asia. Later that year, CBS stockholders were informed of the television network's commitment to "bring world-wide events into the American home."[12]

This, however, required more than a short-term reallocation of resources. Times had changed. Radio news gathering had been based on the premise of live coverage and personal initiative. By deploying a single reporter to the scene of an unfolding news event, the networks required little more than a phone call in order to receive and retransmit information, description, and analysis.

Television news gathering was an entirely different affair. Now network coverage required the deployment of entire crews and thousands of pounds of equipment in order to report from remote locations. Live television coverage was clearly the most labor and capital intensive, but even short film reports for the evening news required extensive logistical planning. Moreover, television demanded the standardization of such collective labor. This involved more than editorial control over the spoken word; it also demanded the development of visual conventions of representation. Boundaries for news photography had to be established so as to eliminate the idiosyncratic. For television news film to look "real," it had to be highly conventionalized in a manner that deemphasized the constructed nature of the visual image. News film from one crew had to be shot so that it could be edited together with footage shot by other crews. Furthermore, network news organizations had to synchronize the shipment, processing, and editing of news film. Film that was shot during the day had to be ready for broadcast before its news value expired at midnight. Thus the visual dimension of broadcast news gathering imposed a whole new set of logistical and economic demands on the networks. In 1956 a CBS management consultant recommended that the network establish quantitative measures of performance, implement quality control checks, and apply the "production methods and philosophies of Hollywood."[13] Both CBS and NBC had been slowly moving in this direction since the early 1950s.[14] But both moved slowly because the costs were high, and it became clear that a limited number of television news programs could not justify the tremendous investment necessary to set up such an international news-gathering operation.[15]

Yet as CBS's growing news film operation gathered momentum in the late 1950s, it began to move the news division toward a more formal and hierarchical structure. The cumbersome organizational logistics of visual news were replacing the more loosely structured relationships that obtained during the days of radio reporting. The "Murrow boys," who achieved their fame reporting from the far-flung hot spots of the Second World War, often operated in a relatively independent fashion, and their news analyses were marginally influenced by the editorial oversight of superiors. In fact, most of the time their reports were broadcast live in their entirety. On the other hand, television news placed a premium on standardized, prerecorded, and edited material. Television news organizations therefore required tighter management controls in order to facilitate the integration of their increasingly global operations.

The mission of the network news operation was changing as well. News always had been financed at CBS as sustaining programming. That is, the budget for the news division was based on a percentage of the overall operating budget of the network. News generated some revenues on its own, but the overall income from commercial programming was used, in part, to subsidize the public information mission of the news division. In 1958 CBS shifted the designation of news from a "staff operation" to an "operating division." With this change came the presumption that news would be judged like any other operating division. That is, news now was expected to generate a positive cash flow.[16]

With these developments in mind, CBS news management sought to utilize its news-gathering potential most efficiently. In a presentation to network executives in 1960, news chief Sig Mickelson reasoned that since the news-gathering infrastructure represented a relatively fixed cost, an increasing use of those facilities by more news programs could reduce the fixed cost per show. Mickelson pointed out that more than a third of his division's budget was devoted to infrastructure. Thus, he argued that an expanded schedule of news and documentary programming would be a more efficient utilization of these fixed costs.[17] In other words, the intensive investment required by international news coverage demanded that the costs be spread across a greater number of programming hours in order to recoup a greater share of fixed costs. It might have been logical to expand the nightly newscast, yet local affiliates objected to network attempts to expand further the significant amount of airtime they already controlled. Consequently, the networks did not move to a half-hour news program until 1963. Another option would have been to expand the number of news hours during off-peak periods in the schedule. And yet, such a strategy would not bring in the sorts of revenues that the news division needed in order to operate in the black. As a result, the best alternative seemed to be an expansion of news programs during prime evening hours.

While CBS apparently adopted this logic, Mickelson was not the one to implement it. As if to emphasize the network's commitment to reorganizing the news division and making it more competitive, Mickelson was fired reportedly because of sagging ratings. Fingers were pointed primarily at the 1960 presidential campaign coverage, in which CBS took a drubbing from NBC. Top brass at CBS allegedly were disturbed by the continuing slide of the news division's reputation. Shortly after the election, Mickelson was replaced by Richard Salant, who moved over from his post as corporate vice president for legislative and political affairs. The number two slot in news went to Blair Clark. Unlike

Mickelson, neither Salant nor Clark had any television news experience; both were outsiders. Perhaps it was reasoned that their detachment from the egos and infighting of the news division would be an asset. But Salant's close ties to Capitol Hill did not go unnoticed, nor did the fact that Clark was reputed to be a friend of FCC chairman Newton Minow's and a Harvard classmate of JFK's.[18] Many attributed these appointments to increasing regulatory oversight, but it is just as important to note that both men were well connected to Washington news sources at a time when network news was growing more competitive. With both prestige and profitability of the news division at stake, CBS may have been seeking to improve its access to government news makers.

Moreover, at the time of the shake-up, it was reported in the trade press that Paley and Stanton were on the "warpath" over ratings and earnings. They not only wanted news, they wanted "numbers." According to widely circulating rumors, they even considered putting the news division under the purview of James Aubrey Jr., president of the television network. Aubrey was known for his insensitivity to matters of content or "quality," and his fixation on ratings and profitability was legendary. According to accounts in the trade press, Paley and Stanton balked at the appointment of Aubrey only because it would create organizational problems. Reportedly, it would have been difficult to place the news division, which served both television and radio, under the direction of the television network's president.[19] Nevertheless, CBS brass made it clear that they would not tolerate the recent slide in news ratings.

As they began to revamp the news division, one of the things that worried top executives at CBS was the stuffy image of its reporters. In a comparative analysis commissioned by the network, researchers found that audience respondents in key consumer groups were attracted to the more spritely pacing and irreverent commentary offered in the *Huntley-Brinkley Report*. They also related their perception that NBC had a more extensive news-gathering operation because of the greater number of remote reports, both live and on film.[20] Thus, for CBS to reverse such perceptions and regain its news leadership would require a major retooling of both news programming and news-gathering operations. As part of the organizational shake-up, CBS established regional news bureaus across the country, more than doubled its news budget, and expanded the hours of nighttime news and public affairs by 40 percent.[21]

The flagship of this network effort, however, was to be the prestigious *CBS Reports* series. Despite indications that its convention coverage and its nightly news were lacking, there was no doubt that CBS held the high ground in documentary. Thus the commitment to *CBS Reports* involved more than a response to public criticism, government regulation, or network expansion overseas. It also was part of a larger network strategy to improve staff morale, expand television news coverage, and make effective use of excess production capacity in the news and public affairs division. Furthermore, the network pinned its hopes on the possibility that documentary could develop as a money-making genre with broad audience appeal.

NBC News

NBC's emerging claim to news leadership grew out of its 1956 convention coverage featuring Chet Huntley and David Brinkley. Capitalizing on the popularity of the anchor team, the network fashioned a nightly news program that steadily grew in ratings and sponsor appeal during the latter part of the 1950s.[22] This same duo improved on its convention performance in 1960, when NBC attracted more than half the audience for the Republican and Democratic conventions. Such an accomplishment was, in the words of NBC chairman Robert Sarnoff and NBC president Robert Kintner, "unmistakable proof of the emergence of NBC News as broadcasting's foremost news organization."[23]

Building on this momentum, NBC set out to increase the number of public affairs offerings and announced a special series of documentaries featuring solo performances by Huntley and Brinkley.[24] Not satisfied to challenge CBS solely in the domain of breaking news coverage, NBC news now was expanding on all fronts. By 1961 NBC announced that advertising time for all of its informational programming, including documentary, was sold out for the upcoming season. It now claimed to be number one in sponsor appeal, and that same season revenues were projected to reach $28.6 million, putting the news division several million dollars in the black.[25] This announcement was a marked departure from the sustaining tradition of network news organizations. And just as surprising, NBC management made it clear that its horizon of expectations was still growing. Profits from the news operation were to be plowed back into *further* expansion, especially in the areas of news interpretation and analysis.[26] Such a remarkable transition in such a short span of time bears careful consideration. The ratings success of the Huntley-Brinkley anchor team clearly justified a major commitment to live news coverage and regular nightly news programming. But why would the network make such an expansive commitment to documentary production when it was nightly news that was generating all the excitement?

First of all, NBC's claim to news leadership was more than a prestige issue. Network executives argued that news leadership had the potential to calm restless station managers who were growing impatient with the lackluster ratings performance of NBC's entertainment programming. As we have seen in chapter 3, this was not a minor consideration. By the late 1950s, ABC was challenging the ratings dominance of the two leading networks in the area of entertainment programming. Overall, NBC was more susceptible to this challenge, since it consistently ran second behind CBS in the national Nielsens. Furthermore, NBC felt pressured by ABC's campaign to lure VHF affiliates away from the peacock network in markets where ABC either had no affiliate or an underperforming UHF affiliate. Some NBC affiliates were intrigued by such enticements, since ABC could demonstrate that the performance of its entertainment programming often outstripped NBC in major metropolitan markets where the two networks competed on equal terms. A loss of even a few key affiliates could seriously hamper NBC's national ratings while significantly enhancing the fortunes of its competitor.

NBC responded to this challenge by distinguishing itself as a network with "balanced" programming and a tradition of significant public service. In a keynote speech at an affiliates' convention, NBC chairman Robert Sarnoff dismissively referred to ABC as a "narrow gauge" network with little to offer beyond its action/adventure fare.[27] The architect of NBC's counteroffensive was network president Robert Kintner, an executive whose thinking about television news would be an important force from the late 1950s through the mid-1960s. Although Kintner was truly a "news junkie" who assiduously advanced the cause of informational programming, he was no stranger to the commercial imperatives of network programming. Kintner's first commitment at NBC was not in the area of news but in the realm of prime-time entertainment. Here he was known as an aggressive programmer who was profoundly aware of the commercial implications of his every maneuver. This awareness grew from Kintner's earlier experiences as president of ABC when the network first hatched its plans to develop a steady schedule of action/adventure telefilm. Despite the commercial success of that strategy, Kintner left the network in 1956 as the result of an internal feud with chairman Leonard Goldenson.[28] Kintner's departure quickly attracted the attention of both NBC's Robert Sarnoff and CBS's Frank Stanton. With offers

NBC president Robert Kintner, a compulsive TV viewer, was tuned to all three networks throughout the working day. (Courtesy of Photofest)

from each, Kintner opted for NBC, according to one confidant, because "he reasoned that CBS had too much executive bench strength and that there was more opportunity at NBC for a new pitcher."[29]

The opportunities at NBC were accompanied by a host of problems, however. Most prominent, the network's entertainment programming was not competitive with front-running CBS. Thus Kintner assiduously applied his action/adventure strategy to program development, a strategy that led to a parade of such profit makers as *Wagon Train* and *Bonanza* at the expense of programs such as *Omnibus* and *Wide World*. Such maneuvers earned Kintner the enmity of critics who referred to him as a "skillful and relentless peddler."[30] Indeed, the new NBC television president was characterized as something of a lowbrow who was known to chide his fellow executives by carping, "[T]he trouble with you guys is you don't watch television."[31]

Kintner, on the other hand, was a compulsive television viewer. In fact, he made a reputation for himself within the industry for having three television sets running simultaneously in his office throughout the workday.[32] Furthermore, he claimed to watch every program on a competitor's schedule at least once each season.[33] Reportedly the same was true for Lucky, Kintner's collie and viewing companion during the boss's evening regimen. In fact, it was a standing joke among NBC executives to ask what Lucky thought of the program schedule the night before. Whatever canine wisdom they may have divined from such repartee, it took little imagination to decipher Kintner's thinking. "We're looking for shows we can sell," Kintner would snarl unabashedly.[34]

Yet it was this same "relentless peddler" who exploited the commercial potential offered by the 1956 Huntley-Brinkley convention coverage. While NBC was dishing up new action/adventure entertainment, it also was revamping its news operation. Wrote Jack Gould:

> The good night kids [Huntley and Brinkley] came along when he needed them most. NBC was nursing a lackluster theatrical image, so Mr. Kintner directed attention to news and public affairs, gave [news vice president William] McAndrew more authority than any other network news head and established corporate morale that permeated all phases of NBC. In television, it may stand as the most striking instance of what can happen in the medium when the top officer has a sense of passionate commitment and uses his power. It's the occasional thing.[35]

While Gould may have been right that Kintner exploited his advantage in news, it is not clear that Kintner's "passionate commitment" would have been so torrid without the ratings to back it up. Nevertheless, Kintner seemed to understand enough about both the entertainment and news aspects of the medium in order to make his formula work. No other network president at the time had such a keen grasp of the news industry as did the NBC chieftain.

This awareness grew out of Kintner's career path, which began with a stint as a newspaper reporter and nationally syndicated columnist during the 1920s and 1930s. He also coauthored two best-selling books with Joseph Alsop, one of which was named *Washington White Paper*. After serving in the War Department Bureau of Public Relations, Kintner changed tracks by joining ABC in 1944 as vice president for programming, public relations, and advertising. He was named network president in 1949, making him a broadcast executive whose experience bridged the worlds of news, public relations, and broadcast entertainment.[36] But in his scramble to the top of the television trade, Kintner never lost his reputed passion for news. Fred Freed, one of NBC's top documentary producers, later lauded Kintner for the extensive resources he made available to his documentary producers, but Freed also cited the intangible moral support that Kintner lavished on his news employees.[37] Kintner paid attention, said Freed:

> The great thing about Bob Kintner was that he watched every documentary program that went on the air. And he told you about every program and whether he liked it or not. He didn't wait until the show was reviewed by Jack Gould in the *Times* to tell you. One of his eccentricities was about the supers that go up on the screen at the bottom of the pictures, telling who the people are. He called them "labels." He wanted them up over everybody. Any producer sitting in the studio as his show went on the air could count on calls from Bob Kintner growling, "Where the hell are the labels?"

Although NBC's news division made most of its money from its nightly news program, Kintner's appetite for different news formats and expanded coverage was not quickly satiated. During this period of rapid growth in television news, NBC management displayed an enthusiasm for informational programming that was unequaled. With the news division's lock on advertiser commitments and its positive cash flow, there seemed no sure bets as to what the future might hold, and Kintner wanted to secure a competitive position for NBC in a period of rapid growth. Thus the development of documentary had to do with an overall network strategy that was tied in with issues of prestige, programming strategy, affiliate loyalties, and a competitive battle for position in the growing arena of television news.

As a result, whenever Kintner talked about the future of television news, he traversed the discourses both of the marketplace and of liberal politics. Even though he was "looking for programs he could sell," Kintner also emphasized his commitment to enlighten the body politic. Here the documentary was considered of prime importance, for Kintner, an ardent Democrat who later left NBC in 1966 to join LBJ's White House staff, never lost faith in what he saw as the documentary's potential. "While I am opposed to editorializing on a network basis," he said, "I am convinced there must be more and more intelligent interpretation, for which a news department must take responsibility, so that complex local, national and international events may be better communicated to the public."[38]

Therefore, in its commitment to build on the momentum of Huntley-Brinkley, NBC management sought to beef up the production staff of its documentary unit. Conscious of morale problems at CBS, Kintner set out to lure away some of his competitors' most talented news workers. The two documentary producers with the hottest reputations in the industry at this time were Irving Gitlin and Fred Friendly. Their competition for resources and recognition at CBS spanned the decade of the 1950s and came to a head in 1959 when the network announced its *CBS Reports* series. According to David Yellin, Gitlin had made it widely known for some time that he wanted to produce a series like *Reports*, and it was assumed by "nearly everyone, including Friendly and especially Gitlin," that Gitlin would be put in charge of the new program.[39] Moreover, Gitlin had just been named head of creative projects at CBS News with supervisory control over programs such as *The 20th Century* and *Face the Nation.* His staff of producers included Burton Benjamin, Perry Wolff, Albert Wasserman, and Fred Freed. It seemed a logical choice to offer Gitlin the program, since his star seemed to be rising at the very moment that the Murrow-Friendly team was clashing with network management. Therefore, when the job was offered to Friendly, Gitlin reportedly "took it quite personally." He quit CBS within a year and quickly was scooped up by Kintner, who made it clear that NBC wanted to compete with CBS head to head in the area of documentary and public affairs.[40]

Gitlin soon was joined by a number of CBS news staffers who saw greater opportunities at NBC as well. Among those making the jump were Wasserman and Freed, both of whom signed on as documentary producers.[41] Thus Kintner had a direct hand in marshaling the talent and logistical support for a flagship documentary series that would bear a title apparently derived from the book he coauthored with Joseph Alsop: *NBC White Paper.* Like its competitor, this new documentary series was not a simple response to the industry image crisis or to RCA's corporate expansion overseas. Rather, its birth was also the product of a complex set of internal dynamics at NBC.

ABC News

By the mid-1950s, both NBC and CBS had committed themselves to a gradual buildup of their television news operations, and the growth of these news organizations escalated rapidly at the end of the decade owing to a convergence of factors. Meanwhile, at ABC the situation was considerably different. News had been a very low priority throughout the 1950s because of the relatively uncompetitive status of the network's entertainment programming. After taking over ABC in 1953, Leonard Goldenson spent most of his time attending to the development of the network's prime-time schedule. Here he showed less concern about "balance" than he did about ratings. It was not until late 1959, amidst charges of rampant commercialism, that Goldenson committed ABC to a substantial increase in the area of informational programming.[42] Yet the resources that were allocated were so meager that one year later ABC News still had only one-fifth as many staffers and one-half as much public affairs programming as its competitors. In fact, during the 1959–1960 season, ABC offered little more than a Sunday schedule of talking heads and an occasional documentary.[43]

Although Goldenson announced his intention to commit greater resources to the news division, the network's sluggish beginning may have been linked to his search for new leadership in the news division. John Daly, then vice president for news, was, like Robert Kintner, a holdover from ABC's previous ownership under Edward Noble. But unlike Kintner, who left in 1956, Daly held on to his post until the end of 1960. As for Goldenson, he seemed content to ignore the news division while focusing his attention on the entertainment schedule. By the end of the decade, however, this strategy was no longer viable, and the power struggle between Goldenson and Daly came to a head.

Controversy over the future of the ABC documentary unit was widely credited as the final straw that hastened Daly's departure. According to newspaper accounts, Daly had been a longtime advocate of "serious" informational programming and was known as a jealous defender of his departmental prerogatives as well. When Goldenson announced in 1960 that ABC was turning to an independent producer in order to purchase a documentary for network prime time, Daly protested that production of such "actuality" programming should exclusively fall under the purview of his division. He contended that only network news professionals could assure a fair and balanced treatment of contemporary social issues. When Goldenson refused to relent, Daly resigned.

There are also indications, however, that Daly may have chosen to resign over this matter of "principle" rather than accept his ouster at the hands of Goldenson.[44] Apparently, the ABC chairman quietly had been courting Daly's replacement for several months. His top choice was James Hagerty, then press secretary to President Dwight Eisenhower. Hagerty had started his career in the media as a stringer for the *New York Times* while enrolled as a history student at Columbia University. Always known for his conservative politics, Hagerty would later describe his early years of news reporting as having been spent opposing the "liberal and radical movement of the mid-30s." After leaving the newspaper trade, Hagerty rose to prominence as Governor Thomas Dewey's press secretary. Later, when Dewey gave up his presidential ambitions, Hagerty jumped on the Eisenhower bandwagon in 1952 and rode it all the way to Pennsylvania Avenue.

The father of two sons, both of whom became officers in the U.S. Marines, Hagerty was an unabashed patriot with explicit faith in American global leadership. Within Eisenhower's White House hierarchy, he was widely considered the third most important staffer, behind Sherman Adams and John Foster Dulles. It was Hagerty who was responsible for orchestrating White House news coverage so as to promote the interests of Eisenhower's foreign policy. Known as a master of "news management," he was roundly criticized by his detractors for "manipulating" the media.[45] Hagerty's deft touch with the media in conjunction with his wealth of Washington connections clearly made him attractive to a television network that needed to appease regulators and repair its public image. At the same time, Hagerty's connections could provide the ABC news division with access to important news makers, for like Kintner and Salant, Hagerty had an entrée to the cloakrooms on Capitol Hill.

Goldenson's courtship of Hagerty made it clear that ABC was no longer going to be satisfied with a second-string news operation. If the network was going to invest the necessary resources to build an international news-gathering operation, Goldenson wanted a potential profit return. Although ABC's revenues had risen dramatically as a result of its entertainment programming, it could not afford to finance expensive news programming on a sustaining basis. At a press conference announcing Hagerty's appointment, ratings and sponsorship were clearly on Goldenson's mind: "It is our intention to make the news and public affairs department competitive . . . whatever that takes."[46]

At first glance it seemed that Goldenson's remarks were framed in terms of his two network competitors. But in the months following Hagerty's appointment, it became clear that Goldenson envisioned his competition in *global* as well as national terms. As a result, Hagerty was an appealing candidate for the top slot at ABC News not only because of his Washington connections but also because of his access to power brokers in capitals around the world. He was characterized as a man who could open markets as well as doors. Indeed, newspaper accounts at the time noted that the former press secretary turned aside an offer to run Coca Cola's international marketing operations in order to take on his new responsibilities at ABC.[47] From the very outset, the international aspect of Hagerty's new job was a key priority for him. Time and again, he predicted worldwide TV in five to ten years via satellite and said this was the principal reason he signed on with ABC.[48] Hagerty also claimed that in the near future the most valuable television reporters would speak several languages and announced that ABC was willing to finance language study for interested news workers.[49] Furthermore, he made it clear that ABC News coverage would pay special attention to Latin America, an area of strategic importance to the United States but also a key element of ABC's overseas expansion strategy.[50] Five months after taking the job, Hagerty held a joint news conference with Leonard Goldenson at which they announced an annual increase in the news and public affairs budget of some 67 percent. Noting the link between ABC's growing news operation and its recent investment in nineteen television stations in foreign markets, ABC chairman Goldenson unequivocally told reporters, "We're getting ready for world-wide TV."[51]

This was the climate in which news became a priority at ABC, and between 1959 and 1961 the network news and public affairs budget more than doubled to $7.63 million.[52] Department growth continued into 1962 along with prophetic pronouncements by the ABC news chief. "Television news," said Hagerty, "as is true of the entire TV industry, is on the brink of scientific progress so startling it will pale by comparison most advancements to date. In about five years, earth encircling communication satellites will bring world-wide television to reality."[53] Hagerty left little doubt that his plans for the news operation were tightly integrated with the larger ambitions of the ABC network. As *Variety*'s George Rosen put it, "[Hagerty] has been building ABC's news operation to meaningful levels of vigor on an expanded worldwide basis, as boss Leonard Goldenson has spearheaded the drive to acquire strategic positions of minority ownership in foreign tv stations."[54]

Although Hagerty expressed his ambitions in terms of market compe-

ABC News chief James Hagerty (opposite) and ABC chairman Leonard Goldenson (above): "We're getting ready for world-wide tv." (Courtesy of Photofest)

tition, he also characterized them in terms of journalistic professionalism. At the same time he promoted global expansion, he also expended a tremendous amount of time and energy refiguring the *image* of ABC News from a ragtag band of "also rans" to a first-rate television news-gathering operation. And the emphasis here was on *news* rather than television. As Hagerty bolstered the staffing of the network's correspondent corps, he openly favored print journalists over "handsome faces and well-modulated voices." Similarly, he stressed the importance of interpretive skills as opposed to a simple recitation of people, places, and events.[55] In testimony before the Federal Communications Commission in 1962, Hagerty claimed to have transformed ABC News into a professional, independent corps of journalists.

> The underlying goal is to present to the American people an ever increasing flow of information and to assist them in understanding better the human events of our times. In pursuit of that goal, we report the news whenever it happens anywhere in the world. We report the hard news of what happened, but we do not fear—indeed we feel we have an obligation—to present the hows and whys of news occurrences through informed analytical and interpretive reporting by experienced members of our news staff and by outside experts who have intimate knowledge of their fields. . . . We are not partisans; we are newsmen practicing our profession, doing our best to bring the truth to our listeners and viewers.[56]

Thus the interpretive and the analytical were characterized by Hagerty as an important mission of television news, and during the early 1960s this mission was most prominently delegated to the prime-time documentary, such as ABC's *Bell and Howell Close-Up!* series. These programs seemed the most likely site for such overtly interpretive work, since evening newscasts of fifteen minutes allowed little time for commentary or analysis and Sunday interview programs, such as *Meet the Press,* largely provided a forum for the views of government officials. By comparison, it was assumed that a thirty- to sixty-minute documentary had the leisure and the resources to produce in-depth analysis of important public issues. And here, ABC, like the other networks, staked a tremendous amount of time and energy during the early 1960s.

Editorial Control

All three networks, then, expanded their documentary efforts dramatically, broadcasting close to four hundred documentaries in 1962 alone. Independent producers also began to produce many documentaries during this period, yet few of them would ever be broadcast on network television.[57] The reasons behind this prohibition are centrally connected to questions of journalistic professionalism. By way of introduction to these issues, it is instructive to consider the experiences of two of the most prolific and influential independent documentary producers of the period, David Wolper and Robert Drew.

Wolper was more than a nonfiction filmmaker; he was an entrepreneur who ran a large, independent production house that produced eight documentaries for the 1961–1962 season alone.[58] Furthermore, Wolper's "Race into Space" (which was produced on film) became the first TV program nominated for an Academy Award, and it drew praise from various critics, among them Jack Gould, who lauded the program for its professionalism.[59] Yet even though it was hailed by critics and by the Hollywood community, the program was rejected for broadcast by all three networks, and Wolper was forced to syndicate the program independently.

The networks might have justified their decision for commercial reasons, arguing that the deal did not make economic sense. Or they might have said it was based on their desire to defend themselves from potential lawsuits that might result from the broadcast of third-party documentaries. Yet neither of these lines of reasoning played a significant role in the controversy that ensued. The debate did not revolve around questions of business judgment, nor was it a matter of safeguarding the airwaves from scandalous behavior. Rather, the networks claimed exclusive prerogative to control access to the public airwaves based on the *professional* judgment of their news personnel. One's right to speak about public issues on television, they argued, should best be regulated by network news professionals.

This debate over access to the public airwaves has troubled commercial broadcasters since the early days of radio in the 1920s. During that time, government regulators chose to organize the radio spectrum as discrete parcels of property that would be entrusted to private interests so that they might develop airwaves both for the public good and for the welfare of their investors. Yet it was the latter group that took control of the nascent medium, and the industry matured under the control of an alliance of broadcasters, manufacturers, and advertisers. As a result, broadcast programming—during both the radio and television eras—developed largely according to principles of the marketplace, and access to the airwaves was largely a matter of commercial viability. Yet legally the airwaves still belonged to the public, and critics of the medium periodically would complain that broadcast audiences were not being served, that the industry only thought of audiences as groups of consumers and paid little attention to their needs as citizens.

Government regulators at the Federal Communications Commission occasionally criticized broadcasters along similar lines. In a series of rulings that became known as the Fairness Doctrine, the FCC encouraged broadcasters to provide a forum for the discussion of important public issues from diverse perspectives. Regulators emphasized the audience's "right to know," but at the same time, the FCC failed repeatedly in its efforts to establish a clear-cut set of standards for determining who should have the right to speak about public issues over the airwaves.[60]

As network documentaries grew in prominence, this very issue became a significant concern. Who should have the right to speak? To whom? And about what? When the networks rejected the Wolper documentary about the space race, their decision was based neither on determinations of quality nor on commercial viability. Rather, it was a question of professionalism. As ABC vice president John Daly wrote in March 1960, "The standards of production and presentation which apply to a professional network news department would not necessarily apply to, for instance, an independent Hollywood producer [such as Wolper]."[61] Despite this seemingly unambiguous declaration, the issue was far from settled, especially at ABC.

Only months later, unbeknownst to Daly, network chieftain Leonard Goldenson tapped the services of independent documentarist Robert Drew, contracting him to produce a documentary about the Communist threat in Latin America. When Daly found out, he was reportedly livid and tendered his resignation from ABC with a dramatic flourish. Although the resignation received quite a bit of coverage in the newspapers, some argued that the real reason for Daly's departure was that he found out Goldenson was aiming to replace him with James Hagerty. Still, it is significant that Daly chose to cloak himself in the mantle of news professionalism as he exited the network. He argued that only network news workers were qualified to select and present public issues in a balanced and responsible manner.[62] Moreover, Daly's appeal to principle was supported by news executives at both CBS and NBC, who, in commenting on Daly's resignation, said it was necessary for news professionals to maintain complete editorial control over the content of all informational programming.[63]

At NBC, Robert Kintner declared that all documentaries were to be produced by the network or under network supervision from beginning to end. He claimed the network could best discharge its public responsibilities by entrusting the analysis of important social issues "to its own staff of professional broadcast newsmen who [were] disciplined to NBC's standards of fairness, balance, and the application of conscientious news judgment; and who [were] directly accountable to the management of the NBC News Department."[64]

Despite such sentiments, ABC's Goldenson went ahead with the Drew project and broadcast "Yanki No!" in December 1960. Goldenson justified the decision by claiming ABC had indeed maintained editorial control from the very outset. Yet control over the documentary was in the hands of neither Daly nor other news professionals. Rather, it was in the hands of top management. Leonard Goldenson, then in the midst of planning the international expansion of his network, claimed personal credit for conceiving the project and commissioning the production crew. Once Drew accepted, ABC executives maintained close involvement throughout. *Variety* wrote, "Goldenson is reportedly active in scrutinizing both topic and product by the outside producer—frequently suggesting, accepting and rejecting material." In fact, Goldenson cabled suggestions for the program to Drew while on a tour of fourteen Latin American markets where ABC was pursuing its expansion plans. He even took personal care to oversee both the scripting and editing of the program.[65] As we saw in chapter 4, the final product was deeply contradictory, with narration and actuality film footage often generating opposing sets of meanings. The narrator cautions against the charismatic attractions of Fidel, while the film footage documents the rapid progress made by peasants after the revolution. Throughout the program, one senses the heavy hand of ABC management molding the documentary to make the case for a more active foreign policy to take on the challenge from Fidel and make Latin American markets safe for American free enterprise.[66]

In many ways, "Yanki No!" proved to be the limit case of network documentary, both because of the controversy about independent production and because of network management's direct intervention in the program itself. "Yanki No!" stretched the boundaries of news professionalism. Nevertheless, critics hailed the program's visual appeal and commented extensively on its cinema verité style.[67] It was argued that Drew's work broke dramatically with the conventions of network documentary up to that time, conventions based on the written word and the talking head. Although some reviewers expressed reservations about the "impassioned" or "emotional" appeal of the program, most saw it as a welcome departure from the norm.[68] Marie Torre of the *New York Herald Tribune* wrote, "Perhaps the other networks would do well this morning to reopen the question of whether public affairs presentations should be kept under the sole purview of the network itself."[69]

Such reconsideration never came to pass, however. Rather than seeing ABC as a trendsetter, executives at other networks saw it as something of an aberration, a product of ABC's unique circumstances. As pointed out earlier, the establishment of a global news-gathering operation was both expensive and time consuming, and many saw that ABC's tiny staff was at a distinct disadvantage during this era of rapid growth.[70] For that reason, competing news organizations may have muted their criticism as ABC commissioned documentaries by Drew and Wolper on several occasions over the next few years. Yet once James Hagerty came on board in early 1961, ABC's policy started to move in the same direction as the other networks. This change probably resulted from three things. First, Hagerty's stature became intertwined with the fortunes of the news division. For Goldenson to go around him to commission independent productions or for Goldenson to protest that the division was incapable of producing significant work would have been contradictory. ABC had gone to great lengths to recruit Hagerty and was therefore committed to enhancing the status of the news department. Second, as the network committed more resources to news, the department became more dependent on commercial sponsors. In order to attract these sponsors, ABC had to tout the quality and professionalism of its news staff. Finally, the network confronted severe recruitment problems. If James Hagerty was to entice talented news workers to join ABC, he would have to guarantee them the status and autonomy that was comparable to what they enjoyed with other news organizations. This was no small consideration.

At the time, the demand for qualified television news employees was far outstripping supply, and as expansion plans at all three networks picked up, the demand for correspondents and documentary producers exploded. Even before ABC entered the competition, *Variety* noted, "There just aren't enough good men around toiling in the pubaffairs vineyards and it's not exactly a secret that a Sig Mickelson or a Bill McAndrews have to beg, borrow or steal to fill the shortages and gaps in the 'real world' kingdoms they operate at CBS and NBC."[71] Consequently, contracts of reporters as well as producers grew more generous as the networks competed for their services.[72] Not only were they now in demand, but they also were considered the elite corps of broadcast news professionals, those to whom the networks would entrust the right to inquire, to document, and to interpret. But what did it mean to refer to these network employees as professionals?

Richard Salant, the new president of CBS News, probably described the core of this professional identity in early 1961 when defending the network against criticism lodged by the American Medical Association regarding a *CBS Reports* documentary, "The Business of Health." Salant claimed that the network stood by the program as the "product of experienced and professional journalists." These employees spent an entire year researching the medical industry, analyzing the evidence, and editing the film. He endorsed their efforts, claiming that, much like an umpire at a baseball game, the television documentarist must render "his close and objective decisions" without regard to personal preference or the special pleadings of the opposing sides.[73]

In essence, the broadcaster's right to interpret and represent issues of societal concern was based on a professional code of objectivity. Although today the concept is treated with greater skepticism, in the early 1960s the term was widely used by journalists and seems to have been considered much less problematic. Moreover, this faith in objectivity was linked to the resurgent enthusiasm for scientific method and professional expertise in the post-Sputnik era. As a result, the concept deserves careful consideration if we are to understand the meanings that these documentaries circulated, for objectivity, the core of documentary methodology, generated a whole array of audience expectations and extratextual meanings. It also imposed a set of demands on the news workers themselves. Producers were expected to devote a substantial amount of time to research and to be less driven by the conventions of deadline journalism. Documentarists were also expected to search beyond the world of press conferences and official sources, to capture first-person accounts of the impact of major social issues. As we saw in chapter 4, these notions of professionalism sometimes resulted in documentaries that conflicted with the agenda of groups that initially promoted the expansion of the genre. Government and corporate leaders, as well as top network officials, all saw documentary as playing an instrumental role in the education and motivation of viewers throughout the Free World. All assumed that the outcomes of such journalistic endeavors would be relatively unambiguous.

This contradiction between documentary objectivity and internationalist activism manifests itself in many of the programs from this period, especially those that focused on political unrest along the frontiers of the Free World. But this tension between objectivity and activism is not unique to the early sixties and should be placed in a larger historical context. The rest of this chapter traces the development of American notions of journalistic professionalism and relates them to the television documentary of the early 1960s.

The Discourse of Objectivity

The concept of objectivity in news reporting first emerged in the United States in connection with the development of a penny press in the first half of the nineteenth century. Scholars have noted that the sale of newspapers to a growing middle class required that journalistic accounts not be tied to the particular interests of specific groups but to the greater public interest.[74] Consequently, market considerations played a formative role in creating an independent press tradition in the United States.

Dan Schiller further points out that notions of an independent press were intertwined with a growing societal fascination with positivism and science. By suggesting that journalism was in some sense scientific, one implied not only that newspapers should be autonomous but that reporters should operate according to a particular methodology. If they did so, human beings might be able to discern the essential mechanisms by which society functioned. It was for precisely this reason that publisher James Gordon Bennett proudly boasted allegiance to "truth, public faith, and science" on the masthead of his popular *New York Herald*.[75] Yet Bennett's understanding of science, like that of others during this period, probably focused on the principles of description and categorization. Facts were collected and placed in categories in the hope that such procedures would reveal natural laws at work. Scientific method was less a matter of hypothesis and experimentation than an attempt to gather together a collection of facts that might reveal a natural order.

However, the collection of facts often rendered inadequate explanations. Facts did not always seem to speak for themselves, and by the latter part of the century, as the writings of Darwin and Spencer began to capture the public imagination, attention shifted from the collection of facts to the connection of facts. There emerged a new emphasis on the theorization of relationships and the testing of hypotheses. Thus an objective methodology became more important than ever before.[76] This was not only true in the laboratory but, by the turn of the century, in other areas as well, among them the field of journalism.[77]

Ironically, journalism was also growing more politically committed at the very same moment. Herbert Gans contends that many of the leading figures in the Progressive movement were journalists who obscured the partisan nature of their politics by articulating it to core notions of science and expertise. They promoted notions of professionalism and expertise as the means to investigate and eradicate societal ills.[78] The newspaper was to play a crucial role in both educating the public and invoking its support for reform. As Robert Wiebe points out, the Progressive was skeptical about the untutored wisdom of the people. But by disseminating the insights gained through expert analysis, the Progressive demonstrated faith in the infinite educability of the citizen.[79]

Moreover, this mission to investigate, to expose, and to enlighten had an international dimension as well. Wiebe contends that the Progressive campaign, which began at the local level, shifted to the national level and culminated in a campaign to "make the world safe for democracy." United States participation in World War I was, for many Progressives, a logical outgrowth of their political beliefs.[80] If anything, the war laid bare the irrational nature of events leading up to the conflict and beckoned the introduction of expertise and democratic choice into the affairs among nations.

It was in this context that American journalism fostered an objective methodology that could get at the truth and activate reform. However, these two principles coexisted in an uneasy relationship. One implied a reverence for the objective and the empirically specific, whereas the other promoted advocacy and universalism. This is precisely the recurring tension that we observed in so many network documentaries of the middle ground. Thus it is important to recall that the foundations of journalistic practice were rooted in both a method and a movement. Although we shall explore this tension more completely in the next part of this chapter, it should be noted that method was usually given priority. American journalists have tended to see themselves less often as political advocates than as professional practitioners.[81] According to Michael Schudson, this was especially true during the period of the network documentary boom.

> By the 1960s, both critics of the press and its defenders took objectivity to be the emblem of American journalism, an improvement over a past of "sensationalism" and a contrast to the party papers of Europe. Whether regarded as the fatal flaw or the supreme virtue of the American press, all agreed that the idea of objectivity was at the heart of what journalism has meant in this country.[82]

Therefore, when television documentary emerged as part of the professional news-reporting mission of the major networks, it was greatly influenced by print journalism's concept of objectivity. In essence, this concept suggested that facts could be separated from values; findings could be independently validated; and personal preferences could be marginalized.[83]

These seem to be the principles that guided television critic Marie

Torre when she reviewed "Trujillo: Portrait of a Dictator," a production of *CBS Reports* broadcast in March 1960: "Reporter Bill Leonard, who spent two months on the Caribbean island, tackled the story with a probing eye, an open mind, and an economy of words. That is, questions were posed more often than opinions were formulated. . . . The result was an objective study of the Dominican Republic and the man who runs it."[84] Torre's review treats the program as an empirically based analysis that is free of personal prejudice in its methodology and style of presentation. This, however, does not completely foreclose the possibility that Leonard would formulate opinions. Indeed, Leonard chose the term *dictator* to describe an American ally, the leader of the Dominican *Republic*. He therefore unambiguously drew a conclusion about the political propriety of Trujillo's regime. Nevertheless, his conclusion was a by-product of objective inquiry.

Bill Leonard, who later became head of CBS News, seemed to share Torre's assessment of objectivity. Both made the assumption that there is something "out there" in society that the documentary can represent in a faithful manner. They contended that truth can coexist with opinion and truth can coexist with art. But, said Leonard, truth must be dominant in the final product:

> Producing a documentary is a complicated business. . . . [The producer is] somebody you've got to trust. He's got to care about the truth; he's got to care about the truth much more than he cares about the art. More about the truth than what looks pretty. He must be willing to ruin films, ruin stories, not rearrange them or throw them out, because he cares that much about truth. He must be willing to have things a little duller than he'd like them to be because that's the way they are. The trick, of course, is not to have things dull and yet still be right and still make it honest journalism. And that's not always easy.[85]

Both Leonard and Torre therefore held fast to the notion of objectivity despite their awareness of the perils posed by interpretation and artistic representation. In the tradition of Edward R. Murrow, both assumed that television documentary could offer a mirrorlike reflection of social reality.[86]

To some extent this notion marked a distinction between television documentary and the documentary film tradition, which included the inspirational efforts of John Grierson, the controversial "re-creations" of the *March of Time*, and the propaganda films of the Second World War. Indeed, producer Albert Wasserman claimed that the network documentarists of the television era set out to develop a *journalistic* genre that was distinctive from the cinematic heritage of documentary.

The whole history of the documentary film, which of course precedes television, was to a great extent a history of social indignation, allowing people who made films to express points of view about which the film maker felt strongly. With the evolution of the television documentary that is no longer appropriate. It is not appropriate for a television network to take a partisan position and to seem to be trying to force on an audience a predetermined editorial point of view.[87]

According to Wasserman, the television era imposed new and distinctive responsibilities. Documentary journalists represented their employers, who were in turn trustees of the public airwaves, a position that granted them enormous power. Yet that power was to be tempered by professional restraint, for it was feared that, without the canon of objectivity, documentary was indistinguishable from propaganda.[88] Consequently, this boundary between truth and falsehood was marked by the professional values and attitudes that were internalized by network news employees. As correspondent Howard K. Smith put it: "The [documentary] program should follow no line, liberal or conservative, except a rational one. It should be objective in that each issue must be judged on its own merits and without preconception. . . . But no rules can be written about this. The reporter must be trusted for his training and record, or else dispensed with."[89]

Although such a conception of objectivity seems unambiguous and firmly grounded in a professional tradition, it would in practice prove to be much more complicated. Documentaries that tackled difficult social issues often generated controversies and complaints. Documentarists drew conclusions, which is exactly what critics such as Walter Lippmann thought they should do. Lippmann, whose career spanned the Progressive Era and the New Frontier, was especially revered among network news workers.[90] He repeatedly touted the importance of journalistic objectivity, yet he also promoted the importance of interpretation. These conflicting elements proved to be particularly troublesome within the context of network television.

The Discourse of Interpretation

One of Walter Lippmann's focal concerns throughout his career was to emphasize the importance of journalistic analysis. Beginning in the 1920s, Lippmann argued that uncovering the facts simply was not enough, because the flood of information and misinformation that confronts the modern citizen makes it difficult to draw sound conclusions from unprocessed facts. Lippmann was concerned that, confronted by a deluge of information, the "masses" would fall back on "prejudices" and "primitive instincts."[91] He therefore contended that journalists could not simply uncover the facts and present them for public consideration. Rather, the modern era demanded that journalists exercise "trained intelligence," that they gather and organize the *right facts* according to a methodology unencumbered by partisan pleadings or prejudice. The modern era demanded that news workers interpret facts in order to assess their relevance and assign them significance.[92] Thus Lippmann's ideas elevated journalistic practice to a level of expertise that entailed analysis, interpretation, and education of the public at large.

The application of such expertise may have seemed especially important to the television documentarists of this era. Following the Second World War, news topics grew increasingly complicated as the United States assumed a role of global leadership and as Americans witnessed the rise of the national security state. This period also was marked by a trend toward centralization of federal executive power and an increasing effort by the national government to manage the flow of news and information. Indeed, James Reston is credited with coining the term *news management* in 1955 in order to describe the policies of President Eisenhower's press secretary, James Hagerty. Reston and other journalists began to express concern about their own role in the staged news event and to grow worried about the manipulation of information by government officials seeking to invoke the unwitting collusion of the news media.[93]

This concern about news management echoed criticisms raised with regard to press coverage during the McCarthy period as well. Writing thirty-five years after McCarthy's witch-hunt, Robert A. Hackett contends that the senator's tactics had a profound effect on journalistic practice: "[There] is a tension between impartially reporting contradictory truth-claims by high-status sources, on the one hand, and independently determining the validity of such truth-claims, on the other. The media's uncritical amplification of Senator Joe McCarthy's unfounded accusations made journalists aware of this tension, and now the concept of objectivity is sometimes taken to include interpretive and analytical reporting."[94] Indeed, during the post-McCarthy period, references to the senator became a common trope employed by journalists in defense of their interpretive responsibilities. Within the television medium itself, the Murrow-Friendly *See It Now* programs about McCarthy were widely hailed for demonstrating the potential of television journalism to operate as an antidote to the forces of demagoguery.[95]

As a result, many journalists and critics suggested that documentary deserved a special status in television news. Given its interpretive potential, documentary could protect the medium from its own superficiality and defend the profession from the manipulations of demagogic public officials. The documentary could bring the most sophisticated forms of journalistic technique into the domain of television news. Moreover, it could boost the morale and prestige of television news workers, who were often looked down on by print journalists. The documentary genre seemed to promise so much. Upon his appointment as executive producer of the new *CBS Reports* series, Fred Friendly declared the series would "provide interpretation, background and understanding at a time when comprehension [was] falling behind the onrush of events."[96] The other networks assigned this interpretive responsibility to their documentary units as well. Analysis, according to Irving Gitlin at NBC, was put in the hands of "trained and trusted" staffers.[97] These were to be television's public servants.

Although these documentarists, like their predecessors in print, were skeptical about the untutored wisdom of the masses, their primary mission was to educate the public, both at home and around the globe. Uninformed public opinion posed two potential problems for society during the modern era. One was noted by Irving Gitlin: "Our problem is that so much is going on [in the world] that the man in the street gets the feeling that it's too complicated and so he withdraws."[98] On the other hand, those who did not withdraw could be subject to demagoguery and manipulation. As Edward R. Murrow wrote regarding government censorship of reporting from China during the 1950s, "A leadership responsible only to an uninformed, or partially informed, electorate can bring nothing but disaster to our world."[99] The network documentarist therefore had an obligation to truth but also a responsibility to share that truth, to educate. As reporter Howard K. Smith commented, "I have long been interested in educational television because I believe that the nation that wins the Cold War will be the best educated nation."[100] Accordingly, the public must be educated but educated with a purpose.

This tension between the collection of facts and the connection of facts has nowhere been subject to more controversy and debate than with the network television documentary. And as a result, no television genre has ever exerted more contradictory pressures on network executives. In the face of FCC inquiries, public outcry, and organized pressure groups, the executive's only defense of a documentary was to valorize the professionalism of the network's news employees. One might point to the facts, but in the end it was the conclusions, the analysis, that often generated the greatest controversy. And these conclusions, whether justifiable or not, could make life unpleasant for those executives who were expected to respond to public critics and disgruntled advertisers.

As a result, network management kept a close eye on the documentary units, never willing to grant them the full autonomy that documentarists so richly desired. As for the news workers, they jealously defended their expertise. Fred Freed recounted one such instance when he and Irving Gitlin were prescreening a documentary for a dozen NBC executives. The program was about the Berlin situation in 1961. Recalled Freed:

> At the end of it, the lights came on and nobody said anything. Everybody was waiting for [network president Robert] Kintner. Then he growled, "I think it's okay." Then everybody else agreed that it was fine, some even said it was very fine. Everybody congratulated Gitlin. Then somebody said something about he didn't think that the Berlin situation was quite like that. And Gitlin turned on him very sharply and said, "You have absolutely no knowledge about that. You have no expertise and we do, and it's not a subject which you should discuss." Kintner nodded. And that ended that.[101]

Although in this instance the debate was foreshortened, such claims to expertise were tenuous and constantly had to be reasserted by news workers. Given the network's desire to avoid controversy and the documentarist's inability to draw undisputed conclusions, the only salient defense was the claim of expertise. However, the professional tradition on which this claim was built was itself contradictory. Documentarists relied on facts, and yet they manipulated the facts in order to draw conclusions. They were unbiased, and yet they promoted a broadly defined political agenda. They were disinterested, and yet they sought to educate, convert, and reform public sentiment. And in the end, the contradiction that would prove most troublesome was that documentarists were professionals, and yet they were not autonomous. Therefore, at the very moment the major networks were avidly investing in the development of their documentary units, they began to wrestle with the complicated claims of the genre's professionals. The resulting indeterminacy of this debate also affected the programs themselves.

Some critics say the documentaries of this era were timid and cautious. Certainly, one of the reasons that foreign policy topics were so popular was that these programs' analyses were rarely subject to challenge. Communists and foreigners were specifically denied standing before the FCC and therefore could not file "legitimate" complaints or demand comparable coverage for their particular point of view. As a result, the documentary could find refuge in the consensus politics of anti-Communism.

Such criticisms, however, tend to overlook the fact that despite the intense pressure sometimes brought to bear on the genre, it never could completely jettison its complicated journalistic heritage. As we have seen in chapter 4, the documentaries of the middle ground often engendered contradictory meanings. In their search for empirical documentation, network news producers regularly undermined the simple dichotomies of superpower struggle. Indeed, documentaries on Latin America frequently created sympathetic portraits of potential and actual Communists. Documentaries on Vietnam questioned the wisdom of U.S. counterinsurgency techniques and presented troubling images of America's client "democracy" in Southeast Asia. On the domestic front, the discourse of documentary professionalism made a number of controversial issues similarly irresistible. The networks produced programs on birth control, automation in the workplace, and cigarette smoking (television's number one advertiser at the time). They even took on the touchy subject of television ratings. Although none of these efforts produced fundamentally radical critiques of the status quo, they do point to the fact that even though the genre may have been constrained by powerful economic and institutional forces, the programs were far less predictable than one might imagine. In good measure such outcomes were due to the contradictory heritage of journalistic professionalism. And while this heritage gave rise to ideological gaps and ruptures within the documentaries of the middle ground, it created even bigger problems in programs about the homefront.

Chapter Six

Documentaries of the Home Front

Although superpower struggle was undoubtedly the most pervasive single concern in television documentary during the early 1960s, domestic issues were not overlooked. As pointed out in chapter 2, the flagship documentary series of each network took on a wide range of issues from civil rights to cigarettes, from poverty to presidential politics. Each of these topics reflected pressing social needs, but for the purposes of this study what is most interesting is the way in which domestic issues were often linked to foreign policy concerns. Indeed, many of these domestic topics when taken up by network documentarists played an important role in marking distinctions between East and West and in promoting the urgency of competition with the Communist other. They suggested ways in which the concept of the Free World might be constituted at home as well as abroad. For example, programs about race generally contended that discrimination was a problem not only because it generated domestic unrest but because it projected a negative image of the very country that presumed to lead the Free World. Other issues such as space exploration were positioned within a wider global context as well. These documentaries often urged public concern not simply because of the scientific challenges that lay ahead but because the United States needed to maintain its image as the global leader in science and technology. Other nations could not be expected to rally to the cause of the Free World if the United States was faltering in areas of strategic interest. The ideological work of these documentaries was therefore to circulate a vision of America that secured its preeminent role in the Free World community.

On the other hand, these concerns also imposed certain logical imperatives on the ways in which network documentary dealt with domestic issues. That is, institutional racism had to be challenged if the United States was to promote its affinity with African states, and due process had to be upheld if the United States was to distinguish itself from authoritarian styles of government behind the Iron Curtain. Furthermore, home front documentaries—like the documentaries of the middle ground—had to wrestle with diverse and often conflicting evidence, thereby engendering alternative and even oppositional meanings. Part of this was due to the nature of the filmic evidence that was gathered, but it also was a product of the internal institutional forces described in chapter 5. Network news workers took pride in their professionalism and reputed autonomy. They were optimistic that a public enlightened by unbiased information and expert commentary could muster the necessary willpower to take on the great issues confronting the Free World. Moreover, these news workers were highly competitive, vying to be the first one to bring a unique issue or perspective to the airwaves. Although they undoubtedly were influenced by the broader agenda of corporate and government leaders, they also found it necessary to account for oppositional viewpoints, thereby bringing images and ideas to prime-time television that were disturbing and even disruptive to the ideological project of the New Frontier.

The significance of these tensions helps to explain why an instrumentalist argument—that documentaries reflected the dominance of powerful interests—needs to be tempered by analysis that takes into account multiple levels of practice. It is indeed true that the converging interests of business leaders, politicians, social critics, and network executives all played a central role in promoting the documentary as a Cold War education project, but none could determine the explicit outcomes of the programs without jeopardizing their legitimacy. That is, because of documentary's peculiar status within network organizations and within the larger public debate over television, the genre could only fulfill its mission so long as it maintained its aura of dispassionate, professional expertise. As we have seen in the preceding chapter, such professionalism was dearly cherished by network news workers, who aspired to join some of their print counterparts by producing sober analysis rather than superficial news spots. They aspired to explain and interpret a vast range of social experience within the framework of New Frontier ideology. In so doing, they encountered complexities that engendered tensions and contradictions within the texts themselves.

The first part of this chapter examines programs about U.S. space exploration efforts. As we shall see, network documentarists enthusiastically promoted such efforts as a key component of the Cold War, but at the same time they had to deal with widespread public ambivalence about the wonders of modern science. This uncertainty is also manifest in documentaries about automation, the focus of the second section. Not only did the wonders of technology generate an employment crisis, but they also encouraged a passive, "push-button" lifestyle that was reportedly robbing the nation of the physical vigor needed to meet the Soviet challenge. Finally, the third section of this chapter looks at documentaries about the underside of the American dream. Throughout the 1950s documentary images of poverty and racism rarely, if ever, disrupted prime time's celebration of middle-class consumerism. Yet some of the most compelling documentaries of this New Frontier era fix an intense gaze on the inequities of the American system.

The Space Race

The *CBS Reports* series showed an early fascination with space research and exploration. The series premiered in October 1959 with "Biography of a Missile" and followed up with three more space documentaries during its first two seasons.[1] Commissioned in the wake of the Soviet Sputnik launch, "Biography" details the step-by-step planning, construction, and launch of an American missile. Here expertise and precision are engaged in the struggle to meet the Communist challenge. Yet the program's acknowledgment of Soviet preeminence in the aerospace field generates some confusion, for if the Russian people are blinded by ideology and subjected to coercive controls, how have they managed to produce such sophisticated scientific knowledge? This confusion is further compounded by the fact that the scientists who head up the American space effort honed their expertise in the Nazi rocket program during the Second World War. The documentary navigates these contradictions by largely ignoring Soviet successes and by casting former Nazi scientists in a rehabilitated and democratic light. The implication is that scientists are not really political and that totalitarian forms of government have little effect on actual research. A personable Werner Van Braun comments on the egalitarian nature of his U.S. research team by noting, "I think nothing hurts team effort and any greater development effort than this, you might call it, 'pappy knows best' attitude on the part of the top management." Braun continues, "Pappy just doesn't know best. He gets the best answers when he asks the man who has to do the job." Later, during the countdown, correspondent Edward R. Murrow comments on the tight discipline in the launch area, but one of the German scientists revises this assessment by commenting that discipline among the staff is voluntary. Despite this democratic point of view, the U.S. scientists nevertheless fail to launch the missile at the climax of the program. Murrow visits the crash site to survey the charred and twisted wreckage, commenting in a direct address to the audience:

> The disappointment is not the loss of money, the twisted metal or the man hours involved. It is rather the fact that, had it succeeded, it would have pushed back the frontier of man's knowledge just a little. That payload would have been one of the reaching fingertips of science that would have brought to man a little bit of knowledge that he never before had. So this is the end of this particular project. There will be another and when it is done we will hope to report it to you.

Murrow's eulogy is interesting for its celebration of "pure" science. Missing is any trace of politics or strategic concern. Gone is any recognition of the purpose behind government funding of the project or of military cooperation with the documentary crew. Instead, Murrow obscures the contradiction between politically motivated research and the concept of pure science. In the end, the failed launch attempt is a setback for the process of free inquiry, and it is therefore interesting to compare Murrow's commentary with the highly politicized meanings associated with the Sputnik launch only two years earlier.

Even more intriguing are the tensions generated by the documentary investigation itself. Certainly this documentary was intended as part of the public education campaign envisioned by national leaders and social critics as discussed in chapter 1. Indeed, one of those critics, Edward R. Murrow, is the reporter of record, and he unambiguously grounds the rationale for the rocket research as part of the Cold War. Yet in the act of documenting this urgent project, he must navigate a set of troubling issues, among them the relationship between science and authoritarian regimes, the central role of Nazi scientists in the American space program, and the failure of an expensive government project. It is in fact the very act of empirical documentation that generates an excess of meanings and tensions in the text. Had CBS not brought the U.S. rocket research into the living rooms of millions of Americans, these ambiguities would not have been so widely circulated. In an apparent attempt to address these excesses, the CBS crew returned a couple of months later to film a successful launch and tack that on as an addendum before the show was broadcast. Nevertheless, these anxieties about the superpower space race permeate other CBS documentaries as well.

Three months later, at the beginning of January 1960, another *CBS*

Reports documentary inquires, "The Space Lag: Can Democracy Compete?"[2] The title itself is obviously an allusion to charges by Democrats, especially presidential candidate John Kennedy, that a strategic missile gap existed between the United States and the Soviet Union. Correspondent Howard K. Smith in his introduction echoes these concerns:

> Two years ago, on October the 4th, 1957, our nation suffered a setback in space called *Sputnik*. A stunned, flabbergasted America promised to catch up. We have not. . . . Let it be stated from the outset that this program is not meant to be entertainment. It is a serious program about how a democracy makes decisions in the space age. Much of it is complicated and some of it is upsetting. We do not have the ability or the desire to make this program otherwise. Nor are we persuaded that the public needs to have its television gimmicked up or watered down to make it easy viewing.

From the outset the documentary takes both the challenge of the space race and the mission of network documentary quite seriously. As many contemporary critics of television had hoped, the program attempts to shake Americans from their complacency by confronting them with stark, unvarnished news of the superpower space race. Smith therefore begins the program in voice-over by briefly narrating a sequence of stock footage that tracks the history of U.S. and Soviet space efforts, concluding with the image of a *Sputnik* replica that "hangs at the entrance to the United Nations as the first trophy of the space age."[3]

Why, asks Smith, did the Russians beat us? The program identifies competing interests among the U.S. Army, Air Force, and Navy, each pursuing its own missile program, none seeing the broader picture. This parochialism combined with the cautious expenditures of the Eisenhower administration frustrated U.S. space efforts in both the military and civilian sectors. The problem was not our science, but our bureaucracy. As Admiral Hyman Rickover puts it, "I believe the real contest we are in with Russia is one between two bureaucracies. Some believe that a democracy is always more efficient than a totalitarian state. We should be because our people are free and their people are bound. But the efficiency of the bureaucracy has nothing to do with the form of government." Rather, it has to do with management and coordination of resources. The documentary therefore suggests that competition between the branches of the U.S. military must be rationalized and that private and public sectors must be more successfully integrated. Furthermore, space exploration must become a government priority. Directly addressing the audience, Smith closes the program by urging support for an expensive, long-term investment in the space race.

Smith's explicit endorsement of more tightly integrated relations between government units and high technology corporations is perhaps the logical outcome of his empirical investigation of the "space lag." Starting from the assumption that the United States must compete with Soviet space efforts, the documentary affords lavish attention to proponents of a more intensive rocket program. At the same time, however, it introduces the puzzling notion that authoritarian regimes may be more efficient than democratic ones. This perspective suggests problems with traditional notions of laissez-faire capitalism and further implies that the policies of the Eisenhower era must give way to a more vigorous form of cooperation between capital-intensive corporations and a centralized government bureaucracy. This analysis of the space lag certainly must have been heartening to those business leaders who had grown disenchanted with the provincialism of Republican economic policy. Nevertheless, it also paradoxically recommends a more centralized and authoritarian organization of the nation's productive capacity.

Ten months later, CBS attempted to unravel this seeming contradiction by reporting on a major success story, "Year of the Polaris."[4] Reporter Edward R. Murrow explains that, in the wake of *Sputnik*, a massive infusion of $350 million in government funding enabled the U.S. Navy to initiate a crash program to produce a nuclear missile that could be launched from submarines at sea. Murrow marvels at the complex challenge of accurately firing a long-range missile that must travel through three distinct pressure zones: water, air, and high atmosphere. The success of Polaris accordingly restores the United States to a position of prominence in the space race. But, Murrow informs us, this was more than a technical success; it was a managerial one as well. He then eulogizes "the person responsible for getting together all these incredibly complicated pieces of machinery." As we watch film footage of workers manufacturing a guidance system, of component parts being packed and shipped, of a missile being assembled and installed at the launch site, of the control room during countdown, Murrow intones:

> [One manager] had to have his fingertips on every piece to see to it that they arrived at the right place at the right time and that they fit together properly. You've never heard of this man. He doesn't get his name in the newspapers. He's a civil service employee, doesn't make very much money, but his contribution was in the field of management. Something that is badly needed not

only on the Polaris program, but elsewhere in the country. His name is Gordon Pearson.

Like so much of Murrow's World War II reporting, this segment presents the little picture of heroic individual effort in service of a greater cause. Discussing his responsibilities, Pearson speaks with the earnest enthusiasm one expects from a soldier. He operates on the assumption, he says, that "you can get more out of one man who is overworked than two who are underworked." Thus Polaris succeeded because its staff was disciplined and dedicated, lean and hard. This imagery seems to directly address post-*Sputnik* anxieties regarding American science, morals, and superpower struggle. Moreover, this program, which was broadcast during the fall of the 1960 presidential campaign, shares the Kennedyesque fascination with managerial expertise. To the Democratic candidate, the problem with government was not only that it had lost its sense of purpose but that it failed to apply managerial expertise to the great problems confronting the nation.[5] Pearson is therefore the embodiment of the New Frontier zeitgeist. He is the civilian soldier: a vigorous, dedicated, and self-sacrificing expert. He is not the mindless automaton of an authoritarian regime; rather, he is the dedicated foot soldier of a momentous campaign against what Murrow referred to in another context as the malignant forces of evil.

After showing a series of successful Polaris launches, the documentary closes with Murrow's reflections on the strategic importance of this triumph.

> Polaris is not the ultimate weapon. There is no such thing. Each weapon, in due course, produces a counter weapon. What Polaris has done is to buy us a certain amount of time. Time in which to solve the great problem of our age. And that problem is to determine the conditions, if any, under which the Communist world and the Free World are willing to live together on this minor planet.

In Murrow's formulation, Polaris represents significant scientific progress. Yet this accomplishment will soon be superseded by another. Technological progress is inevitable, and the space race is only the latest manifestation of a seemingly natural process of scientific advance. What seems less certain and more subject to human agency, however, is the outcome of the Cold War. And here, the outcome seems largely dependent on the dedication of anonymous heroes like Gordon Pearson who have taken on the challenge of a disciplined and dedicated foe.

Yet this moment of apparent closure is tenuous at best because the most obvious rationale behind the space program was to enhance the

United States' ability to wage nuclear war. Such a frightening linkage was no doubt apparent to both producers and audiences of these programs. As Murrow noted in the Polaris documentary, "Destruction is [this missile's] final, desperate, ultimate purpose. If it is ever combat fired, it will have failed its purpose and our civilization will have failed its promise." Therefore, even as these documentaries valorize scientific effort and managerial expertise, they also reveal the anxieties of the nuclear age. Not only had science harnessed the awesome power of the atom, but now it had developed missile delivery systems that brought much of humankind within an hour's range of total destruction. Thus the control that expertise afforded on the one hand was undermined on the other by a prospect more daunting and seemingly less controllable. Even the heroic, scientific efforts of citizens like Gordon Pearson could not erase their dystopian opposite, the increasing prospect of nuclear annihilation.

It is not surprising, then, that these space documentaries were soon followed by a series of programs about nuclear disarmament, such as "The Balance of Terror: In Case of War," "The Balance of Terror: Can We Disarm?" and "Reflections of a Soviet Scientist."[6] Clearly motivated by competing disarmament initiatives from Moscow and Washington, the documentaries promote an agenda that clearly favors the U.S. initiative. Yet at the same time they introduce fundamental questions about the rationale behind government-funded research and the missile race between the superpowers. Here again, the act of documenting official government policy produces an unintended excess of meanings. It suggests that complex bureaucracies have not only generated awesome technological advances but also have engendered the irrational prospect of total destruction.

Dystopian Science

Ambivalence toward scientific progress is prominent in other documentaries of the early 1960s as well. Although most of these programs celebrate rationality, planning, and scientific method, they also work hard to negotiate a set of social problems produced by the "advancement of science." Despite the seeming objectivity of scientific method, the application of science was not value neutral, as became only too apparent in ABC's documentary "Automation, the Awesome Servant."[7]

At the very outset of the program Secretary of Labor Arthur Goldberg explains to an interviewer that inescapable problems will accompany increasing automation, but he is hoping that public policy can encourage a humane transition to the new industrial age. Such official pronouncements seem faint hearted, however, as documentary film footage shows new technologies rapidly displacing American wage workers. An opening montage features film footage of a high-speed bottling machine, a petroleum refinery staffed by only six workers, and thousands of envelopes being stuffed and sealed by machine. The program then zeros in on a new Cudahy meat-packing plant in Omaha that reduced its workforce of nineteen hundred by one-third. Although we are told the company's policy is to assist worker relocation, former employees who gather at a nearby tavern sound pessimistic. One woman says she knows that many people think she should not work full-time, but she has to, and losing her job after fourteen years will be a major blow to her family income. A black employee says that, as a minority, it will be tough for him to find another job that pays as well. "If my kids go hungry, what is my choice? To turn to crime?" Another worker bitterly remarks, "I haven't seen any of these new jobs that they say automation is making." He concludes, "Machines are important to the future of the country, but I think we should all benefit from them, not just some."

This vox populi, though stereotypical, attaches human consequences to the cold economic realities of automation, but the documentary then goes a step further by inviting audience identification with one worker in particular. Visiting his home, we listen as he reflects on the fact that after long years of faithful service, he was laid off at the age of fifty. He says he does not want to move in search of a new job, nor does he think it will be easy to find a job at his age. His wife tells us he became severely depressed when they first heard the news, and she confides her own feelings of isolation and helplessness, "I didn't want to let him know, but [when I heard the news] I felt sick inside." Their victimization is rendered in personal, intimate terms inviting audience identification with their plight and involvement with the broader issue.

The program then turns to a more abstract analysis of the problem, pointing out a similar trend taking place in Detroit, where unemployment is the highest in the nation. The increasing mechanization of the automotive industry is blamed for generating half of all job losses in the area. A welfare commissioner says, "The unfortunate part of it is, however, that we haven't even begun to feel the impact of automation." A Ford Motor Company official denies that automation is causing half of all job losses, and he defends the firm's technical innovations, saying that Ford must keep its labor costs low in order to compete in global markets. Despite his denials, the narrator notes that the number of workers at

River Rouge has dropped from forty-seven thousand to twenty-seven thousand during the postwar period while production output has remained steady. At a union meeting, one worker asks: "How does this look to the world situation, to these other countries, these totalitarian governments, where they don't believe in God? This is supposed to be a Christian nation . . . and Ford Motor Company is making all these profits. Why aren't they willing to share any of these profits with the people who helped build this empire?"

The workers seem fully aware that images of technological progress and American prosperity have been used around the world as weapons in the struggle between the superpowers. Countries that join the Free World have been offered the prospect of economic development so that they too can share the bounty of the American Dream. Yet this vision of development is dependent not only on advanced technology and managerial expertise but also on the adoption of certain values, among them dedication, perseverance, and hard work. So it is with bitter irony that these auto workers—who internalized these very same values in the hope that they too would share in the dream—are now being told that the rules of the game have changed and the company owes them no allegiance. Instead of Christian principles of equity and community, these workers see the greedy logic of corporate economics, a logic that seems no less totalitarian than the principles that guide Communist regimes.

Yet these vanishing factory jobs are only part of the picture, for we find out that the biggest impact of automation will be in the office. As we watch workers assemble computer parts, the narrator says:

> These are the tiny bits of metal and wire that have kindled a revolution in the office. Properly assembled, these parts will make a computer, the most awesome servant of all. The machine that made the space age possible. The machine that remembers and measures and files and projects with incredible speed. [Cut to a shot of a Polaris missile being launched.] It would take eight men four hours to work out all the computations that make this possible. The computer does it in two minutes.

We are further informed that such dramatic advances in information processing have spurred the elimination of huge numbers of clerical jobs. A union official informs us that unemployment among office workers has jumped from 2.8 percent to 5 percent. It is further estimated that each new IBM 727 computer replaces 140 workers. The camera then cuts to a shot of dozens of women working at clerical tasks in a large office as the narrator informs us:

> At Mutual of Omaha [insurance], computers are replacing this department, but none of these girls will be laid off. They'll simply be moved. Relatively few of the girls who work in offices depend on their clerical incomes for a livelihood, and the turnover is high, permitting employers to absorb girls through attrition. The office clerk replaced by automation isn't fired, but the job that was there isn't anymore.

This reassuring description of computerization goes unchallenged, as does the underlying assumption that "girls" only work for pleasure or pin money until they start a family. But when they are tied to earlier comments from the unemployed female meat packer and the official from the clerical union, one is left wondering why office workers would unionize and why the unemployment rate would be rising if office "girls" are being "absorbed" by attrition.

The documentary elides this contradiction and turns to Thomas J. Watson, head of IBM, who says computerization is eliminating dangerous and repetitive jobs, thereby upgrading workers in the United States and ultimately all over the world. Like Labor Secretary Goldberg, he says the transition to an automated society must be a humane one and that care must be taken to help retrain those who have been displaced. But he scotches a suggestion that the benefits of automation might be spread equitably by shortening the workday or workweek. Here again, the global situation influences corporate decision making. "In view of the competition that we have with the Soviet Union," Watson says, "we can't afford to have 7 percent of our workforce unemployed, nor can we afford to absorb this 7 percent by . . . shortening the workday or the workweek. . . . I think this would be a very frivolous thing for us to undertake." Watson seems to believe that automation should not encourage the tilt toward a leisure society but should be used instead to enhance America's ability to respond to the Soviet challenge.

Apparently, many workers do not share that view. A union official says his members are willing to work as much as needed to keep the United States strong in the face of global Communism, but "when more than five million wage earners are denied the opportunity to work, we can't just talk about the challenge in the world and have that as the substitute to the answer to their problem."

What is remarkable about this exchange, and the documentary in general, is the way in which the filmed evidence destabilizes middle-class assumptions of pluralism, progress, and science. Both the union officials and the laid-off workers who appear throughout the program repeatedly argue that the application of new technology is benefiting the few at the expense of the many. They openly challenge common notions of progress and argue that their interests are not being represented. Both Watson and the Ford official seek to temper these complaints by reference to the Communist challenge, but the documentation of laid-off workers and wasted lives resists such easy closure.

Almost in desperation, the documentary returns to Labor Secretary Goldberg for a final comment, and he remarks that the long-term solution to the problem lies with education. He advises families to "make every sacrifice that [they] can make in order to keep people in school." This concluding advice offers a classic liberal solution to dislocations generated by larger social forces. Goldberg treats the outcomes of automation as part of an inevitable process, as if it were beyond human control, almost like the weather. He directs attention away from the arena of class conflict and celebrates the virtues of personal improvement and public education. He valorizes higher learning and scientific progress while denying class antagonism. Finally, he imposes the burden of responsibility squarely on the shoulders of the individual. It is an uneasy mediation of the tensions generated by the text, but one that fits securely within the ideological framework of New Frontier documentary. Imbalances in economic well-being were not to be seen as the product of class antagonisms but rather as localized kinks in an otherwise rational system. Technology appears as neutral rather than as the application of resources in the interests of particular groups. The best route to reform is through the adjustment and integration of the dysfunctional elements, not through substantive change in the relations of power. Like the documentaries of the middle ground, this conclusion positions localized problems within the context of the historical project of the New Frontier. It offers an abstract framework with which to understand the narrative of progress and with which to understand the discontinuities of the system. Nevertheless, this process of abstraction only tenuously resolves the class antagonisms exacerbated by technological innovation.

Anxieties about modern technology emerge in other network documentaries of this period as well. Rachel Carson's best-selling book *Silent Spring* spawned a CBS documentary of the same name and a follow-up program featuring results of a special presidential investigation of the pesticide problem.[8] Here we see the dystopian underside of science that raises questions about the "progress" being made in agriculture. In a similar vein, *Bell and Howell Close-Up!* took on the issue of air pollution with "The Silent Killer" and the problem of endangered species with "The Irreplaceables."[9] Both networks also zeroed in on the problems of water pollution and drought, with CBS's "The Water Famine" and

Marine Corps recruits struggle through calisthenics in "The Flabby American."

ABC's "The Vanishing Oasis."[10] All of these programs question assumptions about technological progress by asking, how much is too much?

Anxieties about modern lifestyles also figure prominently in ABC's "The Flabby American."[11] In the opening montage as we watch shots of Americans lounging in front of their television sets happily snacking away on junk food, the narrator warns, "President Kennedy has said that if we waste and neglect our physical vigor, we will destroy much of our ability to meet the great and vital challenges which confront our people." This is quickly juxtaposed with images of lean, muscular Soviet children doing vigorous calisthenics and running track. While Americans have become a nation of lazy spectators, the Soviets are working hard, even at play. "Thus, a question arises, [cut to shot of Americans on an escalator] Can a push-button, ride instead of walk, easy-living society withstand the twin threats from within and without? Can we survive the soft life or will history record us as the flabby American?" Clearly, the concerns articulated at the outset of the program not only dovetail with New Frontier internationalism, but they explicitly respond to a very high profile White House initiative, the President's Council on Physical Fitness. Perhaps the good life is a little *too* good. Maybe machines have made things *too* easy for the younger generation. The program opens at a U.S. Marine boot camp where we learn that a significant and growing number of recruits

A golfer labors to keep up with an automated driving range gone haywire.

fail basic physical fitness tests and have to be put in a special remedial program. Thus questions of survival in a hostile global environment are being linked with anxieties about new technologies. A growing number of Americans with heart disease and back ailments bring the issue even closer to the suburban home. The program concludes on a more whimsical note, however, as the camera takes us to a driving range where a golfer is hitting balls that are teed up for him automatically. As the camera tightens up on the ball feeder, the problems of modern living become only too apparent as the machine goes haywire and the golfer struggles in Chaplinesque fashion to keep pace with the runaway automaton. Finally, with the clang of a bell, the image goes black. Then the credits fade up against a background shot of American commuters chugging along a smoggy, crowded freeway.

These interrogations of technology and modern living anticipate many of the criticisms that would be leveled by leaders of environmental and counterculture movements later in the decade. Although network documentaries certainly attempted to contain such criticisms within the realm of dominant discourse, they nevertheless presented the underside of the American dream to prime-time viewers. This was not only a significant departure from the conventions of fifties television, but it also helped to legitimize issues that were beginning to find their way into public debate. Unlike the preceding decade, the Cold War no longer provided a justification for stifling social criticism and silencing expressions of discontent. On the contrary, the documentaries of the early 1960s suggested that criticism, activism, and reform were all necessary if America was to address its pressing social problems and maintain a position of global leadership. `

Poverty and Race

The disruptive potential of such self-critical analysis was perhaps at no time more apparent than the day after Thanksgiving in 1960, when *CBS Reports* broadcast "Harvest of Shame."[12] The documentary is famous for the ways in which it details the wretched employment and living conditions of agricultural field-workers, those who gather the bounty for the Thanksgiving table. The program charts their seasonal migration as they search for work, trapped in a cycle of employer exploitation. It is they who provide the necessary toil to make cheap produce available in the American supermarket. Early in the program, their plight is explicitly rendered in both words and images as a train rumbles across the screen and reporter Edward R. Murrow intones:

> The vegetables the migrants picked yesterday move north swiftly on rails. [Cut to a shot of a refrigerator truck.] Produce en route to the tables of America is refrigerated and carefully packed to prevent bruising. [Cut to a cattle truck.] Cattle carried to market by federal regulation must be watered, fed, and rested for five hours every twenty-five hours. [Cut to a shot from behind a canvas-covered stake truck packed with migrants.] People—men, women, and children—are carried to the fields of the north in journeys as long as four days and three nights. [Cut to migrants riding in a crowded bus.] They often ride ten hours without stopping for food or facilities.

This blend of spoken commentary and visual imagery represents the migrants as commodified labor par excellence. They are packed and shipped with little regard for their personal needs or human dignity. In interviews with migrant families we learn that many grew up working as field hands from a very young age and few believe they will ever be able to break out of the cycle of poverty. They are productive members of the workforce. They aspire to settle down, to own a home, to find a steady job. Yet they are denied access to the American dream.

Unlike foreign policy documentaries, this program does not present the viewer with the prospect of Communist subversion, although it does

Migrants represented as commodified labor in "Harvest of Shame."

portray victims of exploitation. These are not renegades or rebels; they are the people who have slipped through the cracks in an otherwise rational system. Solidly within the tradition of muckraking American journalism, the program depicts these migrants as victims of big business. They have no protection against those who wield tremendous power in the farming and food-processing industries. Correspondent Edward R. Murrow argues that their "best hope" lies in the education of their children. But we learn it is impossible to keep migrant children in school when the families depend on their labor. Moreover, it is difficult to deliver services to these transients as they constantly cross state boundaries and local jurisdictions in search of work. The answer, Murrow argues, is national legislation to guarantee better education, housing, health care, and work benefits for migrants. We are told, however, that powerful agribusiness interests have conspired to lobby against such reform.

In closing, Murrow directly addresses the audience wielding a bound volume of recommendations made by a presidential committee on the migrant labor problem. He warns, however, that even these expert recommendations have an uncertain future in the face of powerful opposition from the agribusiness lobby: "In fact a hundred and fifty different attempts have been made in Congress to do something about the plight of the migrants. All but one has failed. The migrants have no lobby. Only an enlightened, aroused, and perhaps angered public opinion can do anything about the migrants." Implicit in Murrow's reasoning is the notion that the Free World is distinguished by pluralist democracy and operates as a system of checks and balances. Without unions, there is no check on employers. Without an electoral process, there is no check on the power of elites. Without education, there are no safeguards against predatory labor practices. The documentary does not argue for a socialist command economy; rather, it proposes that balance needs to be restored to the system and that balance ultimately rests with the voice of the people. Thus, even though the documentary presents some of the ugliest images of exploitation ever broadcast on prime-time television, it also proposes a solution that valorizes the quintessential difference between East and West: the power of public opinion.

At the same time, however, the documentary suggests contradictory meanings as well. For example, expertise has been frustrated in its reform efforts by the political influence of agribusiness. Thus the limitations of expertise become only too apparent. Furthermore, it raises questions about American myths of community and equality, for the program provides persuasive evidence that the power of the plutocrats (as well as the plenitude enjoyed by the American middle class) relies on the exploitation of impoverished field-workers. Not everyone is equal in America. Indeed, this implication was considered so disturbing that when Murrow joined the Kennedy administration as head of the USIA shortly after the broadcast of "Harvest of Shame," he tried to block international distribution of the program, arguing that audiences overseas could not appreciate the fuller context of his criticisms and that the program might be used as propaganda against the United States. Although Murrow later backed down when confronted with charges of government censorship, his concern reflects the irony that the very television genre that was intended to promote the national interest abroad could also undermine it as well.[13] Neither Murrow nor his colleagues at CBS were politically radical, and yet the methodology of their profession pressed them to wrestle with the discontinuities of the American system. No doubt they would justify their journalistic efforts by pointing to the American public's right to know, and yet Murrow, as head of the USIA, would later deny that same right to other citizens of the Free World.

Documentaries about race relations raised similar problems for the New Frontier. When Kennedy took office, race issues offered him the opportunity to make a decisive change in government policy after years of presidential indifference. Kennedy failed to take up the challenge, however, preferring instead to focus on international issues during his first two years in office. Indeed, foreign policy concerns led the administration to make behind-the-scenes attempts to temper the rising tide of civil rights protests.[14] Yet race issues were not so easily contained, and black leaders, such as James Farmer of the Congress on Racial Equality (CORE), used the administration's global focus as leverage in their fight for justice. Farmer explained: "We planned the Freedom Rides with the specific intention of creating a crisis. We were counting on the bigots of the South to do our work for us. We figured that the government would have to respond if we created a situation that was headline news all over the world, and that affected the nation's image abroad."[15]

This relationship between civil rights and superpower struggle is picked up in many network documentaries about race relations. For example, ABC's award-winning "Walk in My Shoes" opens with a black orator passionately addressing an enthusiastic audience assembled on a city street corner.[16] "This is no Communist speaking. This is an angry black man speaking. The twenty million black men of America are angry! America won't have to worry about Communism. It'll have to worry about the restless black peril here in America." Although the speaker distinguishes black unrest from Communist unrest, the comparison of the two recalls the documentaries of the middle ground in which civil

Working in the garment district in "Walk in My Shoes."

unrest was usually characterized as an opportunity for Communist infiltration. Such unrest was also an indication of the need for liberal reform.
Similarly, "Walk in My Shoes" focuses on the failure of earlier reforms
and the growing tide of black unrest during the early 1960s.

At the outset we follow the fortunes of a young black man, torn
between the hollow promises of the status quo and the enticements of
militant black separatism.[17] In an imaginative and engaging use of
point-of-view camera techniques, the documentary tags along on his daily
routine and captures his thoughts through first-person voice-over narration. We are invited to see the American promise of liberty through his
eyes. The day begins as an alarm clock sounds and the camera smoothly
pans across a tenement bedroom to find the protagonist as he first
awakens. We follow him as he washes up and eats breakfast in the
crowded and dilapidated family apartment. Then he is off to the streets
and the subway downtown to "meet the man, the white man you work
for." There in the garment district we follow the protagonist pushing
garment racks through the crowded, bustling streets. In voice-over he
reflects, "It's always the same. The Negroes are concentrated in the
worst jobs, the lowest levels. On the average, we're paid only six dollars
for every ten a white man makes."

Yet things are changing for some blacks, according to the documentary. A visit to the suburbs and interviews with black families show that some are making it up the economic ladder. Still, these "successful Negroes" complain that prejudice against them persists, that integration remains a cruel joke for most blacks. This point is then driven home at the Hungry I comedy club where Dick Gregory tells a white audience, "Ya heard what Bobby Kennedy said? He said that thirty years from now a Negro can become President. So treat me right, or I'll get in there and raise taxes on ya." Amid uproarious laughter, he continues, "I mean, don't get me wrong. I wouldn't mind paying my income tax if I knew it was goin' to a friendly country." Such bitter expressions of disenfranchisement have, according to the documentary, engendered a split among African Americans between older, more moderate leaders and younger activists. The young wish to challenge white power directly, whereas older blacks plead for more time to allow legal reforms to bring about integration.

Even those who have played a central role in the legal struggle are growing impatient, however. We learn that black leaders such as NAACP attorney Percy Sutton have begun to argue the case for direct action, and Sutton himself has joined the Freedom Rides. Framed in close-up and speaking dramatically in a rich, melodic baritone, he recounts in detail his ride from Atlanta to Montgomery, a ride that conjured up a tapestry of memories from his earlier life growing up in the South. During this journey, Sutton remembered the petty injuries inflicted daily by racial prejudice. Thus, as he approached Montgomery— where only a couple of days before, Freedom Riders had been beaten by an angry white mob—Sutton's memories began to overwhelm him. When the bus stopped at the depot, he started to stand, he says, but his legs wouldn't hold him. In a hushed stage voice, he leans toward the camera and slowly, dramatically explains, "This was *fear!*" Then, leaning back in his chair, Sutton's cadence quickens:

> Now fear from what? Fear from riding into the bus station? No! Fear compounded from Percy Sutton who couldn't go to the white playground as a kid. Percy Sutton who was put off a train as an [air force] officer, a captain, in Texarkana, in 1945, when he returned from fighting a war for his country. These were fears that come up from over the years. And what have they done to Percy Sutton? They stilled his legs as effectively as if a nerve had been sat upon. And they were *cold,* and I had to massage my legs to get up and get off the bus. And *this* was fear. Fear that no one else would experience except a Negro, fear from conditioning, and it's a *cruel* sort of fear.

Sutton's account of that moment conveys not only the complex emotions at work but also the profound change taking place in black politics. This

NAACP attorney Percy Sutton recalls the Freedom Rides: "This was fear!"

is no longer simply a struggle over civil rights or legal equality; African Americans are beginning to challenge the social and psychic abuses of racism in the United States.

Moreover, blacks are beginning to connect their struggles with events in Africa. We next travel to the United Nations General Assembly, where black representatives from Nigeria are being seated for the first time. Civil rights leader James Farmer explains that the emergence of sovereign nations in black Africa is giving American Negroes a new sense of self-respect. Negroes, he says, are beginning to demand the same rights as their African counterparts. For many this means integration and equality. But the president of the black National Baptist Convention warns that growing frustration and anger is making many blacks turn to "irresponsible" and "violent" leaders.

The camera then cuts on cue to a shot of Malcolm X arriving in a black sedan accompanied by a cadre of assistants and bodyguards. Like the documentary analysis of Soviet politics presented in chapter 2, the visual imagery conjures up a gangster motif. The segment further suggests that radical politics coalesces around charismatic leadership as the camera directs our attention to a fiery speech by Malcolm, who passionately exclaims:

The gangster motif reemerges as Malcolm X arrives at a Nation of Islam gathering.

They say that [I deal] with the emotions of our people. No! When you tell a man that he's Jim Crowed, you're not playing on his emotions. You're telling him the truth. When you tell a black man that his neck is being broken on the tree day in and day out, that he is segregated, spit upon, Jim Crowed, deprived of civil rights, deprived of equal rights, deprived of first-class citizenship, that's not playing on anybody's emotions; that's playing on a man's intelligence.

The purpose of this segment seems to fit with other documentaries that characterize charismatic political leaders as promoting an ideological blindness among their followers. Clearly Malcolm's speech is set up so as to portray him as a manipulative autocrat. But what is perhaps more interesting is the alternative viewpoint one could derive from the extensive coverage given this oration. That is, positioned toward the end of the program, even a white viewer could begin to glimpse the validity of Malcolm's analysis. Although the documentarists may have intended to present the Black Muslims as the violent alternative to peaceful integration, Malcolm's assessment of American racism is not so distant from the overall message of the documentary. Indeed, it might be interpreted as an eloquent summation of the documentary's portrayal of racism in the United States.

Malcolm X represents charismatic leadership in "Walk in My Shoes."

As the camera returns to the young protagonist in whose "shoes" the viewer is walking, the program concludes with an air of uncertainty. Emerging from the subway at the end of a long day, he returns to the darkened streets of his neighborhood and hears the competing entreaties of street-corner orators, each urging a different course of action for the African American. The program frames the available options on a continuum anchored by polar opposites: further attempts at liberal, incremental reform or militant, separatist revolt. One is predicated on a system of laws (however imperfect), and the other is predicated on the charisma of authoritarian leaders. One establishes an agenda of programmatic reform, and the other is steeped in the politics of passion. One resists impulsive action, and the other preys on human gullibility. One seeks to integrate all people into a pluralist, global system, and the other promotes separatism and open antagonism. Although liberal reform is presented as the most "reasonable" alternative, dramatic tension is structured into the narrative by the presentation of a viable case for the other alternative, black militancy. The *reason* white viewers should press for further civil rights reform is that without it, militant black movements will continue to grow.

Thus the narrative logic of the documentary requires that the attractions of militant movements appear viable—so viable, in fact, that as the

In conclusion, the black protagonist of "Walk in My Shoes" turns to the audience, "What do you expect me to do?"

protagonist listens to the sound of competing orators in the streets of his neighborhood, he turns thoughtfully to the camera and in voice-over asks, "Now where do I go and how do I get there? Do you know? What do *you* expect me to do?" These questions are left hanging at the conclusion as he turns and walks away into the night.[18]

Reflecting on the sixties, Michael R. Winston has written, "Television had more to say *about* blacks in American society, but very seldom was any of this said *by* blacks. Even when the messenger was black, in fact, the message was usually from a white point of view."[19] Thus African Americans were not only marginalized on network television, but they were also prodded to speak on command. This ventriloquism is striking in documentaries such as "Walk in My Shoes" because these programs conjure up black nationalism as the impending crisis facing white viewers who do not consent to the more moderate course of integration. That is, black nationalists are allowed to speak, but their words are positioned by a white institution, for a white audience, about an issue that is constructed as a "problem" for the white majority. Scholars such as Jane Rhodes have persuasively argued that such constraints on independent black speech are the outcome of a system based on the logic of majority politics and mass-market institutions.[20]

Certainly, this logic has permeated American television throughout its history. What makes the documentaries of the early sixties so distinctive, however, is that the same forces that imposed limitations in this case created openings as well. That is, those very interests that sought to contain and control representations of "racial unrest" also produced the conditions that brought angry black critiques of American racism to a prime-time national audience for the very first time. Although there is no doubt that documentaries generally tried to position such criticisms within the realm of dominant discourse, these programs also became sites for testing the boundaries and logic of that discourse. They became sites for probing different ways of understanding the world. Network documentarists were given a mandate to explore the most pressing problems of their time, and many of them took that mandate quite seriously. As a result, they often found themselves challenged by the documentation that they gathered. As with documentaries discussed earlier in this chapter, "Walk in My Shoes" is an unstable and ultimately troubling text. Its efforts at ideological containment are repeatedly undermined at both a visual and a discursive level.

All of the documentaries discussed in this chapter pose problems and frame issues within the overarching context of the Cold War. Is the nation physically fit to take on its determined foe? Can we compete in space exploration? Are the fruits of our labors distributed in a manner that will seem equitable to others? Can we resolve the race issue, or will it continue to undermine the legitimacy of our role as leader of the Free World? Thus each investigation takes the Cold War as its point of departure and its point of reference. These programs therefore conform to the New Frontier agenda by urging systematic reforms that will strengthen the United States internally as well as externally. These institutional documentaries therefore register the larger economic and political interests of the era. Yet at the same time, they often elaborate their arguments in unanticipated ways. The reform impetus often pushes the programs beyond the Cold War framework. The empirical documentation introduces unintended and excessive meanings. And the journalistic heritage of the genre invites competing voices to speak in ways that prime-time television had never before experienced. Consequently, the institutional context of network documentary created opportunities as well as constraints. It helped to open the door to a form of self-critical analysis that tempered and sometimes even undermined the Cold War assumptions that dominated this era.

Chapter Seven

Programs with Sales Potential

Although the first three chapters of this book portrayed documentary's "golden age" as largely a response to converging social, economic, and political forces, subsequent chapters have shown ways in which institutional, journalistic, and textual logics mediated this response. Historian Erik Barnouw is therefore correct to say that the network documentaries of this era bore the stamp of the military-industrial complex, but closer analysis has also shown that the programs were more contradictory than this comment might suggest. This chapter looks at two additional mediating influences during this golden age: the commercial and narrative logics of prime-time television. It explains how the pressures to popularize the documentary genre led to the adoption of many of the storytelling techniques of entertainment television. Producers hoped that these conventions not only would enhance the ratings of the programs but would naturalize the message as well. The outcomes, of course, were more mixed. Nevertheless, by considering these conventions, we will get a more subtle sense of the dynamic relationship between form and content in these New Frontier documentaries.

From the very beginning of the documentary boom, executives at all three networks contended that the programs should be able to attract commercial advertising. Indeed, in 1959 when Irving Gitlin took charge of creative projects in the public affairs unit at CBS, top management explicitly told him they were looking for new programs "with sales potential."[1] Television executives therefore must have been pleased when, over the next few years, the proportion of commercially sponsored public affairs programs rose from 46 to 54 percent.[2] Yet the growing number of sponsors was outpaced by the rapidly expanding number of documentaries. This created intense competitive pressures as all three networks feverishly pursued the limited number of advertisers who were interested in sponsoring prime-time documentaries. Sponsorship concerns were perhaps most severe at ABC, which could ill afford to expand its news and public affairs programming without generating revenues to help defray the cost.

Therefore, ABC executives were delighted to announce in June 1960 that Bell and Howell, the camera and electronics manufacturer, had signed on to sponsor the entire season of a new ABC documentary series.[3] Yet the company's interest in documentary was not strictly journalistic. As Charles Percy, Bell and Howell's chairman of the board, put it, "Our objective is to prove that the times in which we live can be just as dramatic, just as exciting as those 'colorful, heroic days of the West,' which, according to historians, were anything but."[4] Thus Percy made it clear from the outset that his corporation wanted to sponsor documentaries that would compete with entertainment shows for audience attention. During a promotional preview of what came to be known as the *Bell and Howell Close-Up!* series, ABC president Oliver Treyz characterized the sponsor's ambitions in the following manner:

> What Charles Percy and his associates said to us, in effect, was: Give us meaningful shows about important issues. Give us the background so that the problems can be seen in a time perspective of national and international events. But give us programs with compelling visual excitement, with drama, even with the passion of human emotions . . . and that is why [these shows] will all be seen on week days in prime viewing time.
>
> We hope, we anticipate that they will be able to meet and compete with sheer entertainment shows on the level of audience appeal and will be seen by many more millions than customarily view so-called educational programs. . . . *Close-Up* will give the *big picture,* but more than that, it will zoom in for revealing intimate glimpses that highlight the true human drama.[5]

Throughout the summer and into the fall, Bell and Howell kept close track of the series' development. At one point it even interceded in network promotion plans for the second documentary of the season, a report on Haiti called "Caribbean Dilemma." Bell and Howell executives were reportedly troubled by a draft of the press release for the program. One ABC executive who met with the sponsor telexed network headquarters with the following assessment:

> Client feels [the press release] is fine, but it doesn't go far enough, and is really in the nature of describing a documentary. We, of course, recognize this is a documentary, but they want it to be exploited. Not only in the documentary vein, but as a provocative spectacular. Consensus suggests ideas developing—

Communist Foothold Western Hemisphere—America's Soft Underbelly—
Castro's and Khrushchev's Delight—Beach-head to Tyranny, etc.[6]

Clearly, this telex suggests that the sponsor envisioned a program that
would be promoted much the same as Hollywood feature films about
World War II. Even after the program was repackaged as "Paradise in
Chains," the sponsor still expressed reservations about the final product,
however. In a letter to ABC headquarters, Bell and Howell's senior vice
president Peter G. Peterson complained that the visual dimension of the
program "did not have this illusory but important thing called excite-
ment." Peterson continued: "You will also remember our extended conversations about the fundamental need for new and we hoped highly
visual (rather than the traditional abstract) approaches to public service
shows. We felt that too many of these shows in the past might be characterized as newsmanship without showmanship."[7]

In response to Peterson's letter, John Daly, then head of ABC's news
operation, rejected the notion that his department would gear its documentary productions toward "showmanship." Nevertheless, network
pressure to find a documentary formula with mass appeal was unmistakable.[8] Within a matter of weeks Daly was forced out by top ABC executives, and shortly thereafter the news division broadcast one of the most
visual and passionate documentaries of the early sixties, "Yanki No!, a
program produced by independent filmmaker Robert Drew.[9] Furthermore, ABC's own documentarists went on to produce many of the most
visually provocative public affairs programs of the early 1960s.

In some respects the situation at ABC News was exceptional. The network appeared willing to cater to the needs of Bell and Howell because it
desperately needed the income to defray the costs of its rapid expansion.
Moreover, the *Close-Up* sponsor, as a manufacturer of amateur and professional motion picture equipment, had a vested interest in the visual
aspects of the documentaries.[10] Finally, ABC's news division was not then
inhabited by a staff of prestigious, well-paid journalists who had the institutional clout to resist the interventions of a commercial sponsor. Despite ABC's exceptional circumstances, however, the other networks
found themselves confronting similar concerns, and none could ignore
the fact that entertainment values, popularity, and ratings were of growing interest to sponsors and network executives throughout the late
1950s and early 1960s. These pressures manifested themselves in the
very components of documentary highlighted by Bell and Howell executives: narrative and filmic representation. The resulting programs were
intended to do more than convey information. They were designed to

attract audiences with dramatic stories and a seamless flow of visual imagery.

Documentary as a Narrative Form

The documentary genre first appeared on television as a form of "serious" journalism. During the early 1950s, most television news reporting was widely disparaged by media critics as a superficial headline service, as little more than radio news bulletins, sometimes with pictures. Documentary, on the other hand, afforded an opportunity for network news workers to demonstrate the journalistic potential of their medium. It allowed them to prove that television could offer more than a fistful of headlines and a smattering of newsreel footage; it could be more than a *Camel Caravan of News.* As described in chapter five, early network documentarists therefore embraced the standards of professional journalism and sought to distance themselves not only from a heritage of newsreel trivia but also from the cinematic tradition of documentary that included advocacy and even propaganda films.[11]

Yet some of the earliest attempts to fulfill this ambition seemed to overcompensate. Not only did they lack the partisan passion of a filmmaker such as Joris Ivens, but they also were stylistically unimaginative. Issues were framed in stilted rhetorical fashion; visuals were limited; and interviews with experts tended to dominate the programs. Even those who would later emerge as top producers tended to follow this pattern. For example, NBC producer Fred Freed later recalled his early experiences working alongside colleague Albert Wasserman: "[Wasserman] didn't have the film sense that he later developed. He was very, very much still—as was almost everybody at CBS—under the influence of Fred Friendly and the radio approach; tell 'em what you're going to tell 'em; tell 'em; and then tell 'em what you've told 'em. And make everything perfectly clear every step of the way."[12]

As we shall see in this section, documentary producers moved away from this style as narrative considerations became increasingly important during the late fifties and early sixties. Although some of the programs were still rhetorically constructed, the most reputedly successful producers were invoking narrative strategies to deal with public issues. They were paying attention to plot and character and to the affective response of the audience. "Anything I do I like to approach from a narrative rather than an interpretive position," commented NBC's Emmy-winning producer Reuven Frank. "Even great issues can be more successfully illuminated than expounded."[13] That sentiment was echoed at ABC, which put John Secondari in charge of its nascent documentary unit. Secondari's sensitivity to narrative concerns grew out of his experiences writing scripts for "The Alcoa Hour" and "Playhouse 90." Furthermore, he came to ABC News with four novels to his credit, among them a book that was turned into the popular Hollywood feature film *Three Coins in the Fountain.*[14] Others at ABC shared Secondari's disposition as well. Producer Edgar Peterson, who was in charge of a special documentary series about Winston Churchill during the war years, likened the Churchill episodes to westerns with a hero, a villain, and a chase.[15]

Therefore, by 1960 a significant transition had taken place in the discourse of documentary professionalism. Network producers now spoke of narrative forms as important tools for organizing information and attracting the attention of audiences. These producers were not arguing that issues naturally lent themselves to narrative structure, nor were they arguing that events and relationships in the objective world would emerge in narrative form on their own. Rather, they were proposing that many of the conventions of fiction be applied to documentary television. Although the implications for journalistic objectivity seemed troublesome, the trend was unmistakable. As Fred Friendly, executive producer of *CBS Reports*, put it, "We hope each show will be just like reading through to the last page of a detective story to discover whether the butler did it. You won't know the outcome of any of our shows until you see it."[16]

Such an approach to documentary indicated that producers were increasingly reflecting on the affective impact on audiences. As Irving Gitlin pointed out to his colleagues in 1955:

> The proper way to view what we are doing is alone, or with one or two people, seated at home, with maybe the coffee percolating in the kitchen and view it through a somewhat badly focused screen, perhaps no larger than this (indicating two feet), and then see what your effect is. . . . What this really adds up to is the overwhelming importance of the element of intimacy and the element of the personalized approach in TV.[17]

Gitlin contended that character and plot were key elements in this "personalized approach" to documentary. The CBS research department confirmed this assessment two years later when it issued a major study of thirty-two documentaries based on responses by twenty-five hundred adults. The study found the respondents to be critical of most network documentaries for a number of reasons: "too much [voice-over] narration, not enough action, not entertaining, no unity or simplicity (too many scenes, characters, etc.), story gets under way slowly, too many issues and statistics." The programs that audiences found most satisfying were programs with "a strong unifying central character, a definite setting, and a strong unifying plot."[18]

This shifting assessment of the documentary not only reflected commercial pressures, but it also reflected the growing influence of the documentary producer as opposed to the network correspondent. Producers—who had overall responsibility for the finished program—tended to emphasize storytelling, whereas correspondents paid closer attention to issues.[19] This distinction is perhaps best understood by noting that many of the top correspondents at the networks during the early 1960s had matured professionally during World War II. They entered the profession at a time when "great issues" commanded audience attention almost regardless of a news program's structure or style. During World War II, the progress of battle campaigns and political developments created larger narrative frameworks into which the accounts of correspondents were positioned. This is not to say that radio war correspondents did not pay attention to stylistic considerations, but issues and events were their first consideration while the dramatic component was often provided by extratextual elements. In contrast, by the late 1950s documentary producers often felt the need to convey or even create a sense of urgency. For example, CBS's Shad Northshield saw this element as crucial: "In a television documentary the most important thing you have to do is induce an emotional response in a viewer. You have to make an emotional penetration first. Having done that, having gotten inside the viewer, then you give him the information. When you've done both things, you've communicated."[20] It is remarkable how much this comment sounds like the patter one would hear from Madison Avenue or the Hollywood hills during this period. Given the tremendous influence these two communities wielded within the television industry, it is not surprising that as documentaries shifted to prime time, the producers saw themselves competing for the attention of audiences with narrative techniques developed by advertisers and feature film makers.

For example, when executive producer Irving Gitlin and his *NBC White Paper* unit set out to do a documentary about welfare, they focused first on the story. "In doing shows of this sort," noted Gitlin, "you must start out, I believe, with a human center—an individual or group of individuals through whom you can tell a story."[21] Thus Gitlin and his colleagues turned to a small city in upstate New York where City Manager Joseph M. Mitchell had been receiving a tremendous amount of

The Weygant family provides part of the "human center" in "The Battle of New-burgh."

national attention for his campaign against "welfare chiselers." The program repeatedly juxtaposed Mitchell's fiery pronouncements with the everyday lives of the so-called chiselers. This gave the documentary a human center and a conflict, and it allowed NBC to deal with the larger (unmanageable) issue of welfare in microcosm.[22] When interviewed shortly before the broadcast, producer Albert Wasserman said, "We're not interested in Newburgh for its own sake, but it's a symbol of one concept of welfare. We are trying to do it on two levels: a factual and a human level."[23] To achieve this goal, the crew made about sixty trips to Newburgh in order to interview subjects, gather information, and shoot about thirty hours of film. The final product offered villains, heroes, a conflict, and even a coda in which a town judge, seated on a park bench, proposed a moral to the story.

Similar considerations affected the production process at CBS. Executive producer Fred Friendly maintained a fastidious attachment to the 35mm film camera at a time when other documentary units had switched over to more portable 16mm equipment. Friendly stuck with the more unwieldy equipment because he wanted a high-quality film image that could compete with the entertainment programming produced by Hollywood studios. While ABC was portering hand-held cameras around Latin America and NBC was sending reporters behind rebel lines in Angola, CBS crews were showing up on location with several station wagons full of gear. Not only was the 35mm camera heavier, but it required a great deal more lighting. Therefore, as Thomas Whiteside noted in a *New Yorker* profile, when a Friendly crew showed up, the filming became an event in itself.

> His business requires him to be accompanied by a tremendous clutter of equipment—one or two thousand pounds of motion-picture cameras, extra lenses, big lights and reflectors, power converters, great coils of cable, bulky boxes of film, microphone hookups, and sound recording equipment. And he must also be accompanied by the people who operate all these devices, at the very least a cameraman, an assistant cameraman, a sound man, and an electrician.[24]

Given such logistical complications, it would have been difficult for Friendly to argue that his crews had filmed average people carrying on their everyday activities. Instead, what unfolded before the camera was a highly choreographed event. Yet Friendly said he was willing to sacrifice impromptu activity for high-quality sound and photography.[25] According to him, the documentary image, like the Hollywood feature film, had to be free of blemishes and full of detail.[26]

The details Friendly most avidly pursued were those of character. He looked for people with strong convictions who would not wilt under the pressures of filming. If he could not find someone who came across powerfully on camera, Friendly was known to drop a project.[27] Thus Friendly's selection process excluded significant subjects and issues because of the technical and narrative considerations that he associated with Hollywood quality. Friendly aspired to more than objectivity; he aspired to the dramatic representation of character within a narrative framework, and he was willing to make journalistic compromises in order to achieve this goal.

Interviews on *CBS Reports* were known for "crispness and pace," despite the fact that CBS documentary crews had one of the highest shooting ratios in the business. Friendly's staff would winnow through endless hours of exposed film in order to select the most salient and dramatic elements of each interview. Therefore the drama in these programs did not simply result from the camera's ability to record controversy in everyday life. Rather, these programs are marked by a number of filmmaking strategies that sought to heighten the effect of a character's statements. Friendly would generate dramatic tension through the editing process by juxtaposing animated interview subjects from opposing sides of a controversial issue.[28] Yet what made Friendly's work particularly compelling was the manner in which he heightened the dramatic impact of his characters and their concerns by the way he framed the interviews. As Thomas Whiteside noted:

> In the flesh, a man's face is, after all, only part of him, but in a close-up it becomes, suddenly, all of him. Every facial movement or gesture is heightened in effect, and every accompanying vocal inflection is correspondingly stressed, with the result that the whole personality of the man is peculiarly concentrated and revealed. This ability of television to accentuate character gives Friendly an opportunity to make his subjects, as he puts it, "larger than life," and it is into the job of encouraging this mysterious magnifying process that Friendly flings the full force of his professional energy.[29]

Through this process of magnification, Friendly accentuated one of the most important components of Hollywood narrative: character.[30] Although his filmmaking strategies were grossly inefficient, critics agreed that Friendly could achieve striking dramatic effects through his ability to project the image of a character locked in conflict. Therefore, unlike the public affairs talk show in which issues are the focus and respondents are framed at an equal and respectful distance, Friendly's interviews would intrude on personal space of the subject in search of physical gestures and inflections that might heighten the drama of the program.[31]

It should also be pointed out, however, that Friendly and the CBS unit were not unique in their use of such interview techniques. Like Friendly, NBC's Fred Freed employed similar strategies, and his assessment of potential interview subjects was similarly couched in terms of drama. Regarding nuclear scientist Robert Oppenheimer, Freed remembered him as having "the finest command of language of anybody [he had] ever interviewed. Not only were his sentences structured precisely, but his delivery was as perfect as any actor [Freed had] ever known. He had a quiet sense of drama."[32]

Indeed, Oppenheimer was the subject for what Freed recalled as the most moving moment of any interview he had ever filmed. The program was called "The Decision to Drop the Bomb," and Freed had asked Oppenheimer what it was like on July 16, 1945, when he witnessed the first atomic explosion. Oppenheimer responded:

> We knew the world would not be the same. Few people laughed. Few people cried. Most people were silent. I remembered the line from the Hindu scripture, the Baghavad Gita: Vishnu is trying to persuade the prince that he should do his duty, and, to impress him, takes on his mutilated form and says, "Now I am become death, destroyer of the worlds." I suppose we all thought that one way or another.[33]

Nuclear physicist Robert Oppenheimer sheds a tear as the camera zooms closer for "the perfect moment in a television interview."

According to Freed's recollection of the interview:

> At the moment he quoted what Vishnu had said, Dr. Oppenheimer reached up and wiped a tear from his eye. And at the same moment, Joe Vadala [the camera operator] had very smoothly zoomed in so that he was on a tight close-up and he held it. That's not something you can plan or direct. It was there and Joe caught it. The perfect moment in a television interview.[34]

Like Friendly, Freed and his camera operator were both conscious of the dramatic intent behind their framing of Oppenheimer's response. Such maneuvers were then considered unacceptable according to the conventions of breaking news coverage or the public affairs talk show; however, among documentarists such as Friendly and Freed it was considered the epitome of interview technique.[35]

Therefore, by the early 1960s documentary representations of important social issues were significantly influenced by the storytelling conventions of popular television, including considerations of plot, character, pursuit of an affective response from audiences, and conscious competition with entertainment programming. Yet these were not the only conventions that pointed to the growing influence of narrative television. Documentary editing and camera techniques also developed according to Hollywood conventions.

Documentary as Filmic Realism

Historically, the visual image has proven to be a crucial component of the television news report. It is widely assumed by network news workers that words and images should work together. The words of the reporter attempt to organize the complex and conflicting meanings of everyday life so as to create a unified, coherent narrative. Meanwhile, images are used to corroborate the words and give viewers a sense of "being there," of watching events unfold before their very eyes. As Robert A. Hackett has noted, "The film stands as the guarantor of the narrative's validity."[36]

Yet filmic images did more than simply provide a form of visual corroboration during this "golden age" of documentary. They also suggested that the stories that were being told were realist texts, that they emerged *naturally* from a given social environment. As executive producer Fred Friendly told one newspaper critic when announcing the season premiere of *CBS Reports*, "We're going to use Thursday night at 10 for realism, for the world about us, for real people, real issues, real controversy."[37] Note that Friendly chose not to mention the ways in which the documentarist creatively shaped the images that would be broadcast. Like his mentor, Edward R. Murrow, Friendly was fond of characterizing documentary work as little more than holding up a mirror to social reality.[38]

Thus the photographic image was not only an important form of evidence in the documentaries of this period; it is also one of the means by which these programs concealed their constructed nature. The visual imagery in these documentaries invite the viewer to enter the world of the narrative without being conscious of the author's efforts to shape that world.[39] There is an illusion of naturalness. Yet the filmic conventions that make this illusion possible were anything but natural. During the early years of television news, these conventions had to be *learned* by news workers who in many cases had come from a print or radio background. In fact, during the early 1950s, when networks first experimented with the documentary form, news workers were often criticized for producing "illustrated radio shows."[40] The visual dimension of these early programs paled in comparison with the realism of prime-time television. By middecade, however, network news organizations were beginning to make changes.

In 1955, at a workshop for network correspondents, CBS producers stressed the importance of visual considerations. For example, one producer reminded correspondents that most business and government offices are indistinguishable on camera. He therefore encouraged reporters to lure their interview subjects out of the office and to position them in a setting that was "natural" to the story. Quoting the producer: "If you had [Prime Minister Pierre] Mendes-France in your [bureau] office, it would be pretty hard to convince the American audience that it was taking place in Paris. This is something extra. If we can prove by the background that it is in California or Kansas City, it helps." Added Jack Bush, production manager of CBS newsfilm, "I do not think you have to get too 'circusey' about it, but the thing is, you do create the *illusion* of realism."[41]

Toward the same end, correspondents were encouraged to keep the technology of filmmaking concealed. For example, there was extended discussion about microphone placement during interviews and the ways in which a microphone in the frame detracted from the illusion of realism. Lighting and image resolution also were discussed in relation to this issue. Said Bush:

> [I]f anything, the technical perfection of television news is the thing that will create the illusion of realism. If you have a poor picture or a poor sound track, you disturb that illusion. At lunch, we discussed the kind of drama we would

like to put into news. Basically, that is creating the illusion of realism, of taking you to the event, and we must maintain this quality to do that.[42]

As we can see, this illusion of realism was not achieved through some objective or "natural" means of representation. Rather, it was an appeal to a set of conventions that many news workers had to be taught. David Yellin has argued that because most network news executives were from a radio background during the 1950s, they deferred to Hollywood's "pretty-picture" approach to realism. Wrote Yellin: "[T]hey were apt to be fastidious about the proprieties of cinematography, timid about experimentation. They were not about to risk being criticized for allowing fuzzy or shaky pictures on the air, for being unprofessional. These men knew what they didn't know and therefore took refuge in the conventional."[43]

The conventions of realism to which Yellin refers are those that David Bordwell, Kristin Thompson, and Janet Staiger have so meticulously detailed as the conventions of Hollywood style.[44] Following that style, network news executives circulated memos that encouraged their staff to observe the standard principles of framing and shooting that prevailed in Hollywood cinema. In addition, the grammar of analytical editing was considered fundamental. Accordingly, camera operators were encouraged to gather establishing shots and master shots for each scene, along with a series of shots from different angles designed to break down space within the master shot. Similarly, interviews were staged and edited within the parameters of shot/reverse-shot construction. Hollywood conventions of framing also were adopted in order to facilitate eyeline matching. And camera operators were reminded to use a tripod whenever possible.[45]

Other practices were borrowed from the conventions of Hollywood style as well. Images were filmed and arranged so as to deemphasize the manipulation of time and space. Therefore editing conventions fostered the notion that televised events unfolded in real time, that actions and events had not been speeded up or slowed down. This convention was invoked so consistently that, as Gaye Tuchman has observed, it came to signify impartiality. "By seeming *not* to arrange time and space," wrote Tuchman, "news film claims to present facts, not interpretations. That is, the web of facticity is embedded in a supposedly neutral . . . synchronization of film with the rhythm of everyday life."[46] I would add, however, that these filmic images were not so much synchronized with the rhythms of everyday life as they were with the rhythms of Hollywood style. They are synchronized with a particular style of representing

Standard shot—reverse shot editing pattern in "Harvest of Shame."

everyday life, and they achieve their "neutral" effect because this style is so standardized. It is therefore the *conventions* of Hollywood realism that confer the status of facticity on edited news film.

We should not be surprised that the documentaries of the early 1960s mimicked Hollywood's editing conventions, since network news executives filled the technically oriented production jobs with film workers rather than news workers. In fact, the skill that seemed to distinguish top-flight documentary producers was their ability as film editors.[47] For example, Albert Wasserman, one of NBC's top documentarists, started out as an educational filmmaker who produced a series of films for the United Nations in the late 1940s, one of which won an Academy Award. It was not until 1953 that Wasserman started working for the networks, and thus his knowledge of filmmaking preceded his exposure to journalism.[48] Nor was his background unique for a documentary producer during the early 1960s. As Wasserman told one reporter for *Variety*, "What we've found is that it often works out better for us to [hire] a talented film worker instead of a reporter, because it is frequently easier to train him in television documentary techniques." Furthermore, it is interesting that both Wasserman and Gitlin left NBC in the mid-1960s in order set up their own production companies and pursue independent feature film projects.[49]

Similarly, ABC's Nicholas Webster, who moved back and forth between the worlds of feature film and documentary, used his storytelling skills to produce several award-winning *Close-Up!* programs. Webster, who grew up in Hollywood, began his career in the film lab on the MGM lot.[50] He joined ABC in 1961 in order to work on a first-person exploration of racism through the eyes of a young black man. An Emmy nominee in 1962, "Walk in My Shoes" was heavily promoted by ABC and has been singled out as one of the best documentaries of this period.[51] In fact, the wide recognition Webster received for his documentary work made it difficult for him to return to feature films, since many perceived him as having an established reputation as a documentarist.[52]

Meanwhile at CBS, the director of operations for the *Reports* series was Palmer Williams, who spent the 1940s in Hollywood working on both feature films and government war propaganda. Under the direction of Frank Capra, Williams worked on the production staff of the Academy Award–winning *Why We Fight* film series. In 1951 he joined CBS as the production manager of *See It Now*, thus having a hand in formulating the early film grammar of network documentary.[53]

Also at CBS was David Lowe, producer of the documentary classic "Harvest of Shame." Lowe's eclectic background included most every-

Producer David Lowe interviewing a grower in "Harvest of Shame."

thing but news. A member of the Army Signal Corps during World War II, Lowe took part in the filming of the Bikini A-Bomb test. Between that time and when he joined *CBS Reports* in 1959, Lowe produced three Broadway plays, managed two theaters, served as an arts critic, and, during the late 1950s, was director of the TV game show *Who Do You Trust?* starring Johnny Carson.[54] Quite clearly, Lowe, like many documentary producers, matured outside the confines of the city room.

Given the backgrounds of these producers and their colleagues, it is not surprising that the conventions of Hollywood realism should figure so prominently in documentary work from this period. These filmmakers married the dramatic realism of Hollywood cinema to the journalistic pretensions of objectivity. Yet the marriage was not natural, nor did it develop unproblematically. One therefore finds traces of these ambiguities in the documentaries themselves.

Telling Stories about the Cold War

Tensions between documentary style and content were not unlike the ambiguities discussed earlier regarding journalistic documentation and interpretation. In both cases the tensions were unresolvable and left the genre vulnerable to criticism from outsiders as well as network insiders. Was the audience being offered facts or interpretations? Was it being asked to identify emotionally with characters or to work rationally through the issues? Such questions were always in the air. Consequently, news workers were easily subject to criticism, especially when they took a strong stand on a contentious domestic topic. Such programs were sure to draw careful scrutiny from many knowledgeable individuals and interest groups. The Catholic Church, the Republican Party, and the American Medical Association are only a few of the many groups that lodged complaints. Foreign policy documentaries, on the other hand, were less likely to invite such passionate criticism. As mentioned in chapter 5, neither foreigners nor Communists were considered legitimate critics in the eyes of the Federal Communications Commission and therefore had little leverage in their complaints to the networks. Furthermore, few "legitimate" viewers were likely to be discerning enough to challenge documentary representations of complex issues in foreign countries. Such factors may help to explain further the popularity of foreign policy topics with network documentarists during this period. The topics were not only of key concern to political and corporate leaders, but they were also less likely to invite informed opposition.

Yet these same factors presented distinctive problems of their own. For example, because audiences knew so little about foreign affairs, it was more difficult to connect the concerns of people in other countries to the everyday interests of viewers in the United States. And given the commercial pressures to attract sponsors and draw large audiences, documentarists were challenged to produce programs about foreign affairs that were as compelling as prime-time entertainment fare. Secondly, the audiences' lack of familiarity with these issues made it difficult to cover a subject adequately within the space of an hour. Consequently, network documentarists employed many of the storytelling strategies discussed in this chapter both to attract audience attention and to convey information effectively.

One of these techniques was to structure information around a tight narrative conflict. Thus documentaries about Brazil and Angola discussed in chapter 4 took very complicated information and deployed it within a very tight narrative structure that revolved around the struggle between East and West. Similarly, Khrushchev's rise to power during the post-Stalin era was explained largely as a power struggle between key characters. In each of these cases, the program is structured from the outset as a struggle between sharply defined competing forces. And these groups or individuals contend for dramatically high stakes. In most all situations, these narratives are life-and-death struggles for power and control. Moreover, these documentaries repeatedly suggest that the fate of the Free World hangs in the balance.

Another strategy aimed at sustaining audience interest was to anchor issues to particular personalities with whom the viewer might identify. Accordingly, the documentary about Brazil begins as the story of President Quadros, the "white knight" of reform politics who steps down in the face of staunch resistance from conservative factions. His personal story is emblematic of the struggle for modernization and reform in Brazil. Dressed in a business suit, he is likened to the middle-class viewer in the United States and contrasted with the bearded revolutionary Fidel Castro. Quadros therefore becomes a point of identification for the intended audience. Interestingly, however, these techniques were not exclusively reserved for public figures who represented a sympathetic political position. For example, Josira Verabizi was made emblematic of the Italian Communist, and the Manzanilla family represented the arduous conditions in a Caracas slum. Because network documentarists sought to personalize abstract issues and foreign cultures, they often presented sympathetic portraits of characters with oppositional or alternative politics. To know about Verabizi's personal history and her everyday concerns is to know why she would be attracted to the Communist Party in Italy. To understand the Manzanilla family's fate is to know why Castro's popularity is growing throughout Latin America. Finally, character construction was used to embody the abstract threat of monolithic Communism. To witness Castro, the messianic antihero, whipping his adoring audience into a political frenzy is to observe the Red threat at work. Similarly, one could come to understand the nature of Soviet foreign policy by watching a narrative about Nikita Khrushchev's struggle for power after the death of Stalin.

These storytelling techniques were further enhanced by a form of filmic realism drawn from the Hollywood tradition. In an attempt to mimic the visual style of entertainment film and television, these documentaries adopted the same shooting and editing style. Emphasis was placed on the production of a seamless flow of images that would emphasize the major story components and obscure the traces of interpretation and representation. Viewers were encouraged to pay attention to the story and suspend their critical distance. Attention was drawn away from the act of narrative construction and focused on the story itself. These programs did not say, "This is one point of view." Rather, they suggested that they were natural representations of people, places, and events. It was implied that the stories told themselves and that the documentarist merely recorded what was going on "out there."

Although these techniques were at work in all documentaries of this period, their impact may have been greatest with the foreign policy programs. Primarily this was due to most viewers' lack of experience with other countries. As a result, the realist narratives presented in these programs could not be measured against the viewer's everyday experience. Agenda-setting research has shown that news reports that have the greatest effect on public opinion are those that deal with issues that are least familiar to the audience.[55] Reports on inflation can, for example, be weighed against the viewer's own experiences, but this is less commonly the case with foreign policy reporting. Therefore televised accounts of a distant civil war achieve a peculiar power given the fact that television creates the illusion that one is seeing and experiencing the conflict firsthand. That illusion is more than visual, however; it is the product of a carefully integrated package of sound, image, and narration that, like Hollywood fiction, encourages the viewer to suspend disbelief and become absorbed in the story. A similar observation could be made about the foreign policy documentaries of the early sixties. The persuasiveness of their analysis was no doubt significantly enhanced by stylistic techniques that encouraged viewers to temper their critical stance.

Furthermore, the storytelling techniques of the foreign policy documentary were probably influential with audiences because the narrative logic dovetailed with Cold War dichotomies that were widely circulated in the culture at large. As a result, the struggle between East and West in these programs was a narrative mechanism that reinforced the analytical categories promoted by New Frontier discourse. These categories were spoken of with a dramatic flourish by heroic young leaders who labored feverishly against a powerful Communist foe. Thus the "mortal danger" and the "historic challenge" to which the administration so often referred were brought to the screen in similarly dramatic form in network documentary. Even though, for example, the most pressing concerns of Brazilians may have been economic and political reform, the structuring narrative of "Brazil: The Rude Awakening" revolved around superpower struggle. The Manichaean abstractions that have played such an influential role in U.S. foreign policy were therefore augmented by the narrative strategies of the television documentary.

On the other hand, it must also be remembered that these conventions did not entirely have a one-sided effect. They did not simply and instrumentally reinforce dominant ideology. In fact, we have seen that on numerous occasions they invited viewers to identify with alternative or oppositional characters. Josira Verabizi, the prototypical Italian Communist, is an entirely sympathetic character. Exploited by a medieval land tenure system, she spent much of her life toiling at low wages on behalf of the rich and powerful few. Her embrace of the Communist Party is therefore poignant, if not seemingly logical. Similarly, the documentary about automation invites the audience to identify with displaced workers from the very outset. The meat-packing employee who lost his job at the age of fifty reminds the viewer of the precarious nature of middle-class prosperity. Neither computer executives nor government officials become similar objects of audience identification within this documentary. Some critics have argued, of course, that such moments of identification merely invite a sympathetic reaction for victims of exploitation.[56] Consequently, the viewers experience the scene from a position of superiority that actually associates them more closely with the expert or the official spokesperson. Although this may be true, two countervailing tendencies must be taken into account. First, the "victims" in the documentaries of the early sixties were not entirely passive. The young black protagonist in "Walk in My Shoes" is constructed as a representative of many African Americans who, frustrated by legal attempts to achieve equality, are now poised for more confrontational actions. Similarly, the Cuban fisher in "Yanki No!" invites our sympathy, but more tellingly he reminds the viewer of the surging popular movements throughout Latin America. Second, in those instances in which viewer sympathy is directed toward a relatively passive victim of exploitation, such as the field-workers in "Harvest of Shame," one still must wrestle with the contradictions of the Free World. Although the viewers may not identify with the characters in the documentary, they still must reconcile assumptions about free enterprise with a personalized representation of naked exploitation.

Such ambiguities were common in network documentaries through this period. Despite diligent efforts by network producers to promote the genre's popularity and to conceal the traces of interpretation, documentary still remained the most contested form of programming in network prime time. Although many originally hoped that the programs would promote consensus, in practice they proved far more unwieldy, owing in large part to the diverse and relatively autonomous forces that shaped the golden age of documentary.

Chapter Eight

The Overdetermined Text: "Panama: Danger Zone"

As pointed out in the introduction, the concepts of hegemony and over-determination are central to my analysis of television during the New Frontier era. They help us not only to understand the emergence of television documentary's golden age but to analyze the programs themselves. Rather than simply reflecting other social forces, these documentaries have been examined as an important site for the production of societal consensus. My analysis suggests that although cultural forms register changes in society, they also help to *produce* connections between diverse groups and social practices and to mediate tensions and contradictions as well. Thus one cannot adequately assess these programs without trying to understand how the texts are articulated to various economic tendencies, political agendas, and institutional logics. These linkages are in no way inevitable, nor do they always operate the same way. Rather, as Stuart Hall argues, power in modern society is exercised through the "not necessary" articulation of practices.[1] That is, the multiple forces at work during any given moment operate according to specific tendencies and logics, but the connections between practices are in no way predictable. Particular groups may achieve power only as the result of intensive effort to bring disparate tendencies into line. Such an approach offers a structured analysis while also emphasizing the contingency of articulations and the dynamic, contested nature of historical processes. It explains the convergence of societal forces while noting discontinuities and ruptures as well.

Accordingly, I have attempted throughout this book to analyze television documentaries in relation to shifting economic, political, social, and institutional forces. As such, we have moved back and forth between the examination of contextual forces and the analysis of texts that demonstrate these forces at work. We have also seen how the discursive logic of these programs resonated with societal forces and helped to circulate an ideology of New Frontier internationalism. Nevertheless, the overdetermined nature of these documentaries still needs to be more fully elaborated so as to highlight the complex relationships between these texts and larger societal forces. This chapter explores the various and sometimes conflicting tendencies at work in one particular program, NBC's "Panama: Danger Zone." I have chosen this documentary not because it is "representative" of the genre as a whole but because the process of analyzing its discursive logic will allow us to pull together various strands of analysis elaborated in earlier chapters.

"Panama: Danger Zone" was produced by Albert Wasserman under the direction of *NBC White Paper*'s executive producer, Irving Gitlin.[2] It focuses on the controversy over control of the Canal Zone, a conflict that escalated in November 1959 to a violent clash between Panamanian demonstrators and U.S. troops. The documentary crew visited Panama as the first anniversary of the incident approached, hoping to explore the factors feeding the conflict and wondering whether street clashes would erupt again. Yet rather than focusing primarily on the issue of Panamanian sovereignty, NBC network publicists promoted the program as an examination of an "anti-American riot in Panama and its meaning for U.S. policy toward all of Latin America."[3] This promotional slant takes the local and the specific and elevates them to a level of abstraction that was of keen interest to New Frontier elites. In positioning the program for the viewer, it suggests connections between the documentary and President Kennedy's foreign policy agenda at the very moment that the new administration was taking office.

The press release also negotiates a complex set of boundary markers regarding the relationship between U.S. viewers and other citizens of the Free World. It first of all hails the audience as U.S. citizens, as distinct from those who live south of the border, and it also folds Latin America into a single generic category. In this way, the program constructs a unified national audience and sets out to explore the connections between these U.S. viewers and their Free World neighbors to the south. Such an approach clearly responds to criticisms of television that were raised by business and political leaders in the post-*Sputnik* era. The program urges audience awareness of foreign policy issues, particularly the problem of civil unrest in other parts of the Free World. In this sense, it expands the boundaries of public concern beyond the borders of the United States and suggests a common destiny for all citizens of the Western Hemisphere. Rather than focusing on specific issues in Panama, it elevates the conflict to a more abstract level of concern for the fortunes of the Free World community.

Another process of abstraction is at work in the program's address as well. The audience invoked by this documentary is a mass audience that spans the United States. The viewers do not physically gather in a single space but are instead drawn together by NBC's prime-time programming, its promotion efforts, and its ratings services. NBC aspires to construct a *national* audience for its programming owing to the logic of networking, a practice specific to the television industry during this period. Consequently, this documentary about U.S. policy in Latin America addresses a national audience not simply for political reasons but also because of the institutional practices of television. The documentary must fit into the logic of the evening schedule if the genre is to survive in prime time. Thus two logics are at work here. One is a political logic that constructs the audience as motivated by a set of concerns about the Free World. The other is an institutional logic that resulted from the development of the television industry during the 1950s as a national advertising and entertainment medium. As we saw in chapter 1, the articulation of these two levels was the product of a public debate over the uses of television that gathered force around the time of the *Sputnik* launch. Although one might say the focus of this documentary reflects elite political concerns, we can see that the process of linking these concerns to documentary content was mediated through political, institutional, and discursive practices as well.

These parameters engender a documentary narrative that constructs Panama as a site of struggle between the United States and monolithic Communism. On the one hand, converging social, economic, and political concerns of the post-*Sputnik* era necessitate a focus on the question of superpower struggle. On the other hand, the institutional logic of network television encourages the producers to create a documentary with a dramatic conflict that might attract a national audience during prime time. This narrative conflict is represented in an opening montage that begins with film footage of daily operations along the Panama Canal. Images of high technology, rationality, and stability are foregrounded here as we listen to a tour guide describe the canal as the "eighth wonder of the world." Chet Huntley's voice-over narration further notes that little has changed along the canal in more than four decades of operation. This apparent equilibrium is then shattered by an edit that juxtaposes footage of the canal with footage of a street riot that broke out in Panama City one year earlier. As the visual imagery portrays chaotic violence and high emotion, Huntley's narration coolly informs us that, unlike in the Canal Zone, things are changing rapidly in Panama because of increasing protests against the U.S. presence. We see an effigy of Uncle Sam weaving through the streets drawing jeers from the crowd, while a huge poster of Fidel is portered about with great enthusiasm. We also see pictures of a street confrontation between rock-throwing demonstrators and heavily armed troops. Huntley says that American officials fear that, as the first anniversary of this "riot" approaches, violence could break out again.

These contrasting images of the orderly operation of the canal and the unruly nature of Panamanian politics are also juxtaposed with shots of a local calypso band that bring the sequence to a close. Huntley explains that the band is singing about last year's riot, which quickly earned a prominent place in Panamanian folklore. Perched on the steps of an ancient ruin while singing to a calypso beat, the band—like the street demonstrators—seems to represent the antithesis of modern society. These Panamanians spread the news of conflict through folkloric music, while American viewers are informed by one of the most advanced media technologies of the era. In essence, the opening scene constructs a narrative frame that features a clash between modern technocracy and Third World "unrest." It is as if North American policy and technology have tamed the jungle but have failed to tame the darker side of Panamanian society. And it is the darker side that is being exploited by the forces of monolithic Communism.

This narrative logic structures the entire program, suggesting an interpretation of the conflict that features many of the same tropes discussed in chapters 2, 4, and 6. Here the masses are protean, faceless, and passionate. They are subject to infiltration by Communist insurgents, and they show a proclivity toward mindless adoration of charismatic figures. The potential for violence is great, and this contrasts sharply with the images of stability and rationality that characterize American efforts in the Canal Zone.

Such notions of stability, expertise, and policy planning are the very attributes that were ascribed to television's documentary genre during the early 1960s. Chet Huntley narrates with a seemingly dispassionate tone and clearly associates himself with the journalistic tradition of objectivity. Shots of Huntley throughout the program feature him seated at a control console, dressed in a business suit, and speaking authoritatively into the camera. He assumes a seemingly neutral, omniscient stance in relation to the filmed images and delivers information in brief, declarative phrases that are almost devoid of adjectives. He makes no reference to the possibility that documentation might have been col-

Images of technology and stability contrast with the emotional politics of the masses in "Panama: Danger Zone."

NBC correspondent Chet Huntley at the controls.

lected and interpreted in alternative ways. Although he acknowledges "two sides" to the issue, there is only one way for a responsible journalist to represent the conflict. These markers of modern expertise are closely aligned in this instance with images of the Canal Zone as the "eighth wonder of the world," which is now besieged by mob violence. Therefore the program implicitly aligns itself with a U.S. perspective that not only celebrates the values of technocracy but also represents the Panamanian situation as a problem to be managed by dispassionate policy planners.

Despite its pretentions to objectivity, then, the documentary takes an interpretive stance from the very outset that is closely associated with elite concerns about growing "unrest" along the frontiers of the Free World. Yet it further obscures this bias by invoking strategies of filmic realism. That is, the editing strategies in this opening sequence closely follow Hollywood conventions of analytical editing. Individual shots are connected by matching actions, eyeline gazes, and character movement across the screen. Bits of film and audio that apparently were gathered at different times and from various locations are edited together so as to create the impression of a coherent and natural representation of a historical event. Moreover, the filmmaking equipment has been carefully concealed so as to suggest that the viewer has traveled to Panama and

Panamanian peasants waiting for the storm that "is almost inevitable."

gained privileged access to what is going on. This omniscient perspective offered to the viewer not only seems to authenticate the analysis, but it also matches the viewing position offered to audiences of telefilm entertainment during this period. The perspective implies that since the camera can go anywhere, it presents the viewer with a base of knowledge that is at least equal, if not superior, to the perspective of characters presented in the program. Thus the conventions of prime time strongly influence the structure of this opening scene and work to align the viewer with the perspective of U.S. foreign policy experts. Consequently, the program is not offered as *one* analysis of the situation but as *the* authentic representation of social reality.

After a commercial, we return to find peasants seeking shelter as they scan the horizon in expectation of the daily storm that, the narrator comments, "is almost inevitable." This motif of the gathering storm recurs throughout the program and suggests an impending deluge. This, of course, is not an objective observation but a visual metaphor. The fact of the matter is that the daily storms in Panama are usually brief and benign. Yet the documentary engages this metaphor in order to conjure up a narrative tension between contending forces. Thus producer Al Wasserman distances himself from a more didactic approach in order to ground his analysis of the Communist threat in a narrative fashion: at a specific location, at a particular moment of crisis, with a tightly structured plotline. He presents a conflict, an enigma—will the riot lead to revolution?—and a cast of characters: the American expatriate community, the indigenous Panamanian society, and the global, monolithic Communist threat.[4]

The documentary turns first to the expatriate community in the Canal Zone, which is referred to as "a tiny slice of America on the ninth parallel." The program elaborates the character of this community by turning first to historical footage of the construction and early operation of the waterway. What emerges from this segment is a celebration of Yankee technology. The documentary shows us how North American ingenuity subdued the jungle and converted it to a resource of great strategic value, not only to the United States but to all nations of the Free World. Moreover, the canal is compared to a public utility, a nonprofit entity serving the commercial needs of all peace-loving countries. It is portrayed as the product of North American ingenuity, rather than as an early chapter in the expansion of Yankee imperial power.

The program cautions, however, that Panamanians have a different story to tell about the canal. They talk of discrimination against Panamanians who worked on the canal, arguing that white Americans were paid much higher wages than their local counterparts. Furthermore, the Panamanians contend that the United States receives most of the benefits from the canal's operation. And they claim that the canal treaty was never intended to grant the United States sovereignty over the Canal Zone. The Panamanian perspective is offered not because the program endorses it but because of the journalistic and narrative conventions at work in the text. As journalists, the producers of the program are compelled to present empirical documentation of "the other side." Moreover, the narrative logic of the program requires the construction of a threatening opponent with clear motivations. These conventions are intended to enhance the strength of the program's argument, but they also engender textual excesses that open the door to alternative readings of the program. That is, despite the producer's attempt to contain the Panamanian perspective within a framework that legitimizes a U.S. presence in the Canal Zone, African American viewers in the United States might see the criticisms leveled by the Panamanians as resonating closely with their own experiences of everyday life in the Free World. Possible alternative interpretations are examined more thoroughly in chapter 9, but suffice it to say at this point that the codes and conventions of network documentary did not always work in the interests of those powerful groups who promoted the genre. As pointed out in chapter 4, once the networks decided to dispatch their documentary units to hot spots around the globe, they lost an element of control over the meanings that the programs might produce. Although the act of gathering information and documenting local conflicts was intended to build a case for U.S. activism overseas, it also invited unanticipated complexities into the texts. Furthermore, one has to wonder if the producers of "Danger Zone" began their project with a set of a priori assumptions that were later challenged by the documentation they gathered on location.

Such a possibility is suggested by the next segment, which juxtaposes images of the American community with images of Panamanian society. For example, we observe American expatriates sitting on the front porch of the Tivoli Guest House, gazing contentedly offscreen into the distance. As we watch them relax in the shade, narrator Chet Huntley comments on a cultural rift between Canal Zone residents and Panamanians by noting that many of these residents have not stepped out of the Canal Zone in years. "Panama," he notes dryly, "is across the street." This observation is followed by an edit to a modern American elementary school where the day begins with the children singing the national anthem. In turn, this scene is crosscut with shots of an impoverished Panamanian school where the children sing their national anthem. Likewise, a visual profile of the prosperous, suburbanlike trappings of the American community is juxtaposed with the wretched conditions in a poor Panamanian barrio. These contrasting visual images clearly tap into a long tradition of journalistic concern about excessive economic disparities between rich and poor, a tradition that dates from the Progressive Era. The documentarists therefore introduce an instability into the text by suggesting American complicity with a regime that impoverishes Panamanians.

Yet this discontinuity is then folded back into the framework of superpower struggle and married to anxieties about Communist infiltration. The specific instance of Panamanian poverty is not analyzed as a local problem but is elevated to the larger context of East-West relations. Concerns over past inequities are to be considered in light of the growing Communist threat. As the viewer surveys specific visual documentation—such as malnourished children playing in the midst of shantytown squalor—the narrator suggests a broader interpretation: "The setting is Panama, but this could just as easily be Caracas, Venezuela, or Rio, Tegucigalpa, Lima, Santiago, Havana. Panama in its basic problems is virtually indistinguishable from any other Latin land." In essence, the implication is that Panama could become Havana unless reforms are instituted.

The documentary then moves into a more specific analysis of the eco-

Children play in shantytown squalor while Huntley intones that Panama "is virtually indistinguishable from any other Latin land."

nomic forces that have engendered such poverty. It points to widespread unemployment, government corruption, and the persistent indifference of wealthy Panamanians to the problems of the poor. The problem of urban poverty is also linked to the country's "underdeveloped" interior, a vast expanse of dense jungle. Pictures of machete-wielding farmers give way to shots of young girls pounding grain into flour with primitive hand tools. Much of the land, we are told, is owned by wealthy absentee landowners. Squatters have tamed the small percentage that is farmed, but the narrator points out that these are subsistence farmers "who contribute nothing to the national economy." By comparison, we then cut to shots of a United Fruit plantation, and we are told that this company, the largest employer in Panama, makes major contributions to the country's international commerce. Although justifiable complaints regarding worker exploitation have been lodged in the past, conditions have improved on the plantation, which now has a clinic and a school. We are furthermore told that those who work for the company are better off than those who do not. And, by implication, these workers contribute to the national economy through the production of an export crop.

This last sequence helps us chart the contours of the reformist impulse at work in this documentary. Subsistence farming—historically the backbone of American democracy—is equated here with underdevelopment rather than political independence. Meanwhile, development is portrayed as wage labor under the employment of an efficient, modern American corporation. Furthermore, such progress is characterized by an export economy operating within the framework of the Free World. One need not contend that subsistence farming is an alluring lifestyle in order to suggest that this construction of scenes produces a highly politicized set of meanings. It denies the possibility that an "underdeveloped" country populated by subsistence farmers might be socially viable and politically stable. On the contrary, it is contended that poverty and civil unrest can be eliminated only through modernization and integration into the global economy. What appears as a progressive reform agenda is in fact closely associated with the ideology of transnational corporate liberalism. The documentary promotes change, but the changes that top the list call for the elimination of a traditional landed oligarchy, the development of a corporate export economy, the introduction of a professional civil service, and the development of modern attitudes and life-styles among the general populace.

As this segment draws to a close, we are reminded that Panama is a metonymic representation of social problems throughout Latin America. Once again, the voice-over narration works to erase the historical specificity of the canal conflict by reminding the viewer that Panama could be "any other Latin land." The documentary then returns to the motif of the gathering storm and conjures up the specter of Fidel before it cuts to a commercial. This concluding strategy brings us back to the suggestion that the real conflict at work in this program is not simply domestic but, more important, a struggle between the Free World and monolithic Communism.

At the beginning of the next segment, the calypso band segues out of the commercial singing the praises of Fidel, and the camera then cuts to Castro speaking at a microphone before an adoring crowd of Cubans. This scene is crosscut with shots of various groups of Panamanians listening intently to their radios. Furthermore, the images are connected by the sound of Castro's speech, which runs uninterrupted throughout the scene. The overall effect is to suggest contemporaneous actions by Castro and his Panamanian audience. We do not know if they are in fact listening to the very speech that is featured in this specific footage, but the editing suggests a bridging of spatial barriers, a growing influence of Castro on the western shores of the Caribbean. From here, an edit to

Besides the United States, only Cuba stands out in this map of the Western Hemisphere.

historical footage of the riot tightens the link as demonstrators carry posters emblazoned with photographs of the revolutionary leader.

As discussed in chapter 3, one of the key missions of documentary during this period was to circulate images of a global geography that suggest a coherence to the contending spheres of East and West. This geography is initially insinuated at the beginning of "Danger Zone" with a map of the Western Hemisphere. Panama has a circle drawn around it, yet the only two countries specifically named on the map are the United States and Cuba. The privileged status accorded the United States and its tiny Caribbean neighbor suggests that the fundamental contending forces in Latin America are East and West, rather than North and South. Cuba is therefore the "foothold," the "beachhead" for Communist expansionism, and this status diminishes other antagonisms within the Western Hemisphere.

Furthermore, what is interesting about the radio sequence discussed above is the way in which the visual images are edited together so as to foster the same perspective offered by the map. The editing heightens the emphasis on Cuba's proximity to the isthmus by suggesting Castro's pervasive presence. Space is stitched together—speaker-audience, leader-led—through the conventions of Hollywood editing. Shots of

Castro expounding to a Cuban crowd are cut together with a close-up shot of a radio receiver and then portrait shots of various Panamanians listening intently. The sequence further elaborates the connection by cutting together numerous shots of streets and alleyways with their apartment windows open and the sounds of Castro's speech seemingly reverberating through the neighborhoods of Panama. Castro's "presence" is thereby made palpable by an editing strategy that creates an illusion of spatial and temporal continuity, an illusion that is based on the filmmaking conventions of Hollywood entertainment.

A subsequent series of interviews with students and politicians then makes it appear that Castro's presence is growing in Panama because of the problems of poverty, underdevelopment, and U.S. policy regarding the Canal Zone. One student draws the link between Cuba and Panama by saying, "We have the same problems and the same enemy." Furthermore, a member of the Panamanian legislature who supports Castro says, "I think the majority of the people support Castro because we understand that if it was not for Castro, the United States would not change its policy in Latin America." Another member of the legislature agrees and argues that the only thing that will truly bring change to the isthmus is some sort of revolution.

Despite the seeming coherence of this argument regarding Castro's growing influence, the journalistic and narrative conventions at work here also engender an excess of meanings. Although this sequence is clearly structured around the menace of Communist infiltration, Panamanian opposition leaders are nevertheless allowed to present part of their case to a North American audience. The "other side" must be heard in order to legitimate the journalistic analysis. Furthermore, storytelling conventions require a narrative tension engendered by an opponent who appears genuinely powerful. Such moments open the door to alternative reading strategies by audiences who might occupy social positions that are at variance with middle-class U.S. viewers. That is, the network may focus its attention on the Communist threat, but a Latino or African American viewer might pay more attention to the duplicitous nature of U.S. policy in the Canal Zone.

Huntley intervenes at this moment of textual instability in an effort to recuperate the evidence of growing anti-American sentiment into the dominant framework. He explains to the television audience in direct address that as the anniversary of last year's protest at the gates of the Canal Zone approached, Latin America "experts" feared the possibility of further conflict. They also warned that, in the wake of the Cuban revolution, another Panamanian uprising could spark similar actions in

Listening to Fidel in Panama City. Spatial relations are stitched together by the editing pattern in this scene.

countries throughout Latin America. We are told that these possibilities caused intense concern in the State Department leading to the installation of a new U.S. ambassador and a new military command inside the Canal Zone. The United States also mounted a sort of integrationist initiative, called "Operation Friendship," aimed at encouraging social and cultural contacts between Panamanians and U.S. residents of the isthmus. Filmed documentation of sports events, jazz concerts, and other social gatherings suggests that these events were successful. And, as part of the same initiative, President Eisenhower ordered that a Panamanian flag be flown at a key location inside the Canal Zone. Huntley informs the audience that these actions marked a significant shift in U.S. policy toward Panama, but they also remind us of larger changes taking place in U.S. foreign policy during this period.

As discussed in chapter 3, the wave of anticolonial agitation that swept the globe during the 1950s and 1960s necessitated a shift away from earlier models of imperial dominance toward a strategy of popular collaboration throughout the Free World. Rather than simply focusing on gaining the allegiance (or subjection) of local elites, U.S. policy makers at the end of the fifties also began to concern themselves with winning the hearts and minds of local populations throughout the Free World. This approach emphasized the importance of media, culture, and ideological struggle. "Panama: Danger Zone" represents that shift by showing how Castro's radio broadcasts were countered by the appointment of a new U.S. ambassador who is widely considered a public relations wizard. Moreover, the repeated presentation of interviews with indigenous Panamanians shows the documentary's profound concern with popular opinion, especially regarding attitudes toward the United States. This concern with popular sentiment suggests that the efforts of U.S. corporations and foreign policy planners during the post-Sputnik era increasingly focused on transforming popular attitudes both domestically and internationally. At home, emphasis was placed on advocating public support for a more activist foreign policy; internationally this agenda sought to promote the image of the United States as a popular leader of citizens around the globe. On both fronts, an attempt was made to foster the notion of a Free World community anchored by free trade and a rational policy process. In essence, it was an effort to advance the hegemonic project of capital-intensive U.S. corporations by winning popular consensus at home and abroad. Yet as Antonio Gramsci argued, such ideological work does have its limitations, and hegemonic consensus building is always complemented by coercive force. Thus the struggle to win the allegiances of citizens throughout the Free World was accompanied by periodic displays of force, and the Panamanian situation was no exception.

As the first anniversary of the "riot" draws near, the documentary shows military and police forces being put on alert, and the program builds to a moment of climactic tension as a parade begins winding through the streets of Panama City and into the Canal Zone. The camera cuts from spot to spot, offering numerous views along the parade route, seemingly inspecting every aspect of the demonstration, but it finds no traces of violence or rebellion. The march culminates in a rally inside the Canal Zone, where speeches are given and, with the Panamanian flag flying overhead, the national anthem is sung without incident. Nevertheless, the documentary is skeptical about this apparent moment of calm, for the fundamental social problems of Panama and the tensions engendered by superpower conflict still have not been resolved.

The status of the structuring narrative is somewhat muddled as the documentary draws to a close. It lacks a resolution; the tensions persist. The program, however, does provide a tentative form of closure in a scene that proposes a solution to the enigma alluded to from the outset. The camera cuts to a darkened street in Panama at night where there is some sort of festival going on. We see a candle-lit float garlanded with flowers and bearing a statue of a Catholic saint, probably the Virgin Mary. As we watch the float haltingly maneuver through narrow streets on the shoulders of dark-skinned Panamanians, we hear them singing and then we hear the narrator commenting in a dramatic baritone as the scene unfolds:

> The people of Panama, the people of Latin America have been slow to change. In their religious rituals they cling to an old Spanish march, two steps forward, one step back. But today, they're on the move, stirring from the darkness of their past. Throughout much of Latin America an explosive force is ready to erupt. They look to us for leadership and help. They no longer can be ignored.

As one of the documentary's concluding moments, this scene strives to mediate a number of tensions that were deployed throughout the hour-long program: primitive versus modern; low-tech versus high-tech; black versus white; darkness versus light; monolithic Communism versus the Free World. The documentary suggests that Panamanians wish to walk in light but are burdened by a cultural baggage that leads them down dark and narrow streets. These are not the broad boulevards of the urban planner; they are the crowded, rough-hewn barrios of the poor and uneducated. Political choices in these communities are steeped in passion, a passion that conjures up the specter of Fidel. This scene mediates a set of conflicting meanings produced by this documentary and by the foreign policy discourse that emerged as part of the New Frontier. It constructs the problems confronting the Panamanian people as genuine but marks them as dysfunctions in the otherwise rational and stable system of the Free World. The Panamanians must jettison the heavy baggage from their past and modernize their society if they are to enjoy the fruits of the Free World system. "They" must join "us," and "we" must care about "them." The unruly masses must be remade in the image of the modern, enlightened citizen lest they fall prey to the seductions of charismatic Communist leaders like Fidel. This project of enlightenment helps to define the global mission of the United States while at the same time producing the image of a Free World community. It subsumes differences under the banners of modernization and reform, and it implies similarities based on a natural human desire for progress.

Furthermore, this documentary suggests another way in which the Free World is united: it is united against Communism. Thus Communist countries mark the outer limits of the Free World by virtue of their unalterable opposition. Governed by subterfuge and determined to exploit any weaknesses in the Western alliance, these countries pose a threat that is so fundamental as to be completely intolerable. Here we see what William Chafe has described as a process of abstraction common to U.S. foreign policy discourse in this century. Rather than casting the canal issue as a self-interested strategic matter, the program constructs a Manichaean struggle between East and West. To lose the canal is to lose Panama, and to lose Panama is possibly to lose all of Latin America. There is no room for accommodation. Once a country slides across the divide, it is lost forever. Patriotic Americans must rally to meet the Communist challenge at this moment of maximum danger.

Consequently, the program constructs geographical relations in two ways. The radical differences posed by outsiders is complemented by significant similarities within the Free World community itself. If on the one hand this documentary was intended to alert the American people, on the other hand it was to perform an integrative function as well, for modern media play an important role in binding together geographically dispersed and culturally differentiated populations. As Benedict Anderson argues, they foster popular imaginings of camaraderie and social commitment. "Panama: Danger Zone" attempts to play this role by constructing an argument founded on the supposition that Panamanians aspire to have more of what U.S. citizens take for granted. This assumption circulated widely in foreign policy circles during this era and was the basis for Walt Rostow's influential book *Stages of Economic Growth: A Non-Communist Manifesto.* Rostow, who later become a key foreign policy adviser during the Kennedy and Johnson administrations, argues that all capitalist societies pass through similar stages in their progress toward modernity, a path that not surprisingly culminates in a social order remarkably like that of the United States.[5] This documentary suggests throughout that Panama's problems are markers of its underdeveloped status. Thus it implies that the differences between North and South are resolvable and will lead to an increasing similarity between the two regions. Panamanians therefore share "our" aspirations, and we must help them realize their dreams or risk losing them to the Communist other.

The connection made here between modernization and the Free World is very similar to linkages drawn during the eighteenth and nineteenth centuries between modernity and the integrative project of the nation-state. The extension and construction of national boundaries—which brought together diverse local cultures—were then justified as a form of progress that would bring benefits to all. The project of integration was presented as a step toward prosperity, enlightenment, and expanded suffrage. The masses would be lifted up, brought into harmony, and the nation would rest upon their shoulders. For example, when the French republic was founded, less than half of its citizens spoke what would come to be recognized as proper French. Changing one's language, culture, and worldview to fall in accord with the new nation was not simply an acknowledgment of the nation-state's growing political power but also an endorsement of a more modern lifestyle, a lifestyle that was modeled in the capital city of Paris. Similarly, this documentary promotes the notion of modern, metropolitan authority. As Chet Huntley remarks, "They look to us for leadership and help."

The program therefore strives to effect a form of closure by offering a solution to the problem of Panama that integrates the rhetorics of liberal reform and staunch anti-Communism. It suggests that the path forward calls for more U.S. involvement rather than less. Such reform-minded activism is not only a significant departure from the politics of the pre-*Sputnik* years; it represents other important changes as well: increasing global investment of U.S. corporations, overseas expansion of the major television networks, rapid growth and competition among network news organizations, enhanced professional status of documentarists, and changes in public discourse regarding the Cold War.

"Panama: Danger Zone" is one of the first in a series of foreign policy documentaries produced by NBC for broadcast to a national, prime-time audience and for syndication in emerging television markets around the world. As an overdetermined cultural artifact it embodies these multiple and converging tendencies. It is both a product of the era and an important site for the production of public consensus regarding the New Frontier. Yet at the same time, we have seen ways in which this complex process of articulation renders a text that is at times contradictory and unstable. These tensions leave the door open for a range of interpretive practices and consequently direct our attention to issues of reception. What were audiences doing with these very complicated portrayals of social reality? How did they respond to such explicit attempts to rally public support behind the agenda of the New Frontier?

Chapter Nine

The Missing Audience

The network documentary enjoyed a privileged status in the eyes of television reformers largely because it promised access to millions of viewers throughout the United States. Americans spent more time watching television than any other pastime activity in 1961, and it was estimated that 90 percent of TV-owning households had their sets running one-third of each waking day.[1] Major advertisers claimed to reap tremendous benefit from their access to this huge pool of viewers, and this was precisely the reason why corporate and political leaders saw prime-time television as an important site for refashioning public opinion as well. It was believed that documentary would mobilize widespread support for an internationalist political agenda by informing viewers about pressing problems throughout the Free World. Yet despite this optimism, it is difficult to know precisely how audiences responded to these programs. Network archives and special library collections contain few systematic audience studies, and those that still exist provide only a sketchy overview of viewer attitudes and behaviors.

A four-month study by the A. C. Nielsen Company during the 1961–1962 season showed that the average rating for a sponsored public affairs program was 10. This meant the average prime-time documentary reached roughly five million homes and almost ten million viewers. The highest-rated documentary in this particular sample reached 20 percent of television homes and the lowest-rated 3 percent. Overall, these are relatively small audiences in comparison with evening entertainment fare, which averaged an 18 rating.[2] Nevertheless, the same study also showed that 90 percent of the homes surveyed watched at least one documentary during a two-month period.[3] Moreover, the regular viewing figures were not insignificant when compared with figures for other national information media. In 1962, for example, *Time* magazine had 2,655,000 subscribers and *Newsweek* 1,529,000.[4] Even after multiplying by a factor of five to estimate the total readership of these periodicals, one is left with the conclusion that documentaries drew about the same amount of attention as the most successful national news weeklies.[5]

This was nevertheless a disappointment for those who initially hoped that network documentary would dramatically expand the number of Americans exposed to thoughtful analysis of important public issues. It was originally envisioned that documentary would reach beyond regular news readers to draw the attention of those who had previously shown little concern about global affairs. Ratings data seem to indicate, however, that "the masses" preferred entertainment over documentary by a factor of roughly four to one. That is, when two entertainment programs were broadcast at the same time as a documentary, each would average almost twice as many viewers as those tuned to documentary. Furthermore, polling data indicate no substantial shifts in public opinion regarding foreign policy while these programs were on the air.[6] Documentary apparently did not reach large new audiences and did not transform popular attitudes. Thus one is left wondering why this genre failed to exploit fully the potential of what was arguably the most powerful form of modern communication. Why could the best minds in television sell lipstick and canned beans but not American foreign policy?

Answering these questions requires moving beyond the broad generalizations of network ratings data into a more speculative realm of analysis. In other words, we need to ask questions about the relationship between the documentary text and audience that were not commonly asked at the time. Such a venture must draw on clues that may prove suggestive but may not provide conclusive answers. When analyzing audiences from a historical perspective, one is not guided by a well-marked paper trail but rather by a number of disparate indicators that point toward tentative hypotheses. With this caveat in mind, this chapter explores possible explanations for documentary's failure to fulfill the expectations of its supporters. Two related threads of analysis are involved. First, we must ask to whom these documentaries were speaking. What groups were included as part of the intended audience? Which groups were excluded or marginalized? How did the address of these programs affect their ability to bring together a mass audience? Second, we must speculate as to how these programs might have been viewed by people from a variety of social locations and experiences. During the early 1960s, the tendency in the television industry was to aim at the largest possible audience with little regard for the diverse composition of that audience. Gross ratings were considered important because they were the most influential factor in determining the amount broadcasters could charge advertisers. Unfortunately, this type of data is of little use to a researcher who wants to explore the socially situated interpretations of audiences. Ethnic and racial diversity was an important feature of the U.S. population during this period, and, as we shall see, African American viewers may have engaged these programs in very different ways than did white, middle-class viewers. Furthermore, this period exhibited early indications of broad-based dissatisfaction among women in suburbia, thus generating another significant fissure within the mass audience. Some historical indicators would seem to suggest that even in mainstream suburban homes, women may have viewed these programs from a very different perspective than their husbands. By asking new questions and venturing some speculative answers, we can gain insight into why documentary failed both as a popular television genre and as a mobilizer of the masses.

Documentary for the Elite

Public officials, business leaders, and educators all agreed that documentaries were good for the typical television viewer. They were reflective and informative. Moreover, the programs emphasized notions of citizenship that linked the mythology of American democracy with a revitalized liberal mission of global leadership. Thus education about the world and about the principles of American democracy was at the very core of this "golden age" of network documentary.

This was in some ways similar to the era of high imperialism in Great Britain when the study of English literature was urged upon women and workers as part of a self-conscious project of public enlightenment. Terry Eagleton writes:

> The era of the academic establishment of English is also the era of high imperialism in England [that] created the urgent need for a national sense of mission and identity. What was at stake in English studies was less English *literature* than *English* literature: our great "national poets" Shakespeare and Milton, the sense of an "organic" national tradition and identity to which new recruits could be admitted by the study of humane letters. The reports of educational bodies and official enquiries into the teaching of English, in this period and in the early twentieth century, are strewn with nostalgic back-references to the "organic" community of Elizabethan England.[7]

Eagleton goes on to describe the ways in which an increasingly influential entrepreneurial class attached itself to a set of values that would not only legitimize its position of power but would also invoke public support for the overseas ventures that were necessary to maintain an imperial economy. These entrepreneurs promoted broad-based public education regarding Britain's national heritage and the distinctive historical mission of the British people.[8]

Similarly, network documentaries of the early sixties aimed not only to inform the average citizen about current events around the globe but also to evaluate those events in relation to an American heritage of democracy, free enterprise, and Yankee ingenuity. Many of the programs about international issues therefore suggested that it was America's mission to serve both as a world leader and as a model of enlightened democracy. They naturalized the call for action and reform by linking it to a heritage of American exceptionalism. Greatness was thrust upon the American people, and it was therefore each citizen's duty to respond to the needs of others within the community of the Free World.

This conception of documentary's mission was in part a response to promptings from influential figures outside the television industry. As with the period Eagleton describes, a transformation in the interests of American capitalists required changes in government policy and popular support for this shift. Thus Charles Percy's interest in an ABC documentary series makes perfect sense given Bell and Howell's growing involvement in the defense industry. FCC chairman Newton Minow was also quite explicit in describing the linkages between television reform and U.S. foreign policy. And within the White House itself, Arthur Schlesinger Jr. more broadly advocated the development of a government "cultural policy" to enhance the quality of American life.[9] It could therefore be argued that the target audience for documentary was not the regular television viewer but the government official, the business leader, the educator, and the cultural critic. These were the groups who were working hard in the post-Sputnik era to alter the terms of U.S. foreign policy and to garner popular support for a more activist international stance. Yet they supported the genre not so much because of their personal enthusiasm for the programs themselves but because of their concern for the education of the masses.

The masses apparently had other things planned for their evenings at home, however, and the programs appeared as an awkward intrusion into a schedule of family entertainment. They reintroduced discipline and public duty into the private sphere of the home, a sphere most commonly associated with personal relationships and leisure activities.[10]

Another reason the programs may have seemed so dissonant was because they failed to invite popular participation. Their content seemed authoritative, distant, and professional. Network documentarists consistently sought out the opinions of experts and treated those opinions with conspicuous reverence. Popular television, on the other hand, often lampooned authority figures and questioned expertise, especially through satirization of the stereotypical egghead. Furthermore, documentary seemed to be out of place in a medium that regularly invoked the illusion of audience presence and participation. Game shows remained popular throughout this period despite the quiz scandals. Soap opera narratives also invited popular participation as viewers speculated among themselves about future plot developments. Sports, which were becoming an increasingly important form of programming at the time, generated similar enthusiasm. During the evening, prime-time narratives encouraged identification with heroes and fantasy figures.[11] Moreover, entertainment television invited popular participation through a culture of consumption. One could be like the characters on television by purchasing particular products, adopting certain fashions, or furnishing the home with specific items. Finally, entertainment television invited its audiences to engage in popular discourse about television. Fan magazines, program guides, and feature stories about particular stars or programs all offered the kinds of information that became part of everyday discussions among viewers and fans.[12]

By comparison, network documentary purported to offer objective renderings of complex social issues. It was the antithesis of popular entertainment, stripping away fantasy and facade in order to interrogate problems of the public sphere. Moreover, it was the domain of experts, a world of cool neutrality. Documentaries did not take passionate stands or engage in partisan politics. As we saw in chapter 5, the networks' desire to maintain control over prime-time programming and to avoid controversy led them staunchly to refuse to broadcast documentaries by independent producers. Network officials said they feared that issues could be distorted by filmmakers with a personal investment in their subject matter. And within the network news departments, employees were equally zealous in their efforts to squelch the appearance of personal opinion or bias. As a result, documentaries often tackled complicated issues in ways that seemed cold and analytical. Rather than openly encouraging feelings of outrage or concern, the programs often left the viewer with ambivalent conclusions. In fact, one of the central controversies that led to Edward R. Murrow's departure from CBS had to do with his famous "tail pieces"—the moments when he would draw together the threads of his analysis and urge public action. These concluding segments, which were considered appropriate in Murrow's World War II reports from Europe, were not considered appropriate when discussing issues closer to home, such as civil rights or migrant workers.[13] And although international topics allowed documentarists wider latitude, the problems of a distant African republic may have seemed overly abstract or remote to the television viewer. Consequently, viewers may have felt less involvement than they did with entertainment programs.

Even those who may have been motivated by the programs encountered other obstacles when they attempted to connect their concerns to some form of political action. Cut off from labor unions and ethnic organizations in the move to the suburbs, many viewers became participants in community organizations that rarely addressed the social problems examined by network documentary.[14] PTA meetings, local school board sessions, and town councils rarely took up problems such as automation in the workplace or exploitation in Appalachia. Racism was seen as a problem for the South or the inner cities, not the suburbs.[15] Even the Cold War was best left to those who had access to top-secret, strategic information. And besides, what could the average viewer do?[16] This is not to say that documentaries were simply ignored. We know from the ratings that they drew millions of viewers, and some of those viewers may have been motivated to learn more about an issue and to discuss it with friends. Some may have become even more actively involved in public issues by joining the Peace Corps or the Freedom Rides or the Green Berets. Yet it seems that many television viewers had trouble connecting the concerns raised by documentaries with their everyday lives; public action was increasingly allocated to the specialties of large institutions, and issues were represented as the domain of experts. A viewer could trust the experts and do nothing, or mistrust the experts, but see little room for personal action. Television viewers therefore may have had good reasons for showing little interest in the documentary genre.

This argument, that documentary represented a high culture intrusion into the domain of popular television, seems to be borne out by the ways in which different newspapers treated the genre. Elite press organs such as the *New York Times* and the *Washington Post* regularly promoted and reviewed the programs. Indeed, Jack Gould of the *Times* was one of the influential critics of television during the late 1950s who helped to orchestrate the initial pressure on the networks to expand their informational programming. The networks responded to this pressure not only by increasing their commitment to documentary but by courting the approval of the *Times* and its readers. All three networks regularly ran display ads in the television pages of the paper announcing upcoming documentaries and touting the network's commitment to public service programming. NBC, for example, promoted "Angola: Journey to a War" with a full-page ad featuring a charcoal portrait sketch of an African man captioned as follows:

> At 9:00 this evening "NBC White Paper No. 7" brings you television's first eyewitness report on Angola, "The Kingdom of Silence." Now in the anguish of revolt against Portuguese rule, Angola has been a land of secrecy, barred to all reporters. NBC Newsmen Robert Young and Charles Dorkins, however, made a bold 300 mile journey on foot into the rebel-held portion of this strange land. . . . What they filmed and what they saw is the basis of this exclusive NBC report. Throughout its second season, NBC's award winning "White Paper" series will continue to point its cameras squarely at the issues and developments which may explode into major threats to America and the Free World. An important part of NBC's program service of diversity and responsibility, it has been cited as "A significant achievement," as "Television at its informative best."[17]

The advertisement speaks clearly and directly to the concerns of highbrow critics. It foregrounds the network's commitment to public enlightenment through program offerings that meet the network's civic responsibility to inform. It also unambiguously endorses the global mission of the United States and valorizes the documentarists' role as the objective eyes of the people. Such ads were not common, however, in papers that did not service the community of East Coast opinion leaders, such as the *Chicago Tribune*. Clearly, the networks prioritized their promotion efforts according to their conception of the primary audience.

It is therefore not surprising that elite papers were also the ones that consistently reviewed network documentaries. Out of twenty flagship documentaries picked at random, the *New York Times* reviewed all but one of the programs. Documentaries were given equally consistent coverage by reviewers from *Variety*, a trade journal read regularly by key industry figures, station managers, advertisers, and government regulators. Like the *Times*, *Variety* had been a critic of network programming practices during the late 1950s and a proponent of reform. Although reviews in both papers sometimes questioned the analysis of particular documentaries or challenged specific strategies of presentation, these reviewers consistently endorsed the importance of each specific topic and generally commended the finished product to their readers.

For example, the *New York Times* carried a large display ad promoting *CBS Reports*' "The Population Explosion" the morning before it was broadcast. The following day, Jack Gould closed his review by noting,

"After being told of all the ramifications of an unrestricted birth rate, with its possible implications for the free world, no viewer of the presentation could doubt the significance of the network's contribution."[18] Meanwhile, the *Variety* review, which gently chided the producer for not proposing answers to the problem of overpopulation, called the program "an encouraging example of what can happen with prime-timed quality programming."[19] This pattern recurs consistently throughout the early sixties.

Even programs that generated negative criticism received respectful attention. Thus a 1962 *Close-Up!* documentary, "Comrade Student," was given a full-page promotional spread in the *Times* that touted it as "characteristic of ABC's total communications effort. In entertainment, in enlightenment."[20] The following day, the *Times* education editor, Fred H. Hechinger, acknowledged the importance of the topic but questioned the program's analysis because of the indirect influence of Soviet officials who facilitated the production: "[The program] faced some of the limitations that impede the view of all visitors [to the Soviet Union]. Even in the absence of censorship, the observer's target is pre-selected. The picture, though interesting, is not panoramic. Thus, the 'typical' Moscow home, grandfather and all, brought to mind the more sweetly corny household of the Andy Hardy series."[21] Thus Hechinger raises questions about objectivity and comprehensiveness. He then concludes the paragraph with a backhand slap at the stereotypical representation of a Moscow home. Similarly, *Variety* wondered if the producers might have been too gullible regarding Soviet claims about the quality of their educational system. Nevertheless, the review hailed the efforts of the ABC crew for taking on "a central question of the day" and providing "an important, absorbing, persuasive documentary."[22] Although both reviews are critical, they do not disparage the *Close-Up!* series as they might a situation comedy. Instead, they suggest ways in which this important topic might have been more effectively addressed. Both elite newspapers therefore share an abiding respect for the genre and a sense of obligation for its continuing success.

This commitment to the documentary genre was not present, however, in newspapers with more general circulation. The *Chicago Tribune*, for example, ran very few reviews of network documentaries during this period, reserving almost all of its attention for entertainment fare. Although the paper's previews of the suggested viewing options—usually a few sentences—would often recommend documentaries, it is difficult to sense an editorial commitment to the genre. Moreover, the networks rarely ran a display ad in the *Tribune* to promote their efforts, suggesting that the paper and its readers were not perceived as key supporters of documentary. This also seemed to be true of newspapers in smaller cities, such as the *Indianapolis Star*.[23] Daily editions of the *Star* exclusively featured brief viewing tips, and in this case they apparently were provided by a national service rather than a staff reporter. The contrast with coverage in the elite papers is perhaps best suggested by quoting the entire preview for "Comrade Student":

> An explosive documentary on Russian education and a "must" for every American from six to sixty. It's simply a visit to a few schools in Moscow and a look at their classrooms, but you'll be talking to yourself when it's over. The handling of the English language by grade school Russians is perhaps the biggest shocker, but the overall picture of minds being carefully and subtly indoctrinated for the future is the big story. Don't forget the kids for this one.[24]

The breezy style effected in this preview is a marked departure from the sober analysis provided by the *Times*' education editor. The function of the *Star*'s preview seems to be an effort to position the program within the context of prime-time entertainment. The program is "a must," "a shocker," "a big story" that should please viewers of all ages. Moreover, the closing line reminds us that, in an era when most homes had one television set, viewing was a family activity and program selection a matter of negotiation.[25] Children's preferences and interests were therefore a matter of concern for parents when contemplating the evening schedule. One of the key advantages of "Comrade Student" is not the quality of its analysis but the way in which it might fit into the family routine. Unlike the elite reviews, this listing shows a greater awareness of the ways in which television was commonly used in the home. Perhaps opinion leaders considered the medium a vital form of communication, but family viewers were more likely to use it for group entertainment and relaxation. One therefore takes notice of the marginal status accorded the documentary genre by these midwestern papers compared with its extensive coverage in elite press organs and trade publications. Although the genre received lavish attention in the popular press when it first emerged in prime time, ongoing enthusiasm for "serious," issue-oriented documentaries was largely sustained by elite newspapers.

As for viewers themselves, an extensive study of popular viewing habits and attitudes conducted in the early sixties by Gary Steiner of the University of Chicago showed a marked contrast between what many people said about television programs and how they actually used televi-

Elite newspapers criticized "Comrade Student," but the popular press referred to it as a "must" for TV viewers.

sion. Perhaps taking a cue from opinion leaders, most respondents said that analytical programs about public issues were an important part of the TV schedule. And 50 percent suggested there was a need for even more such programming. Yet the same respondents who touted the virtues of public affairs shows were no more likely to actually *view* the programs than those who were less supportive of the genre. Furthermore, when Steiner broke down his sample by educational and economic backgrounds, he found the same pattern among all groups.[26] Steiner concluded from this that when asked what they would like to see more of on television, many respondents applied a social criterion, reasoning: "I myself don't need more information from television, but the country does."[27] This was especially true with upscale viewers who were, according to Steiner, more likely to characterize time spent with television as a "waste." "[The upscale viewer's] chief concern is with the social and cultural implications of so much television 'escape' among the masses," wrote Steiner. "To him, the country *needs* a more informative and educational schedule, as it needs speed limits, better public schools, and racial integration—not necessarily for his personal benefit or use, but for the common good when adopted by others."[28]

Steiner contended that the major difference between upscale

viewers and other viewers was not what they *did* with television but what they *thought* of television. For the elite, television represented a guilty pleasure in which they knowingly indulged. They could not seem to believe, however, that others could use it as judiciously. From the perspective of elite viewers, the masses were consuming inordinate amounts of trivial entertainment while losing touch with important issues confronting the nation. The masses needed to know "what a terrible fix we're in," and maybe television could tell them. NBC documentary producer Fred Freed saw a linkage between this attitude among elite viewers and the ways in which his documentaries were reviewed by critics. Wrote Freed:

> Those of us who made documentaries for television were practically exempt from criticism, just so long as our shows exhibited good intentions. The intellectuals pointed out that our shows were a good thing. They were good for people. People ought to watch them. Other people, that is. The intellectuals didn't watch very much because most of them said they didn't have a television set. But they insisted what we did was good for those people who didn't know as much about the world as they did.[29]

Whether good for them or not, most regular television viewers did not make documentary a frequent component in their viewing schedule. Yet they supported the genre just as they did other forms of high culture: quietly deferring to opinion leaders while maintaining the general course of their lives. Indeed, one of the key achievements of the New Frontier may have been its ability to restore the legitimacy of East Coast intellectuals, not its ability to mobilize the masses. Having suffered on the margins of power throughout much of the fifties, intellectuals were now shaping much of the social and political agenda of the nation, and this made it difficult to speak *publicly* against documentary. Yet how one responded to an opinion poll was very different from how one scheduled an evening at home. This distinction between public declarations and private actions suggests that the New Frontier may have been more effective at rallying opinion leaders and shaping public discourse than it was at changing the private behaviors of large segments of the population. Documentary was one of the key sites for the transformation of public discourse, but it failed to connect with the everyday lives of many television viewers. The genre was a high culture intrusion into the domain of popular television. It was tolerated and even revered, so long as it did not disrupt the rest of the prime-time schedule.

The African American Audience

Although documentary may have unintentionally alienated large segments of the white population, it systematically marginalized the African American viewer. Much of this was a product of prevailing practices in broadcasting and advertising at the time. For example, I found no documents or industry trade publications from this period that attempted to track or distinguish television audiences by race or ethnicity. Black viewers were simply not considered a major or distinctive concern of television broadcasters. Primary emphasis within the industry was placed instead on attracting a mass audience of white, middle-class *consumers*. Furthermore, these commercial practices carried over into the domain of public affairs programming. Documentarists, like their colleagues in entertainment, felt ongoing pressure to broaden the appeal of their programs in order to produce maximum ratings. As early as 1957, a CBS study of documentary viewers recommended that the programs address themselves to a mass audience in order to connect with the largest number of viewers. "It is necessary to provide a broad basis for viewer involvement," argued the report. "Therefore, social and political problems pertaining to a minority should always be presented in terms of their importance to the majority."[30] Although this axiom seemed logical to those within a mass entertainment industry, it quite clearly marginalized the African American viewer so that even documentaries about issues of specific concern to blacks were addressed to a white audience. Furthermore, this address implied that the white middle class was ultimately the agent of political change.

One finds these assumptions consistently at work in the concluding segment of documentaries from this period. For example, Edward R. Murrow wrapped up "Harvest of Shame," CBS's documentary about migrant farm laborers, by asserting: "Only an enlightened, aroused, and perhaps angered public opinion can do anything about the migrants. The people you have seen have the strength to harvest your fruit and vegetables. They do not have the strength to influence legislation. Maybe we do." In this closing address note that migrants are not only lacking in political power, they are not even acknowledged as part of the audience. Similarly, documentaries about foreign policy issues imply that the middle-class viewer at home will be a decisive factor in the struggles occurring throughout the Third World. In NBC's "Panama: Danger Zone," Chet Huntley intones, "They look to us for leadership or help.

They no longer can be ignored." Here again the distinction is between them and us—"us" being middle-class Americans who constitute both a powerful consumer group and a decisive political force.

The implications of this formulation become most apparent in documentaries about the struggle for civil rights by African Americans. These programs place the black viewer in a marginal position even as they criticize the segregation and subordination of African Americans. ABC's "Walk in My Shoes" concludes as the black protagonist, torn between lending his allegiance to a "moderate" or a "militant" civil rights group, turns to the camera and inquires of the mass audience: "Now where do I go and how do I get there? Do you know? What do *you* expect me to do?" Thus the politically progressive elements of the program exist in an uneasy relationship to this closing appeal that repositions the black protagonist in a stereotypically subordinate position. CBS correspondent Harry Reasoner also concludes a documentary on racial politics by noting, "Into separation [the Negro] would have to be driven. Into full citizenship he would have to be accepted, in either case by whites." With both documentaries the white viewer's perspective is the target of the narrator's address and the implied locus of political power. Clearly, these assumptions may have been alienating to many black viewers, especially those who were participants in arguably the most potent grassroots political movement of the era. Thus black viewers occupied a peculiar and oblique position in relation to the network documentary text. The programs featured a white narrator speaking from a white middle-class perspective to a white audience, in many cases about racial issues. The black viewer was therefore *eavesdropping* on a discussion of his or her economic and human rights.

African American newspapers of the period offer some further clues as to ways in which black viewers may have regarded network documentaries. Largely, the papers ignore the programs unless the topic is specifically related to race. This is true not only with reviews but with program listings and viewing tips as well. African American newspapers do not show the same deference to the genre as television critics in mass-circulation newspapers. Furthermore, the black press expresses less enthusiasm for television as a whole. More attention is paid to music, nightclubs, and live theater—where black participation in ownership, management, and performance was common—than to television. What little is said about television is often disparaging. One entertainment critic for the *Pittsburgh Courier* unequivocally states, "Everyone knows that jim crow is rampant in television." Quoting one of his colleagues, he continues,

Once every three months or so the powers-that-be graciously allow a "Negro show" to be broadcast. The great event is celebrated with a lot of sanctimonious and self-righteous publicity, but then the TV screen blanches white once more for months. In between times Negro performers are lucky to get 10 minutes of time a week on a variety show in the hundreds of hours of weekly broadcasting. About the only other time a Negro face appears on network television is in a documentary on migrant workers or narcotics.[31]

As this critique suggests, African American newspapers from this period largely focus their attention on those rare moments when racial barriers were breached, and they only occasionally discuss documentaries.

For example, on February 24, 1962, the *Amsterdam News* completely ignores an upcoming *NBC White Paper* about Red China and instead recommends variety shows with guest performers such as Leslie Uggams and local interview programs featuring black leaders such as Roy Wilkins. Moreover, the same page provides excerpts from congressional testimony of Frederick O'Neal, president of the Negro Actors Guild. O'Neal points out that black consumers spend eighteen billion dollars each year on the products advertised by broadcasters. "Although we feel that we have a moral right to employment in the theatre, variety, opera, etc.," says O'Neal, "we also have, in the case of radio and television, an economic right as well, since our purchases help to pay the cost of this type of entertainment."[32] Such reasoning continued to fall on deaf ears, however. Prime-time television throughout this period was remarkably white, and the black viewer had little incentive to tune in the documentary efforts of the major networks.

Another reason African Americans may have paid little attention to network documentaries was because black communities may have viewed international politics from perspectives that were quite different from those of the network documentarists. We can glimpse this in the international reporting of African American newspapers of the period. Unlike the *New York Times* or the *Washington Post*, black papers tended to be less concerned about the Soviet challenge and instead focused on race as a central concern in foreign policy deliberations.[33]

In 1960, for example, when Fidel Castro traveled to New York City to speak at the United Nations, midtown Manhattan hotels refused to accommodate him, but the Hotel Theresa in Harlem welcomed the Cuban delegation.[34] Castro, in turn, embraced his hosts by publicly proclaiming himself an "African American" and by staging a press conference at which he barred the white American media establishment.[35] He also invited Gamal Abdel Nasser, Jawaharlal Nehru, and Nikita Khrushchev to visit him at the Theresa at various points during his stay. Thus Castro drew local and global attention to the link between the struggles of Harlem's African American community and other struggles by people of color against Western regimes.

As for the response from the local community, one reporter for the *Amsterdam News* wrote, "Castro's arrival at the Hotel Theresa . . . was greeted with curiosity and mixed emotions by most uptowners."[36] Many Harlem residents were reportedly happy that the visit cast a global spotlight on the uptown neighborhood, noting that the mainstream American media otherwise tended to ignore their community. Some even embraced Castro, such as the owner of the Hotel Theresa, who announced he would visit Cuba as Castro's guest along with three hundred other Harlem residents.[37] Yet other prominent black New Yorkers, such as the Baptist Ministers' Conference of Greater New York, condemned the visit as an effort to make Harlem "a battleground for [Castro's] ideologies."[38] The *Amsterdam News* negotiated this split in its readership by navigating a middle course that was hospitable but cautious. Apparently wishing to avoid becoming a pawn of either superpower, the *News* editorialized:

> The [white] folks downtown are still puzzled. They know that Harlem didn't blow hot—and they know that Harlem didn't freeze. They can't understand it. What they don't know downtown is that Harlem has long ago found a midpoint between boiling and freezing a man. They call it "Playing It Cool" and we recommend it to our State Department diplomats who could learn a lot from Harlemites when it comes to getting along with people.[39]

Indeed, the *Amsterdam News* and the *Pittsburgh Courier*, two major black press organs that devoted considerable resources to foreign policy coverage, tended to be sophisticated and judicious when dealing with East-West relations. In 1960, for example, one *News* editorial chides the Eisenhower administration for calling Ghana's prime minister a Communist simply because he joined a Soviet official in denouncing the remaining colonial regimes in Africa. "Is a denunciation of colonialism sufficient grounds on which to label one a Communist?" wondered the *News*. "And if we are going to write off an African leader as Communist every time he denounces colonialism we might just as well hand the African bloc of states to the Russians on a silver platter right now."[40]

Similarly, at the time of the Berlin crisis a columnist for the *Courier* questions the ways in which anti-Communism set the terms for foreign policy deliberations regarding Germany. He challenges the wisdom of American brinkmanship on this issue and states, "I wouldn't want a son of mine to give his life for Berlin." Furthermore, he exclaims, "It is amazing to me that most media which have to do with shaping public opinion use their influence to press or push the leaders of our Government into a position from which they can't retreat."[41] Whether this critique reflects the majority of black opinion at the time is perhaps less important than the simple fact that African American journalists and editors apparently felt less compelled to fall in line when the specter of Communism was conjured up during debates over foreign policy issues.

Some of this may be attributable to the close coverage these papers devoted to Africa. Simple dichotomies between East and West were often problematic when considering the most important issues confronting these newly independent states. For example, in early 1961, when tensions flared in the Congo, both the *News* and the *Courier* provided extensive coverage as the competing political factions vied for United Nations recognition of their respective governments. The group backed by Western powers and led by Joseph Kasavubu received ample coverage from the black press. The same was true of his rival, Patrice Lumumba. However, it was the death of Lumumba that shifted the coverage off center and ignited impassioned criticism of the West. Lumumba, who was supported by several prominent African leaders (including Ghana's Kwame Nkrumah) as well as the Soviet Union, was out of favor with the Western bloc. Therefore, when Lumumba mysteriously died while being guarded by Belgian soldiers under U.N. command, the black press exploded with criticism.[42] As columnist James L. Hicks argued, "His death was the international lynching of a black man on the altar of white supremacy. . . . For here was a man chosen by his people as Prime Minister. And he was duly performing his official duties until he was deposed in an effort by the United Nations community 'to save' his nation from 'chaos.'"[43] Hundreds of black protesters also joined the fray by picketing the United Nations. Reportedly, the U.S. ambassador to the United Nations, Adlai Stevenson, dismissed the demonstrators as "Communistic." Nevertheless, the *Amsterdam News* provided front-page coverage of the protest that included a thorough rebuttal of Stevenson's allegations.[44] Clearly, the news frame applied by these African American newspapers transcended Cold War dichotomies and focused instead on race and colonialism. Within the context of global politics at the time, one would most likely associate the editorial perspective of these newspapers with the policies of nonaligned nations such as Ghana and India.

It is not surprising, then, that the African American press did not tend to revere network documentaries with the same regularity as elite press organs in the United States. As for programs that dealt with foreign policy issues, they were discussed only if they related to race. For example, an ABC documentary about political repression in Haiti was previewed in the *Chicago Defender* as an examination of poverty and corruption in "the world's oldest Negro republic."[45] Similarly, the preview of a CBS documentary about American volunteers working in Guinea paid particular attention to "a formal meeting in which leaders of the Mamou Politburo sharply question the Americans about segregation and other elements of life in the United States."[46] Although such previews helped to frame network documentaries for black viewers, they generally did not provide an in-depth critical assessment. One of the few foreign policy documentaries actually reviewed by a staff reporter was NBC's "Angola: Journey to War." The critique hails the program for providing "a first-hand report of the repulsive punishment Portuguese soldiers are dealing out to a pathetically out-manned, undertrained black people."[47] Part of the reason the program earned such praise was because it undermined Portuguese claims that the rebels were motivated and funded by Communists. Although the premise of the documentary was based on a search for Red insurrectionists, the documentation countered these suspicions and ultimately concluded that the Angolan rebel forces could best be characterized as anticolonialists rather than Communists.

In sum, the African American press of this period seemed to deal with foreign policy questions from a perspective that tended to be suspicious of Cold War dichotomies. It was much more sensitive to issues of race and colonialism throughout the Third World and therefore more understanding of popular movements against exploitative governments. Where the network documentary might represent popular agitation as a threat to the stability of the Free World, the African American press was more likely to represent it as inevitable progress in the struggle to cast off the legacy of colonialism. One would tend to doubt therefore that readers of these newspapers were enthusiastic viewers of network documentaries. Not only were the perspectives of these two media widely divergent, but the social positions of their respective audiences were far apart. Black viewers—having fought for freedom in two world wars only to return to a country where racial prejudice remained largely unchanged—were no doubt more concerned about racism around the globe than they were about notions of superpower struggle.

As for network documentaries that specifically dealt with racial issues, the African American press was largely supportive of these efforts and encouraged the networks to put even greater emphasis on this area. *NBC White Paper*'s "Sit-In," one of the first prime-time network documentaries to deal with the civil rights movement, was hailed by an editorial in the *Amsterdam News* as a television milestone because it "portrayed and captured the dignity, manners and education that accompany the true progress of the Negro today." George E. Pitts, a columnist for the *Courier*, also had high praise for ABC's "Walk in My Shoes," particularly because of the first-person perspective that frames the analysis. "The Negro," he writes, "was permitted to tell his side of the mess and viewers were not forced to swallow some shallow, biased viewpoint presented by a white, so-called 'expert' on Negro life."[48] Pitts's dismissal of white expertise is interesting not only because he challenges the reputed objectivity of policy makers and social scientists but also because he praises a documentary film technique that was disturbing to many white professional journalists. The first-person camera technique was considered too impassioned according to some television critics at the time. It invited audience identification and involvement with documentary subjects supposedly at the expense of more objective analysis. But this is precisely the virtue of the ABC effort, according to Pitts:

> [It] gave the viewer the never-been-done-before experience of living for an hour in the world of the Negro and sharing the frustrating existence of the black man in America. But more important, this documentary served as a warning to white America that the Negro is now sick and tired of his haphazard life and is fast becoming a force to be reckoned with. It also pointed out, to those who noticed, that it is the white man's injustice which is responsible for the emergence and power of such all-black movements as the Muslims.[49]

Although Pitts seemed to share the documentary's perception of the Muslims as an ominous political force, many others in the African American press treated the Nation of Islam quite differently. For example, an article in the *Amsterdam News* detailed the growing number of radio stations carrying a weekly broadcast by Elijah Muhammad. It noted that stations in seventy-three major cities now featured Muhammad, a man "passionately concerned with justice and freedom for the American Negro."[50] The *Courier* also accorded the Muslims respectful coverage. One article described a confrontation between presidential adviser Arthur Schlesinger Jr. and Malcolm X that arose when Schlesinger, speaking to an Atlanta audience, lumped the Muslims in with race-hate groups such as the White Citizens Councils and the Ku Klux Klan. During the questioning period, Malcolm, along with other members of the audience, continuously pressed Schlesinger until he finally conceded that the comparison was inappropriate. Not only did the *Courier* article headline Malcolm's challenge, but it devoted twice as much space to his comments as those of Schlesinger.[51]

This account of the exchange in Atlanta emphasizes some of the differences between the readership of the black press and the intended audience of network documentary. Documentary primarily served a white, middle-class audience with little direct experience of the black community. These programs therefore employed Malcolm X as an ominous symbol of impending black militance should efforts at integration fail. African American newspapers, on the other hand, not only served an audience that had direct experience with the Muslims, but they also served communities in which the Nation of Islam was one of the most forceful and articulate advocates of black independence. The Muslim organization must have been intriguing to many black readers who had grown weary of their treatment by "mainstream" white society.

One senses such weariness and exasperation in Poppy Cannon White's review of the *CBS Reports* documentary "The Harlem Temper." She describes the extensive cooperation that Harlem citizens extended to CBS producers when they learned that their community was to be featured in a network documentary. Yet the project proved to be more exploitative than enlightening. She calls it "the old sensationalism with a new civil rights twist." According to White: "The picture of Harlem (no pun intended) was black, black, black. No glint of hope, no trace of comfort, nor common horse sense or humor. . . . To judge from this program, all of Harlem lives in the streets. Mostly, one might gather, on relief. (Wonder where all those people go on the subways morning and evening.)"[52] Although the program provided an empirical account of life in Harlem, that account was developed primarily for a white mass audience. Consequently, a huge difference existed between CBS's stereotype of Harlem and the diverse African American community represented in the pages of the *Amsterdam News*. The documentary offers a reductive representation intended for a white audience with little direct experience of the Harlem community and even less interest. Harlem is important to the documentary as a symbol of social unrest that might ultimately prove threatening to a middle-class lifestyle. The network viewer need not linger on it for long, since the prime-time schedule would quickly blanch white again after the documentary was over.

In short, institutional assumptions about a singular national audience made it extremely difficult for documentarists to address their work to the interests and concerns of African American viewers. As a result, blacks probably watched few network documentaries and agreed with even fewer.[53] As for other racial minorities, they had an even more oblique relationship to these programs, since most of them were rarely, if ever, referred to by network news organizations of this period. Consequently, the ambitious Cold War education project of the New Frontier systematically marginalized large segments of the potential viewing audience.

Documentary's Gendered Address

A similar assessment emerges when one considers network documentary in relation to gender issues. Not only was the white documentarist speaking to a white audience, but it was a *male* documentarist speaking the masculine language of public life.[54] Indeed, during the early sixties, the only woman working on network documentaries with the status of full-fledged producer or reporter was ABC's Helen Jean Rogers. Her position seemed so exceptional and even disruptive that network promotional efforts and newspaper biographies lavished a great deal of attention on her femininity. Framed as the equal of her male peers, Rogers was nevertheless consistently repositioned within more conventional codings of woman. For example, one story, which describes Rogers as "dark blonde, well-assembled and winsome," also explains her strategy for dealing with government officials in South Africa who tried to seize her film footage when she was leaving the country. "I screamed and I threatened and I beat on the sides of the plane with my fists," said Rogers. "Indeed, I became so hysterical I'm afraid I was hardly coherent at all. In short, I was acting like a woman. And it worked."[55] Another article, which likens her physical appearance to that of actress Barbara Bel Geddes, describes how she coped with the arduous demands of travel in Africa. "If everything else failed, I wept," said Rogers. "I cried myself into some countries and out of others. It seemed to be the only way."[56] Although other producers no doubt had to use imaginative ploys to achieve their objectives in the field, Rogers's gendered ruses were consistently singled out in biographical newspaper accounts.

These stories seem to have served at least two functions. First of all, they made it clear that although Rogers was exceptionally well educated and fluent in several languages, she was, after all, accepting of her "natural" status as a woman. This made her appear less threatening to conventional gender relations despite her accomplishments in a conventionally masculine field of endeavor. Secondly, these accounts suggest that Rogers was a *modern* woman, not unlike Jacqueline Kennedy, a testament to the progress brought about by a democratic consumer society. Unlike women in many other parts of the world, Rogers had choices and opportunities.

The apparent contradictions at work here point to the conflicting ways in which network documentaries addressed female viewers. Although ratings data suggest that documentary audiences were equally divided between men and women, the style and content of documentary were primarily skewed toward a masculine perspective. Thus the programs touted their social significance and beckoned women to pay attention, but at the same time they privileged "hard" public issues and tended to marginalize topics that were conventionally coded as feminine.

In part, this was a product of the debates about television reform that began in the late 1950s. As discussed in chapter 1, many opinion leaders contended that the networks' growing commitment to documentary represented the long-delayed fulfillment of the medium's public service responsibility. Public service in this context was pitted against private leisure. It was also tacitly associated with conventional distinctions between a masculine public sphere and a feminine private sphere. Consequently, news analysis of "hard" issues was contrasted with the "soft" entertainment of Hollywood telefilm. And the high cultural capital of public affairs programming was pitted against the low cultural capital of television fiction and fantasy.

Although these distinctions should not be mistaken for absolute boundaries, they do map out some of the implicitly gendered oppositions that shaped the debate over television reform. Entertainment television was regarded by many critics as little more than a meaningless distraction that supposedly turned the viewer into a passive homebody who was ignorant of public issues. It was further suggested that television invaded the domestic realm and seduced the viewer. It manipulated the masses for commercial gain, turning viewers into hysterical consumers who were irrationally driven to purchase useless commodities. A number of scholars have observed that these images of penetration, seduction, passivity, hysteria, and irrationality have been associated with mass entertainment throughout the modern era.[57] Moreover, they have been associated with the feminine, a gendering that accorded lesser status to popular media.

It is therefore not surprising that during the late fifties and early sixties, the antidote to television's entertainment squalor was the introduction of masculine order to network prime time. The television networks would, for the first time, seriously explore the medium's potential to inform and enlighten. Most crucially, this also involved a reconceptualization of the audience. Whereas industry executives and advertisers had characterized prime time's target audience as the mother-homemaker-consumer, the target audience for the documentary would be the father-citizen-producer, the family's key link to the public sphere.[58] The distinction here between the productive labor of the documentary audience (learning/acting) and the otherwise passive consumption of prime-time entertainment (receiving/relaxing) is not unlike the distinction Tania Modleski points to in gendered stereotypes of book readers from earlier eras. She writes, "The well-educated eighteenth-century minister of Calvinism . . . read 'dense argumentative tracts' that 'forced him to think, not to read in our modern sense; metaphorically speaking, he was producing, not consuming.'" Victorian women, on the other hand, idly reclined on chaise lounges passively consuming "worthless novels."[59]

During the early sixties, this dichotomy between information and entertainment was explicitly echoed by network officials such as Fred Friendly, executive producer of *CBS Reports*. "We have stuck our ostrich heads into the sand of entertainment and creature comforts," said Friendly. "Day in and day out for decades we have been living in a world of fiction—how the favorite ball team made out, the latest escapades of a movie idol or singing star, the latest scandals of the entertainment world."[60] Friendly dismissed these popular pleasures as distractions from the more serious struggle against the global Communist threat. Television must inform, he argued, if the Free World was to survive. At the vanguard of this effort was the network documentarist, whose mission was to activate the viewer's thinking in relation to pressing social concerns and to reconnect "him" with public life. Thus the viewer's relation to the documentary was intended to be an active one, with audiences being spurred to action after learning about important issues. Indeed, many of the programs conclude by urging public concern or activism.

Yet these neatly gendered distinctions suppress a set of tensions at work within the network documentary itself and more generally within network news organizations since the 1950s, for although the documentary was strongly influenced by the standards and conventions of journalism, it also employed many of the conventions of representation common to entertainment television and Hollywood film. While network *reporters* touted objectivity and analysis, documentary *producers* (most of whom were trained as filmmakers) argued that the programs would only work if news workers paid attention to character, plot, and affect. Moreover, their adoption of the editing grammar of Hollywood studios further accentuated links to the storytelling techniques of prime-time entertainment.

This tension between journalistic method and filmic representation was at work not only in the textual strategies of the programs but also in the institutional relations of documentary production teams. Network correspondents and producers actively struggled over program content as well as the professional conventions that governed documentary production.[61] One side leaned toward pretensions of objectivity, whereas the other valorized many of the filmmaking techniques of Hollywood. The outcomes of these struggles varied at each of the networks. A reviewer for an industry trade paper once described *CBS Reports* as the *Atlantic* magazine of television, *NBC White Paper* as the *Harper's*, and ABC's *Bell and Howell Close-Up!* as the *Cosmopolitan* or *Redbook*.[62] The latter earned its designation because of the importance it accorded to character, affect, and visualization. For example, the largely positive reviews of the ABC documentary "Yanki No!" (an examination of Castro's influence in Latin America) referred to the program as passionate and dramatic. The negative assessments turned these virtues against the filmmakers, saying the program was impassioned rather than reasoned, that it was *too* emotional. Although *NBC White Paper* was perhaps not as committed to visualization as its competitor, its producers also emphasized the importance of character and plot, arguing that documentaries about social issues must have a human core, a point of identification for the viewer at home. Moreover, they contended that documentaries should evoke feelings as well as ideas. The most staid of the three network flagship series was *CBS Reports*, which was very conservative in its style of filming. It also was the only network that prohibited producers from using nondiegetic music or sound effects to enhance the visual image.[63]

CBS producer Fred Friendly's austere sense of journalistic purity can be gleaned from a speech he delivered to the convention of American Women in Radio and Television in 1964. Discussing a *CBS Reports* documentary marking the twentieth anniversary of D-Day, Friendly illustrated the distinctions he made between news and entertainment. In a crucial scene of the program, the producers were using film from one of the landing craft during the Normandy invasion. According to Friendly:

> The scene lasts about four minutes, but there is no sound because nobody recorded any sound [at the time]. Now the first temptation was to say, "Well, let's take those sounds which are available to us in the libraries and let's put sound into it. . . ." Then we tried sound effects and it was remarkably better, much more dramatic. But suddenly we were aware that we were doing something phony. We were putting something together that people would see on June 6, 1964 or June 6, 1984—and they would never know that they were looking at something that wasn't real. . . . Sometimes we are less dramatic. Sometimes we are so honest it costs us at the box-office. But if we want to be journalists, that's what we have to do.[64]

This reference to the temptations of the box office is telling, for *CBS Reports* had an exceedingly difficult time attracting advertisers and large audiences. But this was not true of all documentaries. In 1962 network documentarists began to experiment with new approaches, and by the spring of the following year it became apparent that large audiences could be tapped by actuality programs if they steered away from the topics and formats that initially dominated the genre. As *Variety* put it, network documentarists were looking for programs with "jazzier themes" and were placing new emphasis on audiences rather than critics.[65] They were also beginning to jettison their earlier preoccupation with the Cold War.

This shift can be traced to the February 1962 broadcast of "A Tour of the White House with Mrs. John F. Kennedy." The program is arguably a watershed because it was the first television documentary to make it eminently clear that the genre *could* draw huge audiences. Not only did it score the highest ratings of the season (entertainment included), but it was also estimated that its international distribution brought the total number of viewers to several hundred million. Obviously, the documentary traded on its star appeal and its privileged access to lifestyles of the rich and famous. But it also foregrounded a set of tensions that, by the early 1960s, were chafing at what historian Elaine Tyler May has described as the postwar ideology of domesticity.[66] These tensions, I would suggest, were a significant part of the program's appeal.

Here was Jacqueline Kennedy fulfilling her domestic duty by providing visitors a tour of her home. Yet she also was performing a public duty as the authoritative voice of the documentary: providing details on her renovation efforts, informing the audience about the historical significance of various furnishings, and even assuming the position of voice-over narrator during extended passages of the program. In fact, this was the only prime-time documentary from this period in which a woman narrated large segments of the text. Kennedy's authoritative status is further accentuated by her position at the center of the screen. This framing is striking in retrospect because correspondent Charles Collingwood, who "escorts" Kennedy from room to room, repeatedly walks out of the frame, leaving her alone to deliver descriptions of White House decor and its national significance. Only at the very end of the program, when President Kennedy "drops in" for a brief interview, is Jacqueline repositioned in her role as wife and mother. Sitting quietly as the two men talk, she listens attentively while her husband hails her restoration efforts as a significant contribution to public awareness of the nation's heritage.

The ambiguities at work in this program seem to be linked to widespread ambivalence about the social status of the American woman at the time of this broadcast. Here is Jacqueline Kennedy positioned in her home, which is at once a private and public space. It is her family's dwell-

Jacqueline Kennedy bridging private and public life in "A Tour of the White House."

ing but also a representation of the nation's home. Furthermore, Jacqueline Kennedy is presented both as a mother—indeed, the national symbol of motherhood—and as a modern woman: a patron of the arts, a historical preservationist, and a key figure in producing the nation's collective memory. In these respects, she might be seen as symbolic of female aspirations to reenter the public sphere, and I would suggest that these aspirations were a crucial component of this documentary's popularity with female viewers.[67]

The White House tour was soon joined by a number of similar productions, each of which drew prime-time audiences as large as those for fictional entertainment. For example, "The World of Sophia Loren" earned an 18 rating, "Elizabeth Taylor's London" a 23, and "The World of Jacqueline Kennedy" a 19.[68] Perhaps most remarkably, the programs about Loren and Kennedy garnered roughly a third of the viewers then using television, and the Taylor documentary drew close to half of all viewers watching television at the time of its broadcast.

In general, elite television critics reviewed these programs skeptically, noting that entertainment values were privileged at the expense of a more critical assessment of their subject matter.[69] Yet the appeal of these programs may have had less to do with the dichotomy between entertainment and information per se. Rather, these documentaries may have drawn such large audiences because they tapped into women's fantasies about living a more public life while largely maintaining their conventional feminine attributes. As numerous feminist scholars have argued, one of the fundamental appeals of television programming is the opportunity it affords for the viewer to fantasize about situations and identities that are not part of one's everyday existence. In the early 1960s, such fantasies may have been important not only for women who chafed at the constraints of domesticity but also for women who were imagining new possibilities. Writes feminist critic Ien Ang:

> Women are constantly confronted with the cultural task of finding out what it means to be a woman, of marking out the boundaries between the feminine and unfeminine. This task is not a simple one, especially in the case of modern societies where cultural rules and roles are no longer imposed authoritatively, but allow individualistic notions such as autonomy, personal choice, will, responsibility, and rationality.[70]

The popularity of television documentaries about the lives of famous women therefore seems to fit within the broader context of emerging debates over gender roles and the ideology of domesticity. These programs afforded women the opportunity to imagine themselves in public roles outside the home.

Yet fantasy was not the only way in which women deliberated on their changing circumstances. Issue-oriented articles in women's magazines during the early sixties reflected these concerns as well. *McCall's*, the women's magazine with the largest circulation at the time, featured articles such as "Women in Politics: The Coming Breakthrough," "Child Care in Russia: Better than Ours?" and "The Fraud of Femininity" (adapted from Betty Friedan's best-seller *The Feminine Mystique*).[71] Even advertisers and broadcasters were beginning to interrogate the dilemmas facing the modern woman. One advertisement for a series of NBC daytime specials began by describing its target audience as "the most privileged woman in the world." The ad went on to explain, "She can vote, drive a car, speak her mind. She has club memberships, college degrees and a kitchen full of conveniences. Yet, a great number of her kind are in distress. . . . She feels trapped in a role society has forced upon her."[72] These *Purex Specials for Women* were produced under the guidance of Irving Gitlin, who had first pioneered the format in 1959 while working at CBS. Many of these programs dealt with family issues such as raising children and caring for aging parents, whereas others offered reassessments of conventional femininity, for example, "The Trapped Housewife," "The Working Mother," "The Single Woman," and "The Glamour Trap." The programs proved to be widely popular with female audiences during the daytime. Yet prior to 1962, gender issues rarely appeared in prime-time documentary.

It was not until 1963 that ABC brought some of these concerns to the evening schedule with "The Soviet Woman" and "The World's Girls."[73] The former examines how women fare in a Communist society in which, according to the narrator, they are "economically and socially more emancipated than any other land on earth." Over the course of the hour, viewers are introduced to women scientists, editors, ironworkers, and bricklayers. Given the Cold War politics of this era, one would not expect an outright celebration of this equality. Therefore, the program persistently pits equality against femininity, suggesting the balance has tipped toward the former in Soviet society at the expense of the latter. Nevertheless, the documentary takes the issue of equality quite seriously, noting that even though the Soviet working woman still bears primary responsibility for homemaking and child care, the government provides a support infrastructure of nurseries, public laundries, and convenience foods. Moreover, we are told that Soviet women receive four months' paid maternity leave and are eligible for a one-year leave of absence

"The Soviet Woman" playing a prominent role in the workforce and in public life.

without losing their job. Whether and how well this Soviet infrastructure actually performed is less of a concern than the fact that it received prime-time exposure during an era when American women—a significant and growing percentage of whom were working outside the home—were beginning to raise these very issues.

In the fall of 1963 ABC also broadcast "The World's Girls," an examination of the changing status of women around the globe that included interviews with Betty Friedan and Simone de Beauvoir. Like the other ABC documentary—both of them written and produced by men—the riddle of feminine sexuality in a changing social climate plays a prominent role throughout. Once again, however, this masculine perspective struggles to contain and explain expressions of female discontent with existing gender roles. The program shows housewives complaining of boredom and onerous child-raising responsibilities, young women leaving their villages for employment opportunities in the cities of post-colonial Africa, and female college graduates criticizing their limited job prospects despite high levels of academic training.

It is of course impossible to know what female viewers thought of these programs, but their very existence suggests that the networks were beginning to reconsider many of their earlier assumptions about documentary. The potential audience for the genre was far from the homogeneous mass envisioned at the beginning of the decade. Despite the assumption that documentaries took on the "great issues" facing all Americans, actual viewers tended to define their concerns quite differently. As with race issues and African American audiences, gender topics seemed far more connected to the everyday lives of many women than the supposed Communist threat in some distant quarter of the globe. Particular topics drew particular kinds of viewers; not everyone agreed about the urgency of superpower struggle. Thus the effort to promote a singular notion of public duty to a huge national audience proved to be an elusive goal. And what initially was intended as one of the most masculine genres in the early history of television became in practice a form of programming that adopted many of the same conventions as its entertainment counterparts.

In summary, television documentary failed to live up to its promise to reconnect the mass audience with public life and to earn its allegiance to a reinvigorated foreign policy. As we have seen in this chapter, the notion of the mass audience that was so fundamental to the success of entertainment television proved to be an elusive mirage for network documentarists. Instead of huge national audiences, documentaries seemed to appeal to audiences that were modest in comparison with their entertainment counterparts. Part of this may have been due to the ways in which the programs focused their address on a male, white middle-class viewer, thereby marginalizing viewers from other social backgrounds. African Americans occupied perhaps the most peculiar position in this regard. Although their civil rights were often the subject of documentary examination, network documentaries were produced by whites for a white audience. As for foreign policy issues, the programs privileged the question of superpower struggle often at the expense of questions of racial politics and colonialism. It is therefore little wonder that blacks were not outspoken supporters of the genre.

Similarly, women's concerns were not a major consideration for network documentarists. If anything, the documentary was implicitly characterized as a masculine genre of programming intended to displace soft entertainment with hard news about "serious" social issues. With their focus on the Cold War, prime-time documentaries largely overlooked women's growing frustrations with existing gender roles. The programs addressed issues of the public sphere while largely ignoring the fact that more than half of the potential audience was systematically excluded from full-fledged participation in public life. As with black viewers, women had little reason to embrace the documentary genre.

Finally, network documentary fell short in its efforts to reach the American masses because it sought to introduce elite concerns into a medium of popular entertainment. Both the content of these programs and their stylistic characteristics marked them as intrusions in a domain of programming that emphasized viewer participation, identification, and affect. During the early sixties when most homes had only one TV set, program selection was the outcome of negotiations over a collective viewing experience. Given that documentary was primarily targeted at only one member of the family, it is easy to see why the genre suffered in the ratings. Although the programs earned kudos from opinion leaders and elites, and even though opinion polls showed strong support for the expansion of public affairs programming, these indices failed to correlate with the private behaviors of audiences at home. Documentaries were not heavily viewed, nor did they transform popular attitudes about the Cold War. After three years of rapid growth, the networks began to reassess their investment in the genre.[74]

Conclusion

The early 1960s were truly the heyday for the network documentary, and the pattern since that time has been one of inexorable decline. In 1967 the combined efforts of the three major networks yielded only one hundred total hours of documentary programming, one-fourth the total only five years earlier. By 1977 the number had shrunk to fifty-one hours, and one decade later the total was down to thirty-one, roughly half an hour of such programming each week.[1] The reasons for this decline have been the subject of ongoing discussion in the trade press and among broadcast journalists for some time.[2] It has been attributed to a number of factors, ranging from the rise of the broadcast news magazine to the declining corporate commitment to public service programming.

Whatever the reasons for documentary's current status, several factors emerged as early as 1963 that precipitated the slackening of network demand and marked the end of the so-called golden age. As we have already seen, one of those factors was the modest ratings performance of these programs. But since audience demand was not a major catalyst behind the emergence of the golden age, we must turn to other elements that might also help us understand the genre's decline.

Commercial Sponsorship

Even though the documentary achieved the status of prestige programming during the early 1960s, its prime-time scheduling exposed it to many of the same commercial pressures as its entertainment-oriented competitors. Although few network executives envisioned these nonfiction series as equal competitors with entertainment fare, they argued from the outset that the programs must be marketable to advertisers. Thus for many executives it was a positive sign that between 1958 and 1962 the percentage of *sponsored* public affairs programs rose from 46 to 54 percent.[3] These numbers were considered quite impressive in view of the fact that the total number of network documentaries had risen dramatically during this same period. On the other hand, these figures are also indicative of the increasing pressure to market the sponsorship of these programs in order to recover the networks' burgeoning investment in the production of public affairs programming. This pressure was further amplified by the fact that the percentage of documentaries slated for prime time had more than tripled.[4] Documentary was not only expensive to produce, but its growing presence on the evening schedule precluded the networks from broadcasting more lucrative entertainment fare during peak viewing hours. Therefore the costs associated with "lost revenue" were coupled with production costs in the minds of many network officials. This created intense corporate pressure to find sponsors for each program.

One of the ways in which the networks sought to do this was by making the documentary audience appear uniquely attractive. Opinion sampling firms such as Sindlinger and Pulse introduced "quality ratings" during this period, arguing that specific genres, especially documentary, might benefit from more precise sampling techniques.[5] It was hoped that demographic data would demonstrate the advantages of sponsoring programs that drew a small, but affluent group of viewers. Network sales executives accordingly promoted the distinction between "image buys" and "gross circulation."[6] Yet despite these efforts, the number of sponsors willing to take on a public affairs program proved to be limited.

Part of the problem seemed to be that television advertisers were more impressed by raw numbers than prestige. During this era, TV was generally promoted as a distinctive advertising venue that reached large national audiences in a timely fashion. Consequently, the sponsors who were attracted to this costly form of promotion were primarily interested in programs with mass audience appeal. It was therefore difficult to find enough advertisers who would pay premium rates for an "image buy." This meant that documentary was forced to compete on the same commercial terms as its prime-time counterparts. The outcome of this competition can be gleaned from an extensive NBC study in 1961 that showed that news and information programming drew only 13 percent of the network's total audience even though it commanded 23 percent of total network airtime. Although some disproportion had been anticipated, network executives were reportedly "unsettled" by the size of the gap. If things were this bad at NBC, whose public affairs shows enjoyed the best ratings record, then it was assumed that the situation was worse at the other networks.[7] Nonetheless, NBC continued to forge ahead with the expansion of its informational offerings during the 1961 season, perhaps bolstered by the fact that it was able to sell all of its news programming to sponsors and thereby realize a profit of four million dollars.[8]

By 1963 the situation had changed, however. News and information programming had grown to 29 percent of network fare, but the NBC news division was now reporting an annual *loss* of five million dollars.[9] The problem, according to salespeople at the networks, was that advertising agencies would talk about the need for documentary programming when addressing public forums but would advise their clients to buy safer, more commercial programming during private consultations.[10] Both agencies and clients were well aware that telefilm entertainment series from Hollywood drew predictably large audiences. Furthermore, despite the efforts of ratings services to identify "quality" audiences, there was an emerging consensus within the industry that these audiences were in fact diminishing.[11] The viewing elite reportedly was spending its "quality time" away from the tube, and this made it even more difficult to justify documentary sponsorship to network clients.

The impact on news budgets was unmistakable. In 1962 it was estimated that the three networks were laying out sixty million dollars a year for news and public affairs programs while recovering less than half that much in revenue.[12] Too many shows were chasing too few sponsors, and revenues were even further depressed as sales representatives for the networks began to sell documentary ad time at a discount in a desperate attempt to attract clients.

Although few would publicly disparage the genre, both television critics and network sales staffers began to ask, "How much is too much?" Like other innovative program formats that had preceded it, the documentary was falling prey to a familiar cycle in the history of American broadcast programming: innovation, imitation, saturation. As the networks vied for competitive position in documentary programming, some critics contended that broadcasters had overextended their commitment to the genre.[13] Much of this reasoning was based on the commercial logic of network television, but critics also were quick to point out that the attractiveness of documentary was further undermined by the controversies that the programs sometimes generated.

Documentary Content

Bob Lang, who sold advertising time for both CBS and ABC public affairs shows during this period, claimed that it was almost impossible to find advertisers for programs that explored deeply controversial issues.[14] Part of the problem was that documentary programs were often marketed on a single-sponsorship basis. In promoting the programs, network sales staffs suggested that one of the benefits of this arrangement was the association audiences would make between the program's sophisticated, public service content and the identity of the sponsor. According to Lang, however, the flip side of this logic was that audiences might also associate the sponsor with any controversial ideas that might be contained in the program. Sponsors worried about both public reaction and the response of powerful government officials. Yet advertisers were not the only ones to express concern about content issues. The networks also experienced resistance from timid affiliates. Fearful of controversy, some stations chose not to broadcast network documentaries, and this further reduced the size of their national audience and therefore made them even harder to promote with advertisers.[15]

Ultimately, these concerns over content were most problematic for the flagship documentary series. Both *CBS Reports* and *NBC White Paper* had the hardest time attracting commercial sponsorship.[16] By 1963 *Reports* was in particularly desperate straits, and rumors within the industry indicated that this was partly the result of complaints regarding documentaries on South Africa and pesticides.[17] Both programs reportedly offended corporations that were prominent television advertisers. Yet these were not the only organizations that worried network officials. Powerful interest groups such as the American Medical Association and the Catholic Church kept a watchful eye on network treatment of topics within their domains of interest. And local governments howled in protest when they became the subject of documentary critique. Indeed, two of the most celebrated complaints filed with the FCC during this period were registered by local politicians in New York and Massachusetts as a result of network investigations that were broadcast in prime time.

A 1962 FCC inquiry found, however, that NBC's "The Battle of Newburgh" and CBS's "Biography of a Bookie Joint" met the commission's standards for journalistic impartiality. Moreover the FCC explicitly "applauded their analyses of controversial situations." This response was widely interpreted as an effort to bolster the integrity of television documentarists and to encourage network support for the genre. Such encouragement should have been the basis for celebration, but Jack Gould, writing in the *New York Times*, noted the broader implications of the report: "The fact remains the Federal agency did evaluate the *contents* of the news presentations and arrived at its own subjective judgment as to their balance."[18] In other words, despite the commission's favorable findings, the inquiry nevertheless perpetuated a distinction between television and newspapers regarding First Amendment issues. The agency seemed to be saying that the networks should freely pursue such controversial public issues but that they would continue to be subject to government oversight. The impact on broadcast executives is perhaps best summed up by one of the most faithful advocates of the documentary, NBC president Robert Kintner, who remarked, "You don't think of broadcasting companies having opinions, like the newspaper greats."[19]

Here, then, was the crux of the problem for the networks: in order to maintain control over all prime-time content and scheduling, they had claimed the exclusive prerogative to interpret controversial issues over the public airwaves. They based this preemptory claim on their capacity to analyze social problems in a professional, balanced, and objective manner. In so doing, they excluded all other interpretations of the issues at hand. Yet having done so, the networks then were forced to deliver on their claims to objectivity. As a result, they either had to silence all opposing points of view, or they had to focus their attention on issues that would not generate "legitimate" oppositional interpretations. As we saw in chapters 5 and 7, network claims to objectivity were subject to challenge for a number of reasons. As the challenges mounted throughout the early sixties, network documentarists began to privilege topics that were less controversial, or they began to treat controversial topics in less controversial ways. As one newspaper commentator noted in 1964, "The public service may be there in form but the exciting bite of a 'See It Now' has been dulled. Documentaries now are wholesome; they don't jar the convictions."[20] As the genre grew more timid, it also became more scarce as networks began to trim their commitment to documentary and focus instead on much less interpretive approaches, such as live coverage and nightly news.

Networks Shift to Breaking News

Breaking news coverage became increasingly attractive to the major networks not only because it was less controversial but because it was commercially profitable. Close to 90 percent of all viewing homes tuned into live coverage of John Glenn's spaceflight around the earth.[21] In addition to making Glenn a prominent national figure overnight, this exposure demonstrated the marketability of such heroism and generated lively competition between the networks in their coverage of the ensuing NASA spaceflights.

Almost equally telegenic was the ongoing saga of the New Frontier. Although Kennedy reportedly harbored negative feelings about the networks during his presidential campaign, relations between the two camps warmed up considerably during his first year in office. As the trade magazine *Variety* commented, "The television consciousness of Mr. and Mrs. John F. Kennedy looms as the major phenomenon of the '61–'62 [television] semester."[22] Little wonder, presidential news conferences had become a prime-time ratings success, and the first lady's televised White House tour was one of the biggest audience draws of the season.[23] Camelot's ratings were sustained in the following season with the president's popular "rocking chair chats."[24]

Kennedy's success with the medium also proved to be a boon to network news organizations. NBC's conquest of the number one ranking in television news began with the network's coverage of the 1960 presidential campaign.[25] This directly benefited Huntley-Brinkley's evening newscast, which not only increased its ratings but also dramatically enhanced its advertising revenues.[26] Consequently, top executives at all three networks expanded their nightly news programs from fifteen to thirty minutes during the 1963–1964 season in order to better position themselves for the 1964 presidential race.[27] Moreover, Huntley-Brinkley's success supposedly proved that, as with entertainment television, "star qualities" drew large audiences for informational fare. News programs increasingly began to focus on personalities in the news as opposed to issues.[28] Networks also began to conduct audience research on the "likability" and perceived trustworthiness of network anchors and reporters. William R. McAndrew, executive vice president of NBC news, unabashedly commented, "If the newsman has the mysterious quality that appeals to the masses, you've got a star."[29] And it was exactly this elusive star quality to which the networks increasingly attributed the profitability of their nightly newscasts. In 1963 these programs generated more than a third of the total revenues at CBS and NBC News.[30]

Such concern with the popularity of television news was not entirely new, however. What was new was the increasing emphasis on the business side of the equation. Given network promotion of the potential profitability of news and given the growing mass appeal of breaking news coverage, it was almost inevitable that the status of the documentary would be diminished. At all three networks, management began to fulfill a greater portion of its public service responsibilities with largely uninterpretive and noncontroversial breaking news coverage.[31]

In sum, several factors contributed to the declining demand for network documentary. Problems with sponsors and program content were two of the most prominent. At the same time, breaking news coverage was emerging as a way for the networks to maintain their public service image while enhancing profitability. Additionally, it should be noted that the "image problems" that plagued the networks during the late 1950s no longer loomed so large. Not only were the quiz show scandals fading from popular consciousness, but Newton Minow departed from the FCC in 1963, and with him went much of the headline-grabbing scrutiny that had worried industry insiders.

National Politics

Other political factors were changing as well. President Kennedy's successor, Lyndon B. Johnson, began his administration on amiable terms with the networks. From the outset he had close ties to the industry because of Lady Bird's ownership of a substantial number of broadcast properties. He also was personal friends with the heads of CBS and NBC, Frank Stanton and Robert Kintner. Closer relations between the executive branch and the broadcast industry were paralleled by a shift in congressional attitudes toward television as well. Criticism from legislators seemed to be cooling off as many members anticipated the extensive television coverage that broadcasters promised for the 1964 election campaigns. Four years earlier, this sort of news coverage had done so much to convince politicians of the medium's powerful effects, and as the next national campaign got under way, few politicians wanted to disrupt their generally harmonious relations with broadcasters.

Finally, the end of the golden age of documentary must be linked to a shift in foreign policy. By 1963 the need for documentary analysis of global issues no longer seemed so pressing because transnational corporate leaders already had achieved many of their goals under the policies of the Kennedy administration: Congress had approved a massive defense buildup; government negotiators were spearheading a round of talks on tariffs and trade; and the United States was increasing its foreign aid as well as its commitment to programs such as the Alliance for Progress in Latin America. Furthermore, the domestic economy was reentering a period of expansion. Consequently, the business community

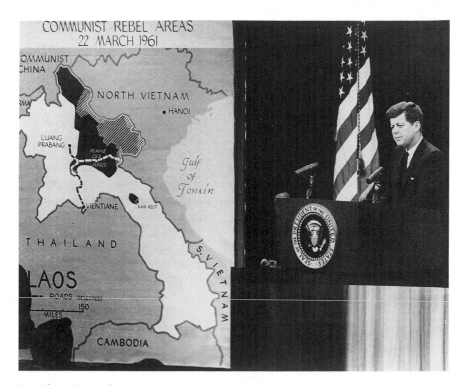

President Kennedy in 1961, when the struggle against Communism in Southeast Asia seemed much more compelling. (Courtesy of the JFK Library)

seemed less alarmed about the prospect of losing access to vital overseas markets. This was accompanied by a change in attitudes among government policy makers as well. Numerous historians have pointed out that after the Cuban missile crisis, the Kennedy administration seemed to rethink its aggressive foreign policy stance and to redirect its attention to domestic issues.[32] Furthermore, media scholar Daniel Hallin persuasively argues that both the Kennedy and Johnson administrations persistently attempted to shift media attention away from their growing military commitment in Vietnam.[33] Although there were complex reasons for this, it should be noted that the very same officials who had entered the White House in 1961 voicing their concerns about trouble spots around the globe were, by 1963, much more cautious about public discussion of American involvement in Southeast Asia and elsewhere.

As a result, the television documentary genre experienced a peculiar crisis of its own. Since programs that tackled contentious domestic issues often generated public disputes, many concluded that the network documentarist had only one "non-controversial arena in which to work—the confrontation of East and West in the sphere of international politics."[34] By 1963, however, this arena no longer enjoyed the stalwart patronage of government leaders. Dramatic East-West showdowns over places such as Berlin and Cuba had tempered enthusiasm for global activism. It seemed the time had come to cool off the rhetoric and direct public attention away from superpower conflict along the frontiers of the Free World. This shift in government policy is best characterized by Hallin's argument that during the escalation of the Vietnam War, U.S. officials repeatedly sought to avoid public alarm and to make intervention appear limited, rational, and inevitable. In such an environment, documentaries about global trouble spots no longer seemed an essential component of the broadcast schedule.

Documentary also lost much of its government patronage because, despite the hundreds of hours committed to the genre, it appeared doubtful that documentary had played a discernible role in mobilizing public support for a more aggressive foreign policy. Popular attitudes regarding the global Communist threat remained remarkably constant throughout this period.[35] Despite the grand enthusiasm for television's educational and transformative powers, important policy makers such as Edward R. Murrow, director of the U.S. Information Agency, found themselves questioning their own assumptions about the political power of television. Traveling across the United States by automobile while on vacation during the summer of 1962, Murrow wrote to the president regarding his conversations with "average citizens." Murrow complained that people had abdicated responsibility regarding foreign policy, most of them saying it was simply too complex and should be left to the leaders in Washington. Wrote Murrow in his letter to the president: "And though I rode my favorite theme, that maybe you should tell them more of what their country is trying to do, explain *why* we do what we do, no one asserted that you had failed in this fashion. (Could it be that I was wrong in our last conversation on this subject?) I do not know, but I *am* shaken."[36] Apparently, Murrow was not alone. By 1963 it was much rarer to find major public officials promoting the documentary as a vital component of American foreign policy. Attention had shifted to television's role as witness to live events rather than as interpreter of important national issues.

Throughout its brief history, fantastic powers of persuasion have been attributed to television. Reformers often wish to use it to change society, and conservatives consistently complain that the medium's liberal bias encourages nothing but change. Yet these assessments have too often been the product of simple, linear analysis. Television is said to be the cause of particular behaviors; or, on the other hand, powerful forces are said to be unproblematically reflected in the content of television programming. Instead, this analysis of documentary's golden age explains television as a site of active social struggle where various groups seek to shape and shift the terrain of public discourse.

During the early sixties the documentary genre was elevated to a privileged status as part of a Cold War education project promoted by corporate executives, New Frontier politicians, and public opinion leaders. Their concerns about public support for a more activist foreign policy were wedded to anxieties about popular culture and a supposedly flagging sense of national purpose. Television documentary was touted as the tonic for a nation adrift in aimless consumerism and passive entertainment. It would help to awaken the nation to its global leadership role and to reconnect the suburban viewer with public life. As such, documentary was promoted as a vehicle for helping the nation reimagine its sense of purpose as inextricably bound up with the community of the Free World.

Yet this group's power to promote the genre and its global perspective was mediated by a complex set of social and institutional forces. The major networks, who also were expanding into foreign markets, initially embraced documentary for many of the same reasons as others outside the industry. This embrace was further encouraged by the changing logic of television news. Increases in the ratings of nightly newscasts suggested that informational television might be self-sustaining, if not profitable, and the networks began to compete in this largely untested domain. News organizations grew rapidly during this era and spread their operations around the globe as the networks experimented with a variety of formats and techniques. These changes set the terms on which documentary would enter prime time. It would be informative and prestigious programming, but it also would be shaped by commercial pressures, audience ratings, and network competition. This was to be more than a public education project; these programs aimed to be commercial, popular, and exclusively produced by network employees.

The latter requirement was intended to sustain the networks' growing control over all components of prime time, but it also was connected to a heritage of journalistic objectivity and to the resurgent celebration of science and expertise in the post-Sputnik era. Consequently, news workers enthusiastically embraced documentary as an opportunity to enhance their status within the broadcast industry and the larger society as well. These were to be television's professionals. Armed with the latest technology and endowed with ample airtime, they would enlighten a nation in a "perilous age." Yet these news workers' engagement with the genre was also fraught with conflicting tensions and pressures. As journalists they were torn between objectivity and activism. As producers they had to balance the competing demands of information and narrative style. As programmers they had to weigh popularity against social significance. And as the exclusive interpreter of major social issues for a national and often international audience, they had to constantly anticipate viewer reaction and the potential for controversy. All of these factors mediated the messages that promoters of the genre initially had hoped to circulate.

As we have seen, the programs themselves register these competing tendencies. On the one hand, many of these documentaries explicitly explore the world of the Communist foe. Others probe the frontiers of the Free World in search of Communist infiltration. Still others turn their attention to the home front and wonder how domestic reforms might enhance the United States' ability to compete with its determined opponent. Thus a priori assumptions about the Cold War are a departure point for most of these programs, and in that sense they fulfill the intent of their promoters. Yet, on the other hand, the programs are also marked by gaps and ambivalences. Documentaries about the Free World allies often prove quite complicated and evade the simple Cold War dichotomies that initially motivated the genre. For example, some programs expose U.S. complicity with dictatorships in other countries, and others represent Communist organizations as more responsive to local populations than the U.S.-backed regimes. Similarly, programs that examine domestic issues such as migrant labor expose inequities that rarely before had been aired in prime time. Steeped as they were in Cold War ideology, the meanings circulated by these programs proved far more complex and troublesome than many anticipated.

Likewise, audience response to network documentary was not what many had hoped. The genre explicitly addressed a white, male, middle-class audience. It marginalized the African American viewer even as it discussed issues of racial segregation. It also failed to take gender issues seriously, even though this was a time when American women were reassessing the gender roles and attitudes that shaped their lives. Finally, the programs failed to connect with the patterns of family life during the evening hours. Skewed toward elite concerns, the programs appeared as an intrusion in the evening's entertainment. Although many viewers publicly endorsed the importance of the documentary, few of them made frequent use of the programs in the privacy of their homes. The genre never delivered on its promise to reach huge new audiences with information that would transform their attitudes and behaviors. In short, despite a massive investment of resources, television documentary did not live up to the persuasive powers that were attributed to it by politicians, advertisers, and social critics. Its messages were highly mediated by complex forces, and its direct effects on popular attitudes proved to be limited.

Nevertheless, we also have seen ways in which documentary played a prominent role in the debates over television and the national interest. Simply the fact that so many powerful groups coalesced around this Cold War education project is indicative of ways in which documentary operated as a site for the production of consensus among key elements of the New Frontier. Furthermore, even if most audience members watched documentaries only occasionally, their status as socially significant programs helped certain groups to define the terms of public debate. This power was further enhanced by the exclusion of alternative perspectives owing to the commercial logic of nationwide network television and the discourse of documentary professionalism.

As we examine the performance of our electronic media today, it is best that we remember such moments from the past, for debates persist as to how information should be produced and delivered in a modern, democratic society. Controversies continue to erupt over the uses of visual imagery, the role of narrative elements, and the involvement of news workers in the stories they produce. The buildup to the Gulf War involved many of the same dynamics we explored in network coverage of the New Frontier. Television reporting from the Persian Gulf concealed many of the economic, political, and social forces that influenced representations of both Kuwait and Iraq. In less than a year, media imagery transformed a politically repressive, oil-rich sheikdom into a pathetic ally for which the American people should be willing to shed blood. Conversely, Saddam Hussein, who had long been a strategic partner in Mideast geopolitics, quickly was remade in the image of a half-mad rogue. As with the New Frontier, American viewers were urged to play a decisive role in restoring order to a distant, "underdeveloped" region of the world.

Corporate television, a medium with its own international ambitions, enthusiastically embraced Desert Storm and labored relentlessly to produce visually engaging representations of the conflict. Dramatic biographies of U.S. combat pilots and exciting video footage of actual bombing runs concealed the fact that the airborne assaults were far less accurate—and the effects on innocent civilians far more severe—than network newscasts suggested. The point is that television was an important site for the production of consensus and the execution of the war. Indeed, so central has television become to the implementation of foreign policy that the conclusion of the Gulf War was carefully staged to feature the retaking of the U.S. Embassy in Kuwait City via helicopter, an inverted image of the chaotic American withdrawal from Saigon in 1974. The embassy in Kuwait could have been retaken just as easily by land, but the figure of a U.S. helicopter hovering over the rooftop in victory was intended for a global audience as if to suggest a reversal of the so-called Vietnam syndrome. Therefore questions of accuracy, objectivity, and professionalism should not distract us from the highly orchestrated connections produced at such moments between powerful institutions and televisual representation. Electronic media play a key role in shaping public images of global relations and consequently are perceived by political and corporate elites as vital to the realization of their transnational ambitions.

On the other hand, we should also remember that such moments of convergence are inevitably marked by gaps and contradictions. Peter Arnett's reports from the CNN bureau in Baghdad caused angry protests from Americans who questioned both his loyalty and that of his employer. In defending itself, CNN—the television network most dependent on a growing clientele around the globe—tried to cloak itself in the mantle of journalistic impartiality and in so doing continued to broadcast from Baghdad with images that formed a distinctive counterpoint to otherwise rhapsodic U.S. media coverage of Desert Storm. Responding to the interests of clients in the Mideast, CNN invoked the very same standards of journalistic professionalism toward a set of objectives at variance with the U.S. government. This cable network kept open a small window of access to firsthand reports of the severe consequences suffered by civilians in Iraq. Its coverage, however, was an exception to the otherwise effective mobilization of political, economic, and discursive forces by the Bush administration. Indeed, official U.S. policy was so compelling as to engender heady proclamations of a new world order.

Yet even at this seemingly triumphant moment of Desert Storm coverage, the television medium itself was undergoing a period of significant change as detailed in Ken Auletta's 1991 best-seller *Three Blind Mice*. Assessing the corporate behaviors that now govern the media industries, Auletta argues that network news is in a dangerous state of decline and that the demise of documentary is indicative of the current dangers posed by economic and technological forces. "Now, frantic for ratings," he writes, "executives too often worry more about giving people what they want than what they need to know."[37] Clearly, Auletta's comment echoes the very rhetoric that fostered documentary's golden age. Like critics of an earlier time, Auletta lauds the professionalism of network news workers and worries that the audience is splintering in an age of proliferating media. "Whatever its failings, a mass medium creates a common set of facts and a sense of community, and that is now at risk," he explains. "If network news dies, so dies a common hearth."[38] In fact, Auletta is so worried by this prospect that despite his weighty volume describing the many problems of the major commercial television networks, he ultimately endorses their prerogative to shape our perceptions of the world.

Others are more suspicious, however, of the giant corporations that have controlled American media for most of this century. They envision a future in which power is more dispersed, in which information flows laterally as well as vertically through high-capacity digital networks. They see the Internet as a model for the future and wax enthusiastically about the development of multimedia, a form of nonlinear information that allows the user far more room for active interpretation. Already, CD-ROM software is being promoted as the documentary format of the future. All of this promises to bring great changes to the genre, in its modes of production, distribution, and reception.

We need not look so far ahead, however, to see some of the changes that are already afoot. The splintering of network audiences has already narrowed the gap between ratings for entertainment shows and reality-based programming. While in the early sixties entertainment programs averaged an 18 rating, today they average close to a 10, not much different than documentaries in their heyday. Today, reality shows are more competitive in the ratings race, and their production expenses are far below those for entertainment. Without going into a detailed analysis of such programs, it is nevertheless hard to overlook the emerging diversity of nonfiction programming sources. Moreover, the low costs and high quality of technologies such as 8mm video have begun to enlarge the population of producers and blur the lines that were so crucial in marking the authoritative voice of the network journalist. This new pool of "documentarists" has provided a range of powerful and compelling moments. *Silverlake Life*, a poignant diary of a gay couple struggling with AIDS, is a good example of how these technologies engender personal forms of expression that previously were excluded from network prime time.

Thus we are poised once again at the dawning of a new media age, and once again various factions are competing to define a vision of the future. Huge corporations with vast resources scramble to contain and control the flow of information and to wed it to their agenda for an integrated global media environment, while grassroots activists struggle to exploit the possibility of a more open architecture of communications. At the same time, opinion surveys are beginning to show that the public is largely ambivalent regarding either agenda. In this current period of uncertainty, many step forward to speak for the people, the audience, the user. They speak not just about what people want but about what they need. They invoke the image of the nation or the global community. They rail against consumerism and superficial imagery. They valorize hard facts and in-depth analysis. And they always anchor their claims on the influential role of electronic media.

By contrast, this volume argues that even the most seemingly unencumbered and analytical forms of communications media cannot magically transform public attitudes. And that media should be studied, not as technologies for the transmission of information, but as sites of social contest over the production of meaning. Ken Auletta is wrong, not because he valorizes the network documentary, but because he essentializes its nature as a preeminent form of modern communication cast in stone by the "fathers" of electronic journalism. Documentary is not by its nature a positive benefit to society. Rather, television documentary, even in its golden age, was a form of communication bound up in the political struggles of its times. It is therefore best not to mourn the passing of the network documentary but rather to understand the convergence of forces that made the early 1960s the documentary's moment of prime time, for this was a unique era when the genre's claim to objectivity achieved peculiar force through its association with the political project of the New Frontier.

Appendix: Network Flagship Documentaries by Season

Flagship documentary series are *CBS Reports, NBC White Paper,* and ABC's *Bell and Howell Close-Up!* Broadcast dates are from Daniel Einstein, *Special Edition: A Guide to Network Television Documentary Series and Special News Reports, 1955–1979* (Metuchen, N.J.: Scarecrow Press, 1987). Einstein also includes a brief synopsis of each program along with production credits.

Key to Topic Categories

*	Specifically about foreign policy issues	e	Environment
†	Superpower struggle is a significant subtext or provides a foundational rationale	p	Poverty
		s	Space race
a	American politics	h	Health
lc	Law and crime	lb	Labor
c	Civil rights	i	Interview

1959–1960 Season

10/27/59	CBS	†Biography of a Missile s
11/11/59	CBS	*The Population Explosion e
12/18/59	CBS	*Iran: Brittle Ally
1/6/60	CBS	†The Space Lag: Can Democracy Compete? s
1/14/60	CBS	*The Population Explosion, Pt. 2 e
2/15/60	CBS	*Nigeria: The Freedom Explosion
3/17/60	CBS	*Trujillo: Portrait of a Dictator
4/21/60	CBS	Biography of a Cancer h
5/27/60	CBS	Who Speaks for the South? c
6/17/60	CBS	*Berlin: End of the Line
7/7/60	CBS	†Lippmann on Leadership i

Season total: 11

By topic: *6 †3 a-0 lc-0 c-1 e-2 p-0 s-2 h-1 lb-0 i-1

1960–1961 Season

9/27/60	B&H	Cast the First Stone c
10/11/60	CBS	†The Year of the Polaris s
10/13/60	B&H	*Paradise in Chains
10/27/60	CBS	Money and the Next President a
11/3/60	B&H	What's the Proposition? a
11/25/60	B&H	The Money Raisers a
11/25/60	CBS	†Harvest of Shame p, lb
11/29/60	NBC	*The U-2 Affair
12/7/60	B&H	*Yanki No!
12/9/60	B&H	Featherbedding? lb
12/10/60	CBS	*Rescue—With Yul Brynner
12/20/60	NBC	Sit-In c
12/26/60	CBS	The Great Holiday Massacre
1/5/61	CBS	Our Election Day Illusions: The Beat Majority a
1/19/61	CBS	Keeper of The Rules: Congressman Smith a
1/22/61	B&H	*The Red and the Black
2/2/61	CBS	The Business of Health h
2/6/61	B&H	†X-Pilot s
2/14/61	NBC	*Panama: Danger Zone
2/16/61	B&H	The Children Were Watching c
2/16/61	CBS	The Case of the Boston Electra
3/1/61	CBS	A Real Case of Murder: People vs. Peter Manceri lc
3/14/61	NBC	The Man in the Middle: The State Legislator a
3/16/61	CBS	*Crossroads Africa: Pilot for a Peace Corps
3/28/61	B&H	†Adventures on the New Frontier a
3/30/61	CBS	*Britain: Blood, Sweat, and Tears Plus 20
4/13/61	CBS	Carl Sandburg at Gettysburg i
4/14/61	B&H	†I Remember
4/16/61	NBC	Anatomy of a Hospital h
4/18/61	B&H	*Ninety Miles to Communism
4/27/61	B&H	*C'est La Guerre
4/27/61	CBS	†Why Man in Space? s
5/9/61	B&H	*Kenya: Land of the White Ghost, Pt. 1
5/11/61	CBS	Censorship and the Movies lc
5/16/61	B&H	*Kenya, Pt. 2
5/18/61	CBS	Who Speaks for Birmingham? c
5/23/61	NBC	Railroads: End of Line? lb
5/25/61	CBS	*The Trials of Charles De Gaulle
5/30/61	B&H	†The Flabby American h
6/13/61	B&H	*The Troubles Land

6/15/61	CBS	†Walter Lippmann 1961 i
6/22/61	B&H	*Our Durable Diplomats

Season total: 42

By topic: *15   †8   a-7   lc-2   c-4   e-0   p-1   s-3   h-3   lb-3   i-2

1961–1962 Season

9/19/61	B&H	†Walk in My Shoes c
9/19/61	NBC	*Angola: Journey to a War
10/12/61	CBS	†Eisenhower on the Presidency, Pt. 1 i
10/19/61	CBS	†The Water Famine e
10/31/61	B&H	The Awesome Servant lb
11/2/61	CBS	*Brazil: The Rude Awakening
11/9/61	CBS	*The Balance of Terror: In Case of War
11/14/61	B&H	*Behind the Wall
11/23/61	B&H	*West of the Wall
11/23/61	CBS	†Eisenhower on the Presidency, Pt. 2 i
11/28/61	B&H	*Heresy in Red
11/30/61	CBS	Biography of a Bookie Joint lc
12/5/61	B&H	Dropout p
12/10/61	B&H	*The Remarkable Comrades
12/13/61	B&H	†It's a Small World
12/14/61	CBS	*The Balance of Terror: Can We Disarm?
12/21/61	CBS	†Walter Lippmann, Year End i
12/26/61	NBC	*Khrushchev and Berlin
1/4/62	CBS	*East Germany: The Land beyond the Wall
1/18/62	CBS	†The Fat American h
1/25/62	CBS	Death in the City Room
1/29/62	NBC	The Battle of Newburgh p
1/30/62	B&H	*The Great Conversation
2/8/62	CBS	Carl Sandburg: Lincoln's Prairie Years i
2/15/62	CBS	†Eisenhower on the Presidency, Pt. 3 i
2/22/62	CBS	†Thunder on the Right a
2/25/62	NBC	*Red China
3/8/62	CBS	†Barry Goldwater: The View from the Right i
3/15/62	CBS	*Can We Disarm: Decision at Geneva
3/22/62	CBS	*Mr. Europe and the Common Market
3/25/62	NBC	*Arms and the State
3/27/62	B&H	*Cambodia: The Peaceful Paradox
3/29/62	CBS	The Beat Majority and the Supreme Court a, lc
4/10/62	B&H	Do Not Enter
4/12/62	CBS	The Taxed American: Prelude to April 15

4/19/62	CBS	The Taxed American: Loopholes of '62
4/17/62	B&H	*Back to Bhowani
4/24/62	B&H	*Britain: Ally on the Verge
4/26/62	CBS	*The Hot and Cold Wars of Allen Dulles
5/10/62	CBS	Birth Control and the Law h, lc
5/15/62	B&H	†The Vanishing Oasis e
5/18/62	NBC	*The Inferno
5/22/62	B&H	*The Overseas Chinese
5/24/62	CBS	*Breaking the Trade Barrier
6/7/62	CBS	†Walter Lippmann, 1962 i
6/12/62	B&H	What's So Funny?

Season total: 46

By   topic: *22   †12   a-2   lc-3   c-1   e-2   p-2   s-0   h-2   lb-1   i-7

1962–1963 Season

9/15/62	CBS	The Teenage Smoker h
9/26/62	CBS	Mississippi and the Fifteenth Amendment c
9/28/62	B&H	*Meet Comrade Student
10/3/62	CBS	*Showdown in the Congo
10/24/62	CBS	The Other Face of Dixie c
10/30/62	B&H	The Big Revolving Door, Pt. 1 lc
10/31/62	CBS	The California Battleground: Nixon vs. Brown a
11/13/62	B&H	The Big Revolving Door, Pt. 2 lc
11/17/62	B&H	*The Turbulent Jordan
11/20/62	B&H	The Lost Neighborhood p
11/27/62	B&H	*India: The Troubled Giant
11/28/62	CBS	*An Hour with the Secretary of State i
12/4/62	B&H	Gamble at the Keyboard
12/11/62	B&H	The Unpaid and the Unsung a
12/12/62	CBS	109 Days to Venus s
12/18/62	B&H	†The Wonderful World of Seven
12/19/62	CBS	*Sabotage in South Africa
1/9/63	CBS	*War at the Top of the World
1/23/63	CBS	†Eisenhower, 1963 i
1/27/63	NBC	*The Death of Stalin: Profile on Communism
2/3/63	NBC	*The Rise of Khrushchev: Profile on Communism
2/6/63	CBS	*Germany since Hitler: Adenhauer Sums Up i
2/20/63	CBS	Storm over the Supreme Court, Pt. 1 lc
3/1/63	NBC	*Who Goes There? A Primer on Communism
3/7/63	B&H	The Irreplaceable e
3/13/63	CBS	Storm over the Supreme Court, Pt. 2 lc
3/20/63	CBS	The Silent Spring of Rachel Carson e

3/31/63	NBC	†British Socialized Medicine h
4/9/63	B&H	The Miners' Lament lb, p
4/14/63	B&H	†The Vatican
4/17/63	CBS	The Man Who Built New York
4/23/63	B&H	A Vanishing Breed: Portrait of a Country Editor
4/28/63	NBC	The Business of Gambling
4/30/63	B&H	Smog: The Silent Killer e
5/1/63	CBS	†Walter Lippmann, 1963 i
5/7/63	B&H	Money for Burning
5/15/63	CBS	The Great Farm Vote of '63 a
5/15/63	CBS	The Verdict of the Silent Spring of Rachel Carson e
5/21/63	B&H	Twenty-third Precinct lc
5/22/63	CBS	†Reflections of a Soviet Scientist i
5/29/63	CBS	Birth Control and the Law h, lc
6/4/63	B&H	Return from Darkness h
6/12/63	CBS	Deadlock: The Railroad Dispute lb
6/19/63	CBS	Storm over the Supreme Court, Pt. 3 lc

Season total: 44

By topic: *11 †6 a-3 lc-7 c-2 e-4 p-2 s-1 h-4 lb-2 i-5

1963–1964 Season

9/18/63	CBS	The Priest and the Politician a
9/25/63	CBS	*McNamara and the Pentagon i
10/23/63	CBS	The Great American Funeral
11/13/63	CBS	*Case History of a Rumor
11/27/63	CBS	†Three Presidents on the Presidency i
12/11/63	CBS	The Harlem Temper c
12/18/63	CBS	†John F. Kennedy: The View from the Cabinet i
1/8/64	CBS	†The Crisis of Presidential Succession a
1/22/64	CBS	†The Business of Heroin lc
2/2/64	NBC	*Cuba: Bay of Pigs
2/5/64	CBS	The Catholics and the Schools
2/9/64	NBC	*Cuba: The Missile Crisis
2/19/64	CBS	The Flight from Hollywood
3/4/64	CBS	†The Legacy of the Thrasher
3/12/64	NBC	Adam Clayton Powell c, a
3/18/64	CBS	Filibuster: Birth Struggle of a Law c
4/1/64	CBS	*Vietnam: The Deadly Decision
4/8/64	CBS	†Walter Lippmann, 1964 i
4/14/64	CBS	Cigarettes: A Collision of Interests h
4/19/64	CBS	*De Gaulle: Roots of Power
5/6/64	CBS	*De Gaulle: The Challenge

6/5/64	CBS	†D-Day Plus Twenty Years: Eisenhower Returns to Normandy i
6/10/64	CBS	Murder and the Right to Bear Arms lc
6/24/64	CBS	*The Education of George Waruhiu

Season total: 24

By   topic: *8   †7   a-3   lc-2   c-3   e-0   p-0   s-0   h-1   lb-0   i-5

Notes

These notes contain the following abbreviations:

JFK   John F. Kennedy Presidential Library, Boston

BRTC   Billy Rose Theatre Collection of the New York Public Library, New York City

SHSW   State Historical Society of Wisconsin, Madison

CNL   CBS News Library, New York City

NMP   Newton Minow Papers, State Historical Society of Wisconsin, Madison

The documentaries cited below were screened at the Museum of Television and Radio, New York City; the Library of Congress, Washington, D.C.; and the UCLA Film and Television Archive. Many of the documentaries are still available for rental from services listed in the *Educational Film and Video Locator of the Consortium of College and University Media Centers* (New York: R. R. Bowker, 1990). Broadcast dates for all programs come from Daniel Einstein, *Special Edition: A Guide to Network Television Documentary Series and Special News Reports, 1955–1979* (Metuchen, N.J.: Scarecrow Press, 1987). Einstein also includes a brief description of each program and production credits.

Introduction

1. Fred W. Friendly, "Television *Can* Open America's Eyes," *TV Guide*, December 10, 1960, 5–7.
2. Raymond L. Carroll, "Economic Influences on Commercial Network Television Documentary Scheduling," *Journal of Broadcasting* 23 (fall 1979): 411–425.
3. Ibid., 415; *Broadcasting*, September 12, 1960, 27, and March 5, 1962, 52–53; *Business Week*, June 9, 1962, 50; *Printer's Ink*, December 23, 1960, 10;

Sponsor, March 26, 1962, 29; David G. Yellin, *Special: Fred Freed and the Television Documentary* (New York: Macmillan, 1973), 107.

4. *Variety,* January 4, 1961, 21, and September 24, 1962, 35.

5. *Variety,* May 16, 1962, 62; Yellin, *Special,* 223; Tim Brooks and Earle Marsh, *The Complete Directory to Prime Time Network TV Shows, 1946–Present,* rev. ed. (New York: Ballantine Books, 1981), 894.

6. *Variety,* February 17, 1960, 22, and September 25, 1961, 31; NBC press release, November 10, 1961, *NBC White Paper* file, CNL; memo to Julian Goodman from Don Meaney, December 20, 1961, Reuven Frank Papers, NBC Collection, box 292, file 20, SHSW.

7. Mary Ann Watson, "The Golden Age of American Television Documentary," *Television Quarterly* 23 (summer 1988): 57–75. Also see Ken Auletta, "Look What They've Done to the News," *TV Guide,* November 9, 1991, 4–7; Burton Benjamin, "The Documentary: An Endangered Species," *Freedom Forum Occasional Paper* 6 (October 1987); Bill Carter, "What Ever Happened to Documentaries?" *Washington Journalism Review* (June 1983): 43–46.

8. Carroll, "Economic Influences," 411–425.

9. Erik Barnouw, *The Tube of Plenty: The Evolution of American Television* (New York: Oxford University Press, 1975), 247; others who take this position include Fred Friendly, *Due to Circumstances beyond Our Control . . .* (New York: Vintage Books, 1967), 99–113; Thomas Whiteside, "The One-Ton Pencil," *New Yorker,* February 17, 1962, 41ff.; and Benjamin, "Documentary."

10. James L. Baughman, "'The Strange Birth of CBS Reports' Revisited," *Historical Journal of Film, Radio, and Television* 2, no. 1 (1982): 28–38.

11. Mary Ann Watson, *The Expanding Vista: American Television in the Kennedy Years* (New York: Oxford University Press, 1990), 135–136. Similarly, the trade press at the time depicted Minow's speech as a direct stimulus to network documentary. Jack Gould noted a "new receptiveness" to public service programming among network affiliates who previously had not cleared network documentaries for broadcast. Clipping, *New York Times,* June 18, 1961, Newton Minow file, BRTC.

    Other explanations for the documentary boom have been offered as well. Fred Freed and David Yellin, in their anecdotal recounting of this era, note the growing competition between the networks in the arena of news and public affairs. The "Friendly-Kintner wars" are often credited with the rapid expansion in both the number and prime-time scheduling of network documentary. See Yellin, *Special,* and Friendly, *Due to Circumstances.*

12. A. William Bluem, *Documentary in American Television: Form, Function, Method* (New York: Hastings House, 1965).

13. World War II is a key exception here, but the resulting documentaries are characterized largely as propaganda and therefore not typical of the genre as a whole. John Grierson's film unit in the 1930s might also be considered

one of the few institutional forms of documentary to draw significant attention. But even he had ongoing troubles with his institutional sponsors.

14. For example, see Stephen Mamber's influential *Cinema Verite in America: Studies in Uncontrolled Documentary* (Cambridge: MIT Press, 1974). Another study of cinema verité that employs an ingenious application of realist historiography is Robert C. Allen and Douglas Gomery, *Film History: Theory and Practice* (New York: Alfred A. Knopf, 1985), 213–241. The literature of film studies has also produced an impressive amount of criticism regarding the nature of documentary, its tropes of representation, and its audience. Much of this work has been published in journals such as *Cineaste* and *Jump-Cut*. Recent volumes of criticism include Michael Renov, ed., *Theorizing Documentary* (New York: Routledge, 1993), and Bill Nichols, *Representing Reality: Issues and Concepts in Documentary* (Bloomington: Indiana University Press, 1991).

15. Erik Barnouw, *Documentary: A History of the Non-Fiction Film* (New York: Oxford University Press, 1983), 227–228. Passing reference is also made to network documentary in Jack C. Ellis, *The Documentary Idea: A Critical History of English Language Documentary Film and Video* (Englewood Cliffs, N.J.: Prentice-Hall, 1989), 189–192, and Richard M. Barsam, *Non-Fiction Film: A Critical History* (Bloomington: Indiana University Press, 1992), 310–311 and passim.

16. William Chafe, *The Unfinished Journey: America since World War II*, 2d ed. (New York: Oxford University Press, 1991), 128–136.

17. Elaine Tyler May, *Homeward Bound: American Families in the Cold War Era* (New York: Basic Books, 1988).

18. Edward Jay Epstein, *News from Nowhere: Television and the News* (New York: Vintage Books, 1973), and Gaye Tuchman, *Making News: A Study in the Construction of Reality* (New York: Free Press, 1978).

19. Herbert J. Gans, *Deciding What's News: A Study of CBS Evening News, NBC Nightly News, Newsweek, and Time* (New York: Vintage Books, 1979).

20. Although oral history can be a productive approach, the uncritical conflation of personal recollections with primary archival research too often favors the interpretations of subjects who have a vested interest in the writing of history. Thus the relationship between personal memories and contemporaneous documentation is a complicated one. For reasons of focus, clarity, and economy, I have therefore chosen to devote my attention to primary and secondary source material from the period. For excellent examples of scholarship that explores the relationship between history and memory, see George Lipsitz, *Time Passages: Collective Memory and American Popular Culture* (Minneapolis: University of Minnesota Press, 1990); Michael Schudson, *Watergate in American Memory: How We Remember, Forget, and Reconstruct the Past* (New York: Basic Books, 1992); and Barbie Zelizer, *Covering the Body: The Kennedy Assassination, the Media, and the Shaping of Collective Memory* (Chicago: University of Chicago Press, 1992).

21. This was apparent not only in television ratings but also in documentation of the only FCC hearings from this period that provided the opportunity for wide public participation. At hearings in Chicago and Omaha, most local viewers, public officials, and business leaders expressed suspicion of, if not outright hostility to, Minow's agenda for television reform. "Omaha" file, box 55, E. William Henry Papers, SHSW; Federal Communications Commission, "Inquiry into Local Television Programming in Chicago, Illinois," docket 14546, boxes 7592–7596, National Archives, Washington, D.C.

22. My approach has benefited greatly from the work of many scholars in the field of cultural studies. I found the following historical studies of media to offer particularly useful approaches: Lynn Spigel, *Make Room for TV: Television and the Family Ideal in Postwar America* (Chicago: University of Chicago Press, 1992), and Robert C. Allen, *Speaking of Soap Operas* (Chapel Hill: University of North Carolina Press, 1985).

23. Clearly such an approach draws on the insights of Antonio Gramsci, *Selections from the Prison Notebooks of Antonio Gramsci,* ed. Quentin Hoare and Geoffrey Nowell Smith (New York: International Publishers, 1971). Regarding the application of Gramsci's ideas to the study of media, see, for example, Stuart Hall, Chas Critcher, Tony Jefferson, John Clarke, and Brian Roberts, *Policing the Crisis: Mugging, the State, and Law and Order* (New York: Holmes and Meier, 1978).

24. Benedict Anderson, *Imagined Communities: Reflections on the Origins and Spread of Nationalism* (New York: Verso, 1991).

25. Louis Althusser, *For Marx,* trans. Ben Brewster (London: Verso, 1979).

One. Opportunities Lost and Found

1. Frank Stanton to John M. Bailey, November 21, 1963, central subject file, box 992, JFK.

2. Frederick L. Holborn, administrative assistant to the president, to Ernest Hall, June 5, 1961, central subject file, box 992, JFK.

3. Gilbert Supple of Shulton, Inc., to Kenneth P. O'Donnell, special assistant to the president, June 27, 1961, central subject file, box 108, JFK.

4. White House route slip to William Brubeck, executive secretary, Department of State, February 11, 1963, asking for guidance in response to a proposal from Anthony Teague and Jack Good, central subject file, box 992, JFK.

5. Memo from Frederick G. Dutton, special assistant to the president, to President Kennedy, March 5, 1961, central subject file, box 845, JFK.

6. Memo from Edward R. Murrow, director of the U.S. Information Agency, to Frederick G. Dutton, March 7, 1961, central subject file, box 845, JFK. Friendly was Murrow's producer on the *See It Now* series and on *CBS Reports*. Dutton's memo cited in note number five recommends that NBC's Chet Huntley be brought on board in an advisory capacity as well.

7. Fred Friendly, executive producer of *CBS Reports,* to President Kennedy, February 6, 1961, central name file, "Friendly," JFK.

8. *Look* magazine, January 5, 1960, 11–15.

9. Memo from Frederick G. Dutton to Pierre Salinger, presidential press secretary, July 6, 1961, central subject file, box 845, JFK.

10. See note 3, introduction.

11. See Carroll, "Economic Influences," 415, and Christopher H. Sterling and John M. Kittross, *Stay Tuned: A Concise History of American Broadcasting,* 2d ed. (Belmont, Calif.: Wadsworth, 1990), 502.

12. Brooks and Marsh, *Complete Directory,* 868.

13. William Boddy, *Fifties Television: The Industry and Its Critics* (Urbana: University of Illinois Press, 1990), 113–127.

14. Christopher Anderson, *Hollywood TV: The Studio System in the Fifties* (Austin: University of Texas Press, 1994), and Tino Balio, ed., *Hollywood in the Age of Television* (Boston: Unwin Hyman, 1990).

15. Boddy, *Fifties Television,* 214–241.

16. Spigel, *Make Room for TV,* 47.

17. Cited in Catherine L. Covert, "'We May Hear Too Much': American Sensibility and the Response to Radio, 1919–1924," in *Mass Media between the Wars,* ed. Catherine L. Covert and John D. Stevens (Syracuse: Syracuse University Press, 1984), 210.

18. Boddy, *Fifties Television,* 214–232. In addition, an example of the debates over commercial mass culture can be found in the symposium "Mass Culture and Mass Media," *Daedalus* 89 (spring 1960).

19. James L. Baughman, "The National Purpose and the Newest Medium: Liberal Critics of Television, 1958–1960," *Mid-America* 64 (April–July 1983): 41–55.

20. Arthur Schlesinger Jr., "How Television Can Meet Its Responsibilities," *TV Guide,* December 12, 1959, 25. Also see Schlesinger, "Notes on a National Cultural Policy," *Daedalus* 89 (spring 1960): 394–400.

21. Vance Packard, *The Hidden Persuaders* (New York: D. McKay, 1957).

22. Mica Nava, "Consumerism Reconsidered: Buying and Power," *Cultural Studies* 5 (May 1991): 161–162.

23. Jack Gould, "Quiz for TV: How Much Fakery?" *New York Times Magazine,* October 25, 1959, 74. Also see Kent Anderson, *Television Fraud: The History and Implications of the Quiz Show Scandals* (Westport, Conn.: Greenwood Press, 1978).

24. Andrew Ross, "Containing Culture in the Cold War," *Cultural Studies* 1 (October 1987): 828–848.

25. Edward R. Murrow, "How TV Can Help Us Survive," *TV Guide,* December 19, 1958, 26.

26. *Variety,* December 2, 1959, 21.

27. *Broadcasting,* January 25, 1960, 70–72.

28. *Sponsor,* November 7, 1960, 29.

29. Newton N. Minow, *Equal Time: The Private Broadcaster and the Public Interest* (New York: Athenaeum, 1964), 50–51.

30. Ibid., 64.

31. May, *Homeward Bound*, 11–13.

32. Ibid., 160.

33. Ibid., 167.

34. Harry Magdoff, *The Age of Imperialism: The Economics of U.S. Foreign Policy* (New York: Modern Reader, 1966); Pierre Jalee, *Imperialism in the Seventies* (New York: Third Press, 1972); and Thomas J. McCormick, *America's Half Century: United States Foreign Policy in the Cold War* (Baltimore: Johns Hopkins University Press, 1989).

35. Other than the works cited above, my synopsis of this period draws on such texts as Frederick F. Siegel, *Troubled Journey: From Pearl Harbor to Ronald Reagan* (New York: Hill and Wang, 1984); Eric Goldman, *The Crucial Decade and After: 1945–1960* (New York: Vintage Books, 1960); Stephen Ambrose, *Rise to Globalism: American Foreign Policy since 1938* (New York: Penguin, 1983); Godfrey Hodgson, *America in Our Time* (New York: Vintage Books, 1978); and Richard J. Barnet, *The Alliance: America, Europe, Japan, Makers of the Postwar World* (New York: Simon and Schuster, 1983).

36. Thomas Ferguson and Joel Rogers, *Right Turn: The Decline of the Democrats and the Future of American Politics* (New York: Hill and Wang, 1986), 46–57; Ambrose, *Rise to Globalism*, 186–244.

37. These same capital-intensive firms financed the political fortunes of Franklin D. Roosevelt. They were a small but powerful bloc during the New Deal era, and by the 1950s they were not only industrial leaders but also household names such as GE, IBM, RCA, GM, Boeing, Pan American, Standard Oil of New Jersey, and Shell. Less well known were the small coterie of banks that helped finance their operations: Bank of America, Chase National Bank, Lehman Brothers, Brown Brothers Harriman, Goldman Sachs, and Dillon Read. Besides their direct effects on campaign financing, these firms also influenced American politics through business associations, the trade press, university research funding, and through their control of major foundations. See Ferguson and Rogers, *Right Turn*, 47.

38. The Rockefeller Brothers Fund brought such powerful public policy figures as Dean Rusk, Chester Bowles, Henry Kissinger, and Adolf Berle together with key industry leaders such as RCA's David Sarnoff, Time-Life's Henry Luce, and Bell and Howell's Charles Percy. Their studies of "the most critical problems facing the nation over the next ten to fifteen years" were published throughout the late fifties as a series of papers and later compiled into a book, *Prospect for America: The Rockefeller Panel Reports* (Garden City, N.Y.: Doubleday, 1961).

39. The same isolationist faction of the Republican Party that rebuffed Rockefeller would later seize control of the party in 1964 after a bitter series of primaries. They not only nominated Barry Goldwater but wrote a party

platform that favored import restrictions while denouncing internationalism, the United Nations, and specifically by name, the Rockefellers. See Ferguson and Rogers, *Right Turn*, 53.

40. Kennedy also borrowed Rockefeller's strategy for deficit financing to implement social programs without the explicit endorsement of taxpayers. Rockefeller argued that, in this moment of national crisis, it was time for youthful, vigorous, and expert leadership. Ferguson and Rogers, *Right Turn*, 46–57; Siegel, *Troubled Journey*, 121–25.

41. Quoted in Siegel, *Troubled Journey*, 125.

42. Arthur M. Schlesinger Jr., *The Vital Center: The Politics of Freedom* (1949; reprint, New York: Da Capo, 1988), 233.

43. Regarding the ambivalent treatment of science in popular film during the 1950s, see Peter Biskind, "Pods, Blobs, and Ideology in American Films of the Fifties," in *Shadows of the Magic Lamp: Fantasy and Science Fiction in Film*, ed. George Slusser and Eric S. Rabkin (Carbondale: Southern Illinois University Press, 1985), 58–72, and Michael Rogin, *Ronald Reagan, the Movie: And Other Episodes in Political Demonology* (Berkeley and Los Angeles: University of California Press, 1988), 236–271.

44. "CBS Television Biography," CBS press release, November 26, 1958, Albert Wasserman file, BRTC. At the time this press release was written, Wasserman was working at CBS. In 1959 he moved to NBC.

I should also point out that my discussion of objectivity should not be received as a sweeping or reductive argument. Both journalists and social scientists are well aware that the notion of complete objectivity is unattainable within their fields of endeavor. As Michael Schudson has argued, many journalists simply see objectivity as an ideal. However, during the early 1960s both journalists and social scientists were striving to perfect their methods so as to produce work that most closely approximated this ideal. Furthermore, as we shall see in chapter 5, when journalists were pressed to defend their work to superiors or outsiders, they tended to draw on the trope of objectivity. It was also common for outsiders to borrow selectively from the findings of journalists and social scientists as if their work provided objective data. Thus politicians often borrowed from newspaper accounts in citing "facts" to support their conclusions. Therefore the concept of objectivity circulated widely in American society during this period even though many expressed their doubts about the very possibility of objective analysis. For my purposes, I simply wish to argue that scientific methodology and objectivity played a powerful role in constituting claims to authenticity in the network documentary. Discussions of the relationship between objectivity, science, and journalism can be found in Michael Schudson, *Discovering the News: A Social History of American Newspapers* (New York: Basic Books, 1978); Gaye Tuchman, "Objectivity as Strategic Ritual: An Examination of Newsmen's Notions of Objectivity," *American Journal of Sociology* 77, no. 4 (1972): 660–680; Gans, *Deciding What's News*; and Dan Schiller,

Objectivity and the News: The Public and the Rise of Commercial Journalism (Philadelphia: University of Pennsylvania Press, 1981).

45. *Variety*, January 23, 1962, Fred Freed clipping file, BRTC.

46. It is interesting to compare this notion of documentary with the more unabashed advocacy style of Edward R. Murrow. The Murrow style emerged out of the World War II era when journalists, seeking to mobilize public support for the war effort, displayed little self-consciousness about offering opinion or commentary within the context of a news report. By the mid-1950s, CBS management began to show increasing concern about this advocacy style, however, particularly in relation to Murrow's work. See Bruce H. Westley, confidential report to CBS, "An Objectivity Study of the Three CBS News Broadcasts," November 28, 1955, and confidential memo from Sig Mickelson, CBS vice president for news, to Frank Stanton, December 6, 1955, Mickelson Papers, box 1, file 11, SHSW.

47. Minow, *Equal Time*, 117. This mission to inform is not exclusively a national mission but also included the larger domain of the Free World. That is, although the target audience was the American middle class, the New Frontier envisioned the global potential of modern mass media. This is discussed in greater detail in chapter 3.

48. James L. Baughman, *Television's Guardians: The FCC and the Politics of Programming* (Knoxville: University of Tennessee Press, 1985), 86.

49. *New York Times*, June 18, 1961, Minow clipping file, BRTC.

50. *Variety*, January 3, 1962, 27; F. J. Kahn, ed., *Documents of American Broadcasting*, 4th ed. (Englewood Cliffs, N.J.: Prentice-Hall, 1984), 214.

51. Quoted in *Christian Science Monitor*, October 7, 1961, Minow clipping file, BRTC.

52. Letters between James Hagerty and Newton Minow, box 2, NMP.

53. Advertisements from the *Washington Post* and the *Wall Street Journal* forwarded to Minow by William R. McAndrew, NBC News executive vice president, box 31, NMP.

54. Minow to Irving Gitlin, February 5, 1963, box 31, NMP.

55. Gitlin to Minow, June 12, 1963, box 31, NMP. This opinion was shared by correspondent Howard K. Smith, who worked at both CBS and ABC during the early 1960s. In the midst of the barrage of industry criticism leveled at Minow after the "vast wasteland" speech, Smith wrote, "I don't know whether you need the assurance or not but let me tell you, you still have numberless friends for you and for your viewpoint inside the television industry." Smith to Minow, June 20, 1961, box 9, NMP.

56. *Broadcasting*, January 22, 1962, 27; *Variety*, December 13, 1961, 25; *Newsweek*, April 16, 1962.

57. *Variety*, April 26, 1961, 184; October 25, 1961, 31; April 25, 1962, 19; *Broadcasting*, May 14, 1962, 146.

58. *Variety*, July 4, 1962, 69.

Two. Documentaries of the Communist Other

1. *Variety*, July 27, 1960, Gitlin clipping file, BRTC.
2. *TV Guide*, December 10, 1960, 6.
3. *Variety*, July 27, 1960, Gitlin clipping file, BRTC.
4. *TV Guide*, December 10, 1960, 6.
5. Anderson, *Imagined Communities*, 9–36; Hermann Bausinger, "Media, Technology, and Daily Life," *Media, Culture, and Society* 6 (October 1984): 343–351; Jesus Martin-Barbero, "Communication from Culture: The Crisis of the National and the Emergence of the Popular," *Media, Culture, and Society* 10 (October 1988): 447–465; David Morley, "Where the Global Meets the Local: Notes from the Sitting Room," *Screen* 32, no. 1 (1991): 1–15; David Morley and Kevin Robins, "Spaces of Identity: Communications Technologies and the Reconfiguration of Europe," *Screen* 30, no. 4 (1989): 10–34; Paddy Scannell, "Public Service Broadcasting and Modern Public Life," *Media, Culture, and Society* 11 (April 1989): 135–166.
6. Daniel C. Hallin, "Cartography, Community, and the Cold War," in *Reading the News: A Pantheon Guide to Popular Culture* (New York: Pantheon Books, 1987), 110. Also see Hallin, *The Uncensored War: The Media and Vietnam* (Berkeley and Los Angeles: University of California Press, 1986). Along related lines, researchers who have studied the "agenda-setting" function of the mass media argue that news reporting on foreign policy issues is generally more influential than reporting of domestic or local issues. They claim news is more likely to shape an individual's opinion regarding issues with which a person is least familiar. See J. P. Winter, "Differential Media-Public Agenda-Setting Effects for Selected Issues, 1948–1976" (Ph.D. diss., Syracuse University, 1980). For an overview of this area of research, see Maxwell E. McCombs, "Explorers and Surveyors: Expanding Strategies for Agenda-Setting Research," *Journalism Quarterly* 69 (winter 1992): 813–824.
7. James W. Carey, *Communication as Culture: Essays on Media and Society* (Boston: Unwin Hyman, 1989), 26–29.
8. "Red Threat Livest Program Theme," *Broadcasting*, January 22, 1962, 27–30. This was true not only for television documentary but also for newspaper coverage of international issues. Daniel C. Hallin writes, "The *New York Times* in the early 1960s was full of outposts of the non-Communist world, near and far. It was very unusual, in fact, for any foreign location, least of all a mountain village in a 'backwater' like Vietnam, to make the *Times* if it could not be described as an outpost in the great struggle between the free world and communism." See Hallin, "Cartography," 134–135.
9. "Ninety Miles to Communism," broadcast April 18, 1961; "The Red and the Black," January 22, 1961; "Troubled Land," June 13, 1961.
10. "The Flabby American," broadcast May 30, 1961.
11. "Walk in My Shoes," broadcast September 19, 1961.
12. Between the premiere broadcast of *CBS Reports* on October 27, 1959, and the end of June 1964, the network produced ninety-six original programs

in this series according to Einstein, *Special Edition*, 112–132. Of those, I would argue that twenty-nine present superpower struggle as a major theme and twenty-six others, such as "Eisenhower on the Presidency" and "Why Man in Space?" use it as an important subtext.

It should also be pointed out that, although superpower struggle may not have been as dominant a theme on *CBS Reports* as on the other network flagship series, this does not mean the network gave foreign policy issues short shrift. *Eyewitness to History*, another weekly documentary series on CBS, almost exclusively focused on the presidency, the New Frontier, and foreign policy. Thus *CBS Reports* may have limited its attention to foreign policy issues so as to avoid conflicts with other news programs.

13. For example, see David Morley and Kevin Robins, "No Place like Heimat: Images of Home(Land) in European Culture," *New Formations* 12 (winter 1990): 1–23; Philip Schlesinger, *Media, State, and Nation: Political Violence and Collective Identities* (Newbury Park, Calif.: Sage, 1991); and Rogin, *Ronald Reagan*.

14. Lucy Jarvis to Pierre Salinger, July 7, 1961, central subject file, box 845, JFK. Jarvis worked with producer Fred Freed, who later reflected: "When I began doing my documentaries at NBC in 1961 we lived in a consensus society. Those were the days of the Cold War. There was an enemy outside. The Communists. Nikita Khrushchev. The Red Chinese. Back in those days we planned our whole season of White Papers well before the season started. We would sit around months before September and agree on the four biggest and most significant stories we could think of, and Al Wasserman would do two and I would do two. In 1962 we knew that unless there was a revolution in the Soviet Union, 'The Rise of Khrushchev' was going to be a story next year and 'The Death of Stalin' was going to be a story next year. In fact, my first six White Papers involved Khrushchev." Yellin, *Special*, 275.

15. Broadcast on NBC, March 1, 1963.

16. Note that these are *reframings* of the more conventional portrait style of the 1800s.

17. Schlesinger, *Vital Center*.

18. "Death of Stalin" drew a 19 rating and a 32 share and "Rise of Khrushchev" a 17/31. See Robert Lee Bailey, *An Examination of Prime Time Network Television Special Programs, 1948 to 1966* (New York: Arno Press, 1979), 283.

19. Broadcast on NBC, January 27, 1963.

20. Broadcast on NBC, February 3, 1963.

21. Robert H. Wiebe, *The Search for Order, 1877–1920* (New York: Hill and Wang, 1967), and *Businessmen and Reform: A Study of the Progressive Movement* (Cambridge: Harvard University Press, 1962).

22. Philip Elliot and Philip Schlesinger, "Some Aspects of Communism as a Cultural Category," *Media, Culture, and Society* 1 (July 1979): 195–210, reprinted in Schlesinger, *Media, State, and Nation*, 92–110.

23. In addition to the program discussed here, *CBS Reports* broadcast "Berlin:

End of the Line," June 17, 1960, and "East Germany: The Land beyond the Wall," January 4, 1962; ABC *Bell and Howell Close-Up!* broadcast "West of the Wall," November 23, 1961; and *NBC White Paper* broadcast "Khrushchev and Berlin," December 26, 1961.

24. Broadcast on ABC, November 14, 1961.

25. This is a distinguishing characteristic of liberal politics during the New Frontier period and the era of Fordism in general. Automation and increasing productivity were yoked to the expansion of union power in developed countries. This combination was characterized as a win-win proposition. So long as productivity gains outran labor costs, corporate leaders of capital-intensive firms were willing to allow unionization and rising worker compensation. These peaceful reforms were widely touted by the leaders of the Free World as the alternative to violent revolution and centralized state control. For an overview of Fordism, see David Harvey, *The Condition of Postmodernity: An Inquiry into the Origins of Cultural Change* (Cambridge, Mass.: Basil Blackwell, 1989), 121–197, and Alain Lipietz, *Mirages and Miracles: The Crises of Global Fordism* (London: Verso, 1987).

26. Broadcast on NBC, February 25, 1962.

27. See discussions of Kennan's analysis in Chafe, *Unfinished Journey*, 54–78; Siegel, *Troubled Journey*, 45–47; and Ambrose, *Rise to Globalism*, 130–147.

28. For example, Walter Cronkite, Chet Huntley, Howard K. Smith, and Charles Collingwood were all war reporters. Others, such as producer Palmer Williams, worked in Hollywood on war propaganda, and most of the rest served in related areas or in combat. Executives also participated in the war effort. For example, Robert Kintner and William Paley served with the Office of War Information.

Three. Going Global

1. Sig Mickelson memo to "files," August 29, 1960, Mickelson Papers, box 4, file 3.

2. Documentary is not the only form of programming that was part of the industry's attempt to deal with television's image crisis. Coverage of the 1960 presidential campaign and the broadcast of the Kennedy-Nixon debates were also part of this initiative. Although I do not discuss election programming in the course of this book, it should be noted that, like the documentaries of this period, much of the coverage focused on questions of national purpose and superpower struggle.

3. This was not the first time that American businesses had ventured abroad. There was a long history of economic ties to Latin America, and by the turn of the century the scope of U.S. foreign investment was beginning to reach out beyond the confines of the Western Hemisphere. However, the First World War attenuated this trend, and the period between the two wars has been characterized as a recessionary period in the globalization of corporate

capital, with the amount of international investment activity during the interwar period actually shrinking in real dollars. See Jalee, *Imperialism*, 68.

4. Ibid., 70.
5. Ibid.
6. Ibid., 70–76.
7. Magdoff, *Age of Imperialism*, 73.
8. Ferguson and Rogers, *Right Turn*, 50.
9. Magdoff, *Age of Imperialism*, 76.
10. Cited in Ibid., 51. Interestingly, CBS chairman William S. Paley was a member of the committee that drafted the report on strategic materials. He also was vice chairman of the Committee for International Development, which played a key role in pushing President Kennedy's first foreign aid bill through Congress. See "Foreign Aid: The Road Ahead," introductory notes and a speech by Paley to the Forty-ninth National Foreign Trade Convention, October 30, 1962, central name file, JFK.
11. Magdoff, *Age of Imperialism*, 50–52.
12. Siegel, *Troubled Journey*, 137.
13. Kwame Nkrumah, *Neo-Colonialism: The Last Stage of Imperialism* (New York: International Publishers, 1966).
14. Ambrose, *Rise to Globalism*, 238.
15. Ibid., 251.
16. Siegel, *Troubled Journey*, 140.
17. Sterling and Kittross, *Stay Tuned*, 640; figures produced by the FCC for this period are slightly different. See *Broadcasting*, June 22, 1959, 64.
18. *Newsweek*, September 11, 1961, 61.
19. *Variety*, January 22, 1958, "Television: Networks," clipping file, BRTC.
20. *Variety*, January 15, 1958, "Television: Networks," clipping file, BRTC.
21. *Variety*, January 22, 1958, "Television: Networks," clipping file, BRTC.
22. Sterling and Kittross, *Stay Tuned*, 329.
23. *Forbes*, June 15, 1959, 17.
24. *Broadcasting*, August 17, 1959, 28.
25. Disney and Warner Brothers were the two Hollywood studios that provided most of the telefilm programming for ABC during this period. See Anderson, *Hollywood TV*.
26. *Forbes*, June 15, 1959, 15.
27. Ibid.
28. Sterling and Kittross, *Stay Tuned*, 658.
29. Although the industry appeared to be incredibly profitable during this period, there was reason for concern. The dissemination of television receivers among the public happened much more quickly than it had during the radio era. Thus there was concern among network executives that television's growth era was over. For a comparison of receiver sales in both the radio and TV eras, see Sterling and Kittross, *Stay Tuned*, 656–658.
30. *Variety*, February 2, 1963, 25.

31. *New York Times*, October 4, 1957, "Television: Networks," clipping file, BRTC.

32. *Variety*, January 15, 1958, "Television: Networks," clipping file, BRTC.

33. *New York Times*, September 17, 1960, "Television: Networks," clipping file, BRTC. It should be noted that option time was first raised as a policy issue in the FCC's 1941 Report on Chain Broadcasting. However, the FCC did not forbid the practice until 1963. Thus the period between the Barrow Report and the FCC ban was fraught with controversy and concern as network executives imagined the impact such action would have on their industry.

34. *Variety*, December 12, 1958, "Television: Networks," clipping file, BRTC.

35. Goldman, *Crucial Decade*, 320; Sterling and Kittross, *Stay Tuned*, 361–363; *Broadcasting*, February 15, 1960, 94.

36. Goldman, *Crucial Decade*, 316.

37. *Broadcasting*, February 15, 1960, 96; *Variety*, May 25, 1960, 31; and *Variety*, June 1, 1960, 36.

38. *Broadcasting*, January 25, 1960, 70–72.

39. *Variety*, December 2, 1959, 21.

40. *Broadcasting*, February 15, 1960, 112.

41. Ibid., 111.

42. Robert Sarnoff at NBC made no dramatic pronouncements on the sponsorship issue, perhaps because his network was not so heavily burdened with sponsored programming as was CBS. Nevertheless, the trend toward magazine-style program advertising was by this point irreversible. *Variety*, December 30, 1959, 19, February 3, 1960, 31, March 30, 1960, 25; *Printer's Ink*, April 1, 1960; *Broadcasting*, May 16, 1960, 92.

43. *Variety*, April 27, 1960, 30, and December 21, 1960, 17; *Broadcasting*, May 16, 1960, 92–94, and October 5, 1960.

44. *Variety*, July 20, 1960, 27.

45. *Business Week*, November 7, 1959, 29.

46. Thomas Knode, vice president for station relations, to station managers, July 19, 1962, Harry Bannister Collection, box 6, file 7, NBC Papers, SHSW; *Television* (March 1962): 74; *Variety*, January 17, 1962, 29.

47. *Variety*, June 28, 1961, 1.

48. *Variety*, April 5, 1961, 25.

49. *Variety*, March 1, 1961, 29.

50. 1963 Annual Report to the Stockholders of the Columbia Broadcasting System, Inc., p. 5, CBS file, BRTC. As one looks at the situation in retrospect, the 1963 report indicated that network performance in 1962 and 1963 was better than expected and management had revised its prognosis, arguing that television was not as "mature" as previously believed.

51. Indeed, television was identified as the primary source of information for most Americans during the 1960 presidential campaign. And in the realm of advertising, network leadership was indisputable by the end of the 1950s.

52. *Broadcasting*, May 14, 1962, 146.

53. Wilson Dizard, "American Television's Foreign Markets," *Television Quarterly* 3 (summer 1964): 61.

54. Dizard, "American Television's Foreign Markets," 58.

55. Dizard, "American Television's Foreign Markets," 58.

56. Ibid., 60.

57. In 1962 Congress passed the All-Channel Receiver Act, which required televisions sold in the United States to be equipped with UHF receivers. This considerably enhanced the national ratings of ABC programming by the end of the 1960s.

58. *Broadcasting*, May 14, 1962, 146.

59. John Frappier, "U.S. Media Empire/Latin America," *North American Congress on Latin America* 2 (January 1969): 2.

60. Dizard, "American Television's Foreign Markets," 63.

61. One reason ABC's international networking effort failed later in the decade is because it tried to forge Latin America into a unified market and did not respond to local needs and cultural differences. See Fred Fejes, "The Growth of Multinational Advertising Agencies in Latin America," *Journal of Communication* 30 (autumn 1980): 46–47.

62. *Broadcasting*, October 22, 1962, 92.

63. *Variety*, February 6, 1963, 25.

64. Frappier, "Media Empire," 3.

65. *Variety*, August 28, 1963, 31.

66. *Variety*, February 24, 1960, 32.

67. See *Poor's Register of Corporations, Directors, and Executives* (New York: Standard and Poor's Corporation, 1964), 52, 347, 1254.

68. *Variety*, February 24, 1960, 32.

69. *Variety*, December 9, 1959, 29.

70. *Variety*, May 10, 1961, 24. Similar thinking existed among other broadcast executives. See Sig Mickelson memo to files, November 15, 1961, and memo from Andrew Heiskell to Wes Pullen, January 4, 1961, Mickelson Papers, box 2, file 12.

71. Annual Report to the Share Holders of the Columbia Broadcasting System, Inc., 1960, CBS file, BRTC; *Variety*, December 9, 1959, 29.

72. Annual Report, CBS, 1963, BRTC.

73. Annual Reports, CBS, 1960 and 1961, BRTC.

74. Report from Martin Codel, March 15, 1962, 10, Mickelson Papers, box 2, file 27.

75. Dizard, "American Television's Foreign Markets," 58.

76. Frappier, "Media Empire," for example, contends that CBS did not expand overseas as much as its competitors.

77. Quoted in Harry Skornia, "American Broadcasters Abroad," *Quarterly Review of Economics and Business* (autumn 1964): 14–15.

78. NBC Year End Report, 1964, NBC file, BRTC.

79. Ibid.

80. News release, Radio Corporation of America, April 5, 1961, NMP, box 35. The utopian discourse of global television at the dawning of the satellite age is analyzed in Michael Curtin, "Beyond the Vast Wasteland: The Policy Discourse of Global Television and the Politics of American Empire," *Journal of Broadcasting and Electronic Media* 37 (spring 1993): 127–145.

81. Newton Minow, "Vast Wasteland," address by Newton N. Minow to the National Association of Broadcasters in Washington, D.C., May 9, 1961, in Kahn, *Documents of American Broadcasting*, 215. For a discussion regarding the FCC and global television, see Curtin, "Beyond the Vast Wasteland," 127–145.

82. Newton Minow, Address to the International Radio and Television Society, September 27, 1962, in Minow, *Equal Time*, 212.

83. Daniel Lerner, *The Passing of Traditional Society: Modernizing the Middle East* (New York: Free Press, 1958), 43–75.

84. Richard N. Gardner, "Countdown at the UN," *Saturday Review*, March 17, 1962, 105.

85. These notions of global community and mutual knowledge also are interesting in light of popular notions regarding "the family of man" during this period, for not only does development theory suggest that all societies progress through similar stages of economic development, but it also suggests that underneath their racial and cultural exteriors, all humans are essentially the same. See Edward Steichen, *The Family of Man* (New York: Simon and Schuster, 1955), a coffee-table picture book that was popular during the 1950s and early 1960s. This book grew out of a museum show that traveled the globe during the 1950s courtesy of the USIA.

86. *Business Week*, December 8, 1962, 58.

87. *Variety*, March 29, 1961, 23.

88. *Variety*, September 7, 1960, 27, and May 24, 1961, 21. In addition, in Eastern Europe there reportedly was an effort to use the programs for propaganda campaigns against U.S. gangsterism, a development that drew pointed concern from the USIA. See *Broadcasting*, May 14, 1962, 146.

89. As program codes began to spread internationally, British television exports, which eschewed violence, began to pick up momentum. In response, the networks reportedly turned back more than a dozen television episodes for reediting in order to curb the violence. *Variety*, July 12, 1961, 30.

90. *Variety*, June 14, 1961, 29, and July 5, 1961, 27.

91. Frappier, "Media Empire," 2; Skornia, "American Broadcasters Abroad," 19; Dizard, "American Television's Foreign Markets," 66–67; *Variety*, February 7, 1962, 33.

92. *Variety*, February 17, 1960, 22, and March 29, 1961, 23.

93. *Variety*, October 25, 1961, 31.

94. *Variety*, March 1, 1961, 27.

95. Anderson, *Imagined Communities*; Anthony Giddens, *The Nation-State and Violence* (Cambridge, England: Polity Press, 1985); E. J. Hobsbawm, *Nations and Nationalism since 1780: Programme, Myth, Reality* (Cambridge: Cambridge University Press, 1991); Hugh Seton-Watson, *Nations and States: An Enquiry into the Origins of Nations and the Politics of Nationalism* (Boulder, Colo.: Westview Press, 1977).

96. Here I use the term *American* to refer to revolutions throughout the Western Hemisphere during the eighteenth and nineteenth centuries. As Benedict Anderson quite rightly points out, revolutions in Latin America were some of the first to base their legitimacy on popular sovereignty.

97. Anderson, *Imagined Communities*, 15.

98. Seton-Watson, *Nations and States*, 77–87.

99. *Variety*, March 7, 1962, 1.

100. Minow, memo to the president, June 26, 1962, NMP, box 24, and memo from Donald Wilson, acting director of the U.S. Information Agency, to Pierre Salinger, presidential press secretary, June 21, 1962, JFK, president's office files, box 91.

101. Watson, *Expanding Vista*, pays particular attention to the media savvy of the Kennedy administration.

102. Tedson Meyers to Ralph Dungan, special assistant to the president, with attached report, May 24, 1962, NMP, box 18.

103. *Variety*, August 29, 1962, 24.

104. Memo from K. R. Hansen, assistant director of the Bureau of the Budget, to McGeorge Bundy, special assistant to the president for National Security Affairs, undated, JFK, central subject file, box 992.

105. Robert Lewis Shayon, "Breakthrough in International TV," *Saturday Review*, January 14, 1961, 35.

106. Holly Shulman, *The Voice of America: Propaganda and Democracy, 1941–1945* (Madison: University of Wisconsin Press, 1990).

107. Regarding USIA funding during the fifties and sixties, see "Annual Budget Message to Congress," *Public Papers of the Presidents of the United States: Dwight D. Eisenhower* (Washington, D.C.: Government Printing Office, 1959–1961), and *Budget of the United States Government* (Washington, D.C.: Government Printing Office, 1960–1963).

108. During the late fifties and early sixties, the USIA began actively to track public opinion in countries around the globe. USIA Report, "A Review of USIA Research," March 4, 1963, JFK, president's office files, box 91. In this same box there are numerous other opinion surveys; see especially "Public Opinion in Italy prior to the Elections," May 9, 1963; "First Effort to Measure World Opinion," July 10, 1963; and "Foreign Reaction to Diem Repression and U.S. Foreign Policy," August 28, 1963.

109. Memo from Edward R. Murrow, USIA director, to the president, July 24, 1961, JFK, president's office files, box 91. The meeting with network heads took place on October 5. On a related front, Minow was urging the presi-

dent to meet with the heads of the twenty-five corporations that spent the most on television advertising in order to encourage their support for public affairs programming. Memo from Frederick G. Dutton to the president, November 6, 1961, central name file, "Newton Minow," JFK.

110. Minow, address to the International Radio and Television Society, September 27, 1962, in Minow, *Equal Time*, 211.

111. *Variety*, December 13, 1961, 25; James C. Hagerty, written text of testimony before the FCC, February 5, 1962, NMP, box 2; *Business Week*, June 9, 1962, 50.

112. *Variety*, March 1, 1961, 25, October 4, 1961, 33, March 21, 1962, 25, 46, April 4, 1962, 25, and May 2, 1962, 141.

113. This context has generally been overlooked by previous scholars. Baughman is the exception here. In *Television's Guardians* he does pay passing attention to the relationship between FCC policy and the Cold War. See pp. 33, 56, and 63.

114. Minow, "Vast Wasteland."

Four. Documentaries of the Middle Ground

1. This was true not only of newspapers but of novels and of "print capitalism" in general. Anderson, *Imagined Communities*, 9–46.

2. Broadcast February 15, 1960.

3. Broadcast April 17, 1962.

4. Chafe, *Unfinished Journey*, 33–35, 66–78.

5. Broadcast November 2, 1961.

6. Broadcast December 7, 1960.

7. Goldenson's role in the production is discussed in more detail in chapter 5.

8. Regarding the administration's concerns, see memo from Donald M. Wilson, acting director of the USIA, to Kennedy, May 9, 1963, president's office files, box 91, JFK.

9. Secondari to Bundy, December 5, 1961, central name file, "Secondari" file, JFK. "Remarkable Comrades" was broadcast on ABC, December 10, 1961.

10. Regarding Hollywood style, see David Bordwell, Janet Staiger, and Kristin Thompson, *The Classical Hollywood Cinema: Film Style and Mode of Production to 1960* (New York: Columbia University Press, 1985), and for a discussion of the style's application to network documentary, see Michael Curtin, "Packaging Reality: The Influence of Fictional Forms on the Early Development of Television Documentary," *Journalism Monographs* 137 (February 1993).

11. See chapter 8 to compare this with the treatment of religious ritual in "Panama: Danger Zone."

12. Broadcast September 19, 1961.

13. Broadcast April 1, 1964.

14. This concept of identity derives from the linguistic theories of Ferdinand de Saussure and the critical work of Roland Barthes. It has been employed

to explain media's role in the construction of national identities by such scholars as Philip Schlesinger, *Media, State, and Nation*, 137–192; David Morley and Kevin Robins, "Spaces of Identity," 10–34, and "No Place like Heimat," 1–23; and Edward Said, *Covering Islam: How the Media and the Experts Determine How We See the Rest of the World* (New York: Pantheon Books, 1981).

Five. Television News Comes of Age

1. Report of the CBS Special Committee, March 3, 1959, Mickelson Papers, box 1, file 26. The committee was composed of James T. Aubrey Jr., Louis Hausman, Kidder Meade, Richard S. Salant, and Arthur B. Tourtellot.
2. Among these offerings, the committee proposed a series of special educational programs targeted at teenagers. It also recommended a series of women's documentary specials designed to counter claims that daytime TV was overly lathered with soap opera serials. Ibid., pp. 23–24.
3. Ibid., p. 23.
4. CBS took its image problems seriously, as can be seen in the internal report, Frank Stanton's public speeches, and the annual report to stockholders, which included a copy of Stanton's testimony to the FCC regarding the quiz scandals. See CBS Annual Report, 1959, CBS file, BRTC.
5. Baughman, "'Strange Birth,'" 27–38.
6. Murrow, "How TV Can Help," 22–27.
7. Sol Taishoff to Sig Mickelson regarding his resignation from CBS in 1961. Undated except for "Wed," Mickelson Papers, box 4, file 3.
8. Boyce Nemec, "Report of Management Survey of the Television News Film Operations of the News and Public Affairs Department," December 1956, Mickelson Papers, box 1, file 2.
9. Special Committee report, p. 48.
10. Sig Mickelson to Frank Stanton, February 20, 1959, Mickelson Papers, box 4, file 3.
11. See memos regarding contract negotiations with Fred Friendly in June and July 1959. Mickelson Papers, box 1, file 10.
12. CBS Annual Report, 1959, p. 17, CBS file, BRTC.
13. Nemec, "Report of Management Survey."
14. Regarding NBC's news film operation, see Kristine Brunovska Karnick, "NBC and the Innovation of Television News, 1945–1953," *Journalism History* 15 (spring 1988): 26–34.
15. To meet the high costs involved, CBS sought to generate income by setting up a global syndication operation for its news film, an industry then dominated by the newsreel firms United Press Movietone and Telenews. By its second year in business, 1955, CBS was syndicating its product to forty-four stations, including four overseas. For CBS news chief Sig Mickelson, the advantages of having an in-house news film operation were obvious, and syndication appeared to be the only way to finance it. Speaking to news

correspondents that same year, Mickelson commented, "I am not sure of the exact economics as of today, but on our overall film job, we are pretty close to the break-even point, and syndication is a pretty important factor in getting us close to the break even point." See transcript of CBS News Clinic, 1955, Mickelson Papers, box 1, file 4, p. 82; see also Annual Review of CBS News, 1960, Mickelson Papers, box 1, file 1.

16. Fred Friendly in *Due to Circumstances* bemoaned the increasing bureaucratization of CBS under the leadership of Frank Stanton during this period. Yet he does not discuss the even more significant shift in accounting practices, which turned CBS News into an operating division. See "Draft, Budget," 1958, Mickelson Papers, box 1, file 2, and confidential notes from budget meeting, January 30, 1958, Mickelson Papers, box 1, file 2; see also CBS Annual Report, 1959, p. 8.

17. Outline for Budget Presentation, November 30, 1960, Mickelson Papers, box 1, file 10, pp. 1–4.

18. *Variety*, December 14, 1960, and February 8, 1961, Mickelson Papers, box 4, file 3.

19. Ibid.; see also *Variety*, November 30, 1960, 25, and December 7, 1960, 27.

20. Sig Mickelson, "Some notes from Eisenberg analysis of Edwards News and Huntley-Brinkley News," December 10, 1960, Mickelson Papers, box 1, file 16; *Variety*, November 2, 1960, 35; and Taishoff to Mickelson, as cited in note 7 above.

21. *Variety*, June 22, 1960, 23, September 27, 1961, 24, and December 20, 1961, 23; CBS Annual Report, 1961, p. 4, CBS file, BRTC.

22. Mickelson, "Some notes from Eisenberg analysis."

23. Memo to "all NBC personnel" from Robert Kintner and Robert Sarnoff, August 4, 1960, Harry Bannister Papers, NBC Collection, box 10, file 6, SHSW.

24. *Variety*, September 21, 1960, 1.

25. *Variety*, May 31, 1961, 20, and June 14, 1961, 19.

26. *Variety*, December 13, 1961, 25.

27. Regarding Sarnoff's pitch to affiliates, see *Variety*, November 23, 1960, 24; one week later, NBC took out an ad in a trade magazine touting itself as the acknowledged leader in news and public affairs. See message to affiliates, *Variety*, November 30, 1960, 32.

28. *Newsweek*, December 20, 1965, Kintner file, BRTC.

29. *New York Times*, October 24, 1965, sec. X, p. 21.

30. *TV Guide*, February 9. 1963, 20.

31. *Variety*, December 24, 1960, Kintner file, BRTC.

32. *New York Times*, October 24, 1965, sec. X, p. 21.

33. *Newsweek*, December 20, 1965, Kintner file, BRTC.

34. *TV Guide*, February 9, 1963, 20–21.

35. *New York Times*, October 24, 1965, sec. X, p. 21.

36. "NBC Biography," July 11, 1958, Kintner file, BRTC.

37. Yellin, *Special*, 213–214.
38. *New York Times*, February 26, 1966, Kintner file, BRTC.
39. Yellin, *Special*, 104.
40. Ibid.; *Variety*, May 25, 1960, 27.
41. *Variety*, June 29, 1960, 28.
42. Confidential memo from John Daly to Simon Siegal, December 16, 1959, John Daly Papers, box 29, file 1, SHSW.
43. *Time*, November 28, 1960, clipping, Daly Papers, box 31, file 11.
44. *Chicago Daily News*, November 17, 1960, 75; also see clippings in Daly Papers, box 31, file 11, including *Washington Post*, November 18, 1960, and *New York Daily News*, November 15, 1960.
45. *New York Post Week-End Magazine*, November 18, 1962, 2; Schudson, *Discovering the News*, 170; for a more detailed discussion of Hagerty's role, see Craig Allen, *Eisenhower and the Mass Media: Peace, Prosperity, and Prime-Time TV* (Chapel Hill: University of North Carolina Press, 1993).
46. *Variety*, January 11, 1961, 18.
47. *Variety*, October 19, 1960, 1.
48. *Broadcasting*, January 16, 1961, 40, and March 6, 1961, 56; see also *New York Herald Tribune*, January 10, 1961, and January 30, 1961, Hagerty file, BRTC; *Washington Post*, July 14, 1962, Howard K. Smith Papers, box 51, SHSW.
49. *Variety*, April 12, 1961, 18.
50. *Broadcasting*, January 16, 1961, 40.
51. *Variety*, May 10, 1961, 24.
52. *Variety*, July 12, 1961, 27.
53. *Variety*, March 1, 1961, 27, and June 6, 1962, 19.
54. *Variety*, August 15, 1962, 25.
55. *Broadcasting*, December 24, 1962, 20; *Variety*, February 15, 1961, 27, and February 22, 1961, 1; *Reporter*, January 3, 1961, 40.
56. Statement of James Hagerty to the FCC, February 5, 1962, NMP, box 2, ABC file.
57. *Variety*, December 2, 1959, 21, March 23, 1960, 25, August 31, 1960, 25, December 28, 1960, 23, and February 14, 1962, 27.
58. *Variety*, April 12, 1961, 23.
59. Undated *New York Times* clipping in Daly Papers, box 31, file 6; regarding Wolper's documentary work, see *New York Herald Tribune Sunday Magazine*, March 21, 1965, 58ff.
60. These debates over ownership of and access to the airwaves are discussed by Thomas Streeter, *Selling the Air: A Critique of the Policy of Commercial Broadcasting* (Chicago: University of Chicago Press, forthcoming); see also Fred W. Friendly, *The Good Guys, the Bad Guys, and the First Amendment: Free Speech vs. Fairness in Broadcasting* (New York: Vintage Books, 1975).
61. John Daly to Erik Barnouw, chairman of the Censorship Committee of the Writers Guild, March 25, 1960, Daly Papers, box 29, file 1; also see Daly

memo to Leonard Goldenson, March 4, 1960, Daly Papers, box 29, file 1; and Erik Barnouw, *The Image Empire: A History of Broadcasting in the United States*, vol. 3 (New York: Oxford University Press, 1970), 159.

62. *Chicago Daily News*, November 17, 1960, 75; *Washington Post*, November 18, 1960; *New York Daily News*, November 29, 1960, 59; Bluem, *Documentary in American Television*, 122.

63. *New York Daily News*, November 29, 1960, 59.

64. Robert Kintner to NBC vice presidents, station managers, and department heads, April 17, 1961, Bannister Papers, box 10, file 6.

65. ABC press release regarding upcoming broadcast of "Yanki No!" undated, Daly Papers, box 31, file 11; *Variety*, August 17, 1960, 27, November 23, 1960, 24, and December 14, 1960, 21.

66. Stephen Mamber also notes the contradictory nature of this documentary. *Cinema Verite in America*, 42–48.

67. *New York Times*, clipping, December 8, 1960, Daly Papers, box 31, file 11; *Broadcasting*, March 6, 1961, 82.

68. UPI wire copy, December 8, 1960, Daly Papers, box 31, file 11; *Time*, December 19, 1960, 54.

69. *New York Herald Tribune*, December 8, 1960, 27.

70. Documentary seemed to be part of a transitional strategy at ABC. The tiny size of its news operation made it difficult for the network to match its competitors on campaign coverage or nightly news. Yet documentary allowed the network to finance information programming without having to rely on a large news-gathering infrastructure. Moreover, ABC's relationship with independent producers was also unique owing to the nature of its management team. Unlike the leadership at other networks, Goldenson's background within the field of movies and television entertainment may have made him more receptive to independent productions.

71. *Variety*, December 2, 1959, 21.

72. *Harper's*, August 1960, 82–90; Yellin, *Special*, 107.

73. Richard S. Salant, president of CBS News, to Dr. Julian Price, chairman of the American Medical Association, February 14, 1961, "CBS Reports: PR and Reviews" file, CNL. In this correspondence, Salant is responding to specific complaints about a particular documentary. Yet he more generally reiterates the argument in the CBS Annual Report, 1961, p. 5, CBS file, BRTC. A similar point of view is expressed by William McAndrew, vice president for news at NBC, in a memo to "News Personnel," October 23, 1960, Bannister Papers, box 10, file 6.

74. Schudson, *Discovering the News*, 60; Schiller, *Objectivity and the News*, 10.

75. Schiller, *Objectivity and the News*, 83.

76. Schudson primarily attributes this to the skepticism of late-nineteenth-century thinkers such as Nietzsche. *Discovering the News*, 120. However, as we shall see, emerging concerns over mass society as expressed by Lippmann also play a role here.

77. Theodore L. Glasser and James S. Ettema, "Investigative Journalism and the Moral Order," *Critical Studies in Mass Communication* 6 (March 1989): 5.

78. Gans, *Deciding What's News*, 204–205; James Weinstein also points to the valorization of expertise during this era by noting that principles of social engineering and social efficiency during this era grew up alongside notions of industrial engineering and efficiency. *The Corporate Ideal and the Liberal State: 1900–1918* (Boston: Beacon Press, 1968).

79. Wiebe, *Search for Order*, 57–58 and passim.

80. Ibid., 224–255.

81. Gans, *Deciding What's News*, 205; also see Tuchman, *Making News*.

82. Schudson, *Discovering the News*, 9.

83. Ibid., 5–6; also see Robert A. Hackett, "Decline of a Paradigm? Bias and Objectivity in News Media Studies," *Critical Studies in Mass Communication* 1 (September 1984): 229–259.

84. It is perhaps also significant that Torre was married to CBS documentary producer David Lowe, the organizing genius behind "Harvest of Shame." *New York Herald Tribune*, March 18, 1960, "CBS Reports PR and Reviews, 1960" file, CNL.

85. Quoted in Yellin, *Special*, 125.

86. Alexander Kendrick, *Prime Time: The Life of Edward R. Murrow* (Boston: Little, Brown, 1969), 318.

87. Interview with Albert Wasserman in *The Documentary Conscience: A Casebook in Film Making*, ed. Alan Rosenthal (Berkeley and Los Angeles: University of California Press, 1980), 99.

88. In many cases it was assumed that television had the power to refashion public opinion and it was only professional restraint that protected society from such manipulation. In 1957 the CBS Research Department reported, "The objective, democratic type of approach—presenting arguments pro and con—will limit the effectiveness of any program designed to sell the audience on an idea or a course of action. In such a situation, a one-sided, propagandistic approach which ignores the opposing viewpoints is generally more effective. Of course, it is *axiomatic* [that] for most programs such an approach is inapplicable." (Italics are mine.) See "What We Have Learned about Documentary and Educational Programs," by the CBS-TV Research Department, Program Analysis Division, September 1957, Mickelson Papers, box 1, file 27.

89. See "Plans for Series," marked in pencil "Shown to Nationwide," November 27, 1961, Howard K. Smith Papers, box 51, SHSW; Freed makes a similar point in Yellin, *Special*, 220–221.

90. Lippmann was the most frequent interview guest on *CBS Reports* during the early 1960s and the subject of admiration at other networks as well. Friendly's *Due to Circumstances* is a virtual paean to Lippmann; especially see pp. 9 and 95–96. Meanwhile, NBC producers reacted to CBS's Lippmann interviews by organizing regular sessions with their own top journalists.

"These would be similar to the Lippmann interviews, except with our own Lippmanns," noted Julian Goodman in a memo to William Monroe, August 9, 1962, Robert Asman Papers, NBC Collection, box 10, file 1, SHSW.

91. Schudson, *Discovering the News*, 127–129; also see Walter Lippmann, *Public Opinion* (New York: Harcourt, Brace and Co., 1922); Ronald Steel, *Walter Lippmann and the American Century* (Boston: Little, Brown, 1980), 180–185.

92. Schudson, *Discovering the News*, 40, 151–154; note that this is the essence of Tuchman's study: "Taken by itself, a fact has no meaning. . . . It is the imposition of a frame of other ordered facts that enables recognition of facticity and attribution of meaning." Tuchman, *Making News*, 88.

93. Schudson, *Discovering the News*, 170. Despite this concern about news management, Schudson claims that news workers did not seriously challenge the assumptions of Cold War policy until after the Cuban missile crisis (p. 177). Similarly, Bernard Cohen says foreign correspondents at the time established little critical distance, characterizing themselves as both observers and participants in the execution of U.S. foreign policy. See *The Press and Foreign Policy* (Princeton: Princeton University Press, 1963), 19–47.

94. Hackett, "Decline of a Paradigm?" 231; Schudson notes the same thing. *Discovering the News*, 167–168.

95. Friendly describes this potential in *Due to Circumstances*, 3–66.

96. CBS News press release, July 20, 1959, Mickelson Papers, box 1, file 10.

97. Gitlin, CBS News Clinic.

98. *New York Herald Tribune*, October 17, 1960, Gitlin file, BRTC.

99. Cited in Kendrick, *Prime Time*, 417–418.

100. *Ft. Lauderdale News*, February 18, 1962, clipping from "News and Comment" file, Smith Papers, box 51. It is curious that Albert Wasserman sought to distinguish his work from earlier film documentarists such as John Grierson, a central figure in the British and Canadian documentary movements, for Grierson arrived at a similar conclusion—documentary must educate—although by different means. The most pressing question that figured in Grierson's work was: How could the masses be educated to understand the complexities of the modern world in order to assume their full responsibilities as citizens in a democratic society? During the early part of his career, Grierson first turned to print journalism for an answer to this question. He was particularly fascinated with the impact of dramatic journalism, such as the popular newspapers of William Randolph Hearst. Although not a fan of Hearst's ends, Grierson was clearly attracted to the means. That is, he applauded the assumption that information should not be dryly relayed to the reader but that it must be creatively shaped. Grierson would later reflect on the lesson that he and his colleagues derived from Hearst's example, "We thought, indeed, that even so complex a world as ours could be patterned for all to appreciate if we only got away from the servile accumulation of fact and struck for the story which held the facts in living or-

ganic relationship to each other." Such was Grierson's fascination with the journalism of Hearst. But in the end it was Lippmann, not Hearst, who proved most influential in shaping Grierson's approach. While studying on a fellowship in the United States during the 1920s, the young Grierson became acquainted with Lippmann, whose writings regarding matters of knowledge and citizenship had already achieved international renown. Indeed, it was Lippmann who turned Grierson's attention away from the press and got him interested in film.

As Grierson's documentary career progressed, his work became distinguished by its emphasis on interpretation and dramatic storytelling. He unabashedly described his work as a form of advocacy aimed at achieving social effects. What is interesting for the purposes of this study is that network documentarists would shun any association to the tradition of Grierson and yet they too were in search of similar goals. See Forsyth Hardy, ed., *Grierson on Documentary* (Boston: Faber and Faber, 1946), 78, 150–151.
101. Cited in Yellin, *Special*, 213.

Six. Documentaries of the Home Front

1. Broadcast on October 27, 1959.
2. Broadcast on January 6, 1960.
3. This concern regarding the effect of the space race on the global image of the United States is conveyed in numerous USIA opinion studies during this period that were forwarded to the president as either "top secret" or "confidential." See memos and reports from Edward R. Murrow to the president, August 13, 1962, and March 7, 1963; also from Donald M. Wilson, acting director of the USIA, to the president, March 4, 1963, May 9, 1963, and July 10, 1963, president's office files, box 91, JFK.
4. Broadcast on October 11, 1960,
5. Chafe, *Unfinished Journey*, 185–192; Hodgson, *America in Our Time*, 95–99; Siegel, *Troubled Journey*, 139–141.
6. "The Balance of Terror: In Case of War" was broadcast on November 9, 1961, "The Balance of Terror: Can We Disarm?" on December 14, 1961, and "Reflections of a Soviet Scientist" on May 22, 1963.
7. Broadcast on October 31, 1961.
8. "The Silent Spring of Rachel Carson," broadcast on April 3, 1963, and "The Verdict of the Silent Spring of Rachel Carson," broadcast on May 15, 1963.
9. Broadcast respectively on April 30, 1963, and March 7, 1963.
10. Broadcast respectively on October 19, 1961, and May 15, 1962.
11. Broadcast on May 30, 1961.
12. Broadcast on November 25, 1960.
13. *Variety*, March 29, 1961, 18; Friendly, *Due to Circumstances*, 122–123.
14. Chafe, *Unfinished Journey*, 205–217. The administration's concern about the international implications of racial issues can be seen in memos from USIA

director Edward R. Murrow to the president, March 7 and 9, 1963, president's office files, box 91, JFK; and in a number of public opinion surveys conducted abroad by the USIA Office of Research and Analysis, box 91, JFK.

15. Quoted in Siegel, *Troubled Journey*, 147.
16. Broadcast on September 19, 1961.
17. Interestingly, the protagonist in this piece is an actor, Ernest Washington, yet this never became a controversial issue. In fact, the program was widely celebrated and even nominated for an Emmy Award for best television program of the year.
18. Other civil rights documentaries during this period made similar claims regarding growing frustrations among African Americans. For example, in *CBS Reports'* "Harlem Temper" (broadcast on December 11, 1963), Harry Reasoner guides the viewer on a trip through Harlem, where he learns that segregation in the North may be worse than in the South. Moreover, he finds that moderate, integrationist organizations such as the NAACP and CORE have little influence in ghettos like Harlem. Once again it is groups like the Nation of Islam, with an emphasis on black pride, that are the most powerful voice in these communities. They are even achieving a level of respectability according to college professors and social workers, who explain the importance of positive self-image. Furthermore, by 1963, groups such as CORE and the NAACP begin to endorse the merits of such movements as well.
19. Michael R. Winston, "Racial Consciousness and the Evolution of Mass Communications in the United States," *Daedalus* 11, no. 4 (1982): 180.
20. Jane Rhodes, "The Visibility of Race and Media History," *Critical Studies in Mass Communication* 10 (June 1993): 184–190.

Seven. Programs with Sales Potential

1. Clipping, *New York Times*, May 20, 1960, Gitlin file, BRTC.
2. "Public Affairs Shows Climb," *Sponsor*, August 20, 1962, 32–34.
3. Memo from John Daly to Leonard Goldenson, August 11, 1960, Daly Papers, box 31, file 16.
4. Clipping, *New York Herald Tribune*, September 23, 1960, Daly Papers, box 32, file 3.
5. Script from closed-circuit promotional screening of "Cast the First Stone," undated, Daly Papers, box 31, file 17.
6. Telex from Jim Beach to John Daly, September 29, 1960, Daly Papers, box 32, file 3.
7. Peter G. Peterson to "Ollie," November 1, 1960, Daly Papers, box 32, file 17.
8. Memo from John Daly to Oliver Treyz, November 11, 1960, Daly Papers, box 31, file 17.
9. Although "Yanki No!" and other direct cinema documentaries have received a great deal of historical and critical attention, these programs (while

influential) were exceptional. Both CBS and NBC showed particular reluctance to adopt this verité style of documentary. Perhaps the key reason they eschewed this style was that it eliminated the need for an on-air correspondent. Both of these networks invested heavily in promoting the star status of their correspondents, and therefore almost all of their documentaries were anchored by a news personality who provided commentary and analysis. ABC, whose tiny news organization had much less star power, was more likely to remove the reporter from center stage; however, it still produced many documentaries with voice-over narration and with a visual style that was more reminiscent of its competitors than it was of the style pioneered by filmmakers such as Robert Drew and Ricky Leacock.

10. Patricia Zimmerman, "Reel Films: A Social History of the Discourse on Amateur Film, 1897–1962" (Ph.D. diss., University of Wisconsin, 1984), 387.

11. I am not suggesting that these earlier films by Grierson, Ivens, Riefenstahl, Vertov, and others had no influence on network documentarists. They may well have. Nevertheless, I have found little to indicate that network news workers talked about these films or drew on them for inspiration in their work. On the other hand, they often did comment about the influence that Hollywood film had on their work. This might be explained by the impact that Hollywood had on television in general, particularly during the late 1950s when live New York productions were being displaced in network prime time by Hollywood telefilm. Thus documentarists, in an effort to compete for ratings with entertainment programs, sought to employ many of the techniques of entertainment television.

One of the few network documentarists who made explicit reference to earlier nonfiction film genres is Burton Benjamin, executive producer of the CBS *Twentieth Century* series. See "The Documentary Heritage," in *The Non-Fiction Film: Theory and Criticism*, ed. Richard Meran Barsam (New York: Dutton, 1976), 203–208.

12. Although many innovations can be attributed to Murrow and Friendly, their programs mostly offered radio-style analysis interspersed with cross-cut interview clips. They do not have the narrative and visual "sophistication" that becomes apparent in the period under study. One of the programs that most closely approximates later stylistic developments is "The Case of Milo Radulovich," a program that focuses on the impact of Mc-Carthyism on a single individual. This program does enjoy a narrative coherence, but it was the exception rather than the rule at *See It Now*. For example, compare it with "Argument in Indianapolis" or Murrow's famous critique of McCarthy.

As for visual characteristics, the Radulovich program is riddled with awkward camera techniques, inconsistent framing of subjects, and technical intrusions, such as poor lighting and microphones in the frame. The programs often lacked the "polish" that would come to characterize the genre. Fred Friendly himself later commented that, with a few exceptions, these

See It Now programs could not have competed in prime-time like their later counterparts. See "The (Fred) Friendly Touch," *TV Guide*, February 6, 1960, 14.

13. Clipping, *Variety*, March 14, 1962, Frank file, BRTC; also see memo from Bob Asman, producer of *This Is NBC News*, to "The Correspondents," September 13, 1962, Asman Papers, box 10, file 1, NBC collection, SHSW. Furthermore, it should be noted that such notions have a continuing influence on the genre. See Carter, "What Ever Happened," 43–46.

14. In 1963 Secondari received an Emmy Award and was named Television Writer of the Year for producing documentary dramatizations of Columbus's voyage of discovery and the drafting of the Declaration of Independence. See Clippings, *Variety*, February 12, 1975; *Newark Evening News*, May 7, 1961; and *Current Biography*, April 1967, Secondari file, BRTC.

15. "Churchill Series: 'Just Like a Western,'" *Variety*, May 18, 1960, 31. In addition, Bob Lang, one of the producers of *The Twentieth Century*, noted that a similar formula had made that program a ratings success. Said Lang, "We built this show for 6:30 p.m. on Sundays, when kids control the sets. So we built in 'cops and robbers' (we called them Nazis and Poles and British and Americans) and the ratings were there. Here we have an outstanding example of thoughtful material, but . . . a review of the subjects treated might suggest certain of the controversial aspects of the subjects remained unexplored." *Sponsor*, March 25, 1963, 75.

16. *TV Guide*, February 6, 1960, 14.

17. CBS News Clinic. NBC producer Fred Freed makes a strikingly similar observation in Yellin, *Special*, 259.

18. It also was noted that audiences preferred fewer and more developed scenes. See CBS-TV Research Department, "What We Have Learned about Documentary and Educational Programs," Mickelson Papers.

19. This is not to suggest that producers were only concerned with filmic issues and correspondents with journalistic concerns. Job responsibilities often overlapped. Correspondents usually were brought in to perform particular tasks—such as scripting, narrating, and conducting on-camera interviews—whereas the producers were assigned overall responsibility for the program from start to finish. Producers not only made decisions about production techniques, but they were also deeply involved in the research and framing of issues.

20. Quoted in Yellin, *Special*, 126. Also see interview with former *NBC White Paper* producer Albert Wasserman in Rosenthal, *Documentary Conscience*, 92. Wasserman recalls: "I think the early concept, particularly in television, was that the function of the documentary was to present simple information and simple content. My whole approach, however, was that film is essentially an emotional medium, not an informational medium. I know it might sound platitudinous but I thoroughly believed one should not pack films too full of substance, but should try to make films that involved people, and

that helped involve the audience in an experience. Then if they came away with one or two ideas, this is as much as can be expected from a film."

21. Clipping, *New York Herald Tribune*, May 1, 1960, Gitlin file, BRTC.

22. Wasserman in Rosenthal, *Documentary Conscience*, 93.

23. *New York Times*, January 28, 1962, 15.

24. Whiteside, "One-Ton Pencil," 42. The cumbersome equipment caused complaints from correspondents as well. See Schoenbrun's comments at CBS News Clinic, p. 67, and Yellin, *Special*, 163.

25. Friendly's filmmaking style was criticized by some of his contemporaries as "old-fashioned." Whiteside wrote, "One of Friendly's critics in the business has called his television 'big head TV'—a world bounded, in Friendly's endless closeups of people, by the chin and the eyebrow—a form of representation in which the camera is accepted as a great, clumsy machine, into whose glassy visual range the subject has to be taken, rather than being made a truly flexible and mobile instrument that can reach out to the subject and readily travel with him." Whiteside, "One-Ton Pencil," 69.

26. This was despite the fact that most people watching on their home set had trouble telling the difference between 16mm and 35mm film stock.

27. For example, Whiteside notes that *Reports* never produced a documentary about Navajo Indians because CBS crews could not find "strong" interview subjects. Whiteside, "One-Ton Pencil," 47–48.

28. Bluem attributes this to the legacy of radio documentary. Bluem, *Documentary in American Television*, 93–111.

29. Whiteside, "One-Ton Pencil," 52; Jack Gould makes a similar point in his review of "Who Speaks for the South?": "As is typical of the Murrow-Friendly team at its best, the fascination of the program lay not only in the sharply conflicting opinions voiced either with moderation or passion but also in the close ups, which reflected the personalities involved." Jack Gould, clipping, *New York Times*, May 28, 1960, "CBS Reports: PR and Reviews" file, CNL. On the other hand, Friendly also was criticized by colleagues and competitors for his cloying and deferential attitude toward certain interview subjects. Harvey Swados conveys the opinions of these critics when he describes Friendly's "'Washington syndrome'—the seductive talk about the national purpose, the awe of the celebrity and the abject reliance on 'the world's leading authority,' the belief that the *New York Times* is the sole criterion not only for news, but for intellectual significance.... Behind all the high-flown talk resides the kind of belligerent low-brow who is fascinated by technique and by the 'wisdom' symbolized by a handful of sages, and who knows nothing of an entire world of art and intellect." Harvey Swados, "Fred Friendly and Friendly Vision," *New York Times Sunday Magazine*, April 23, 1967, 31.

30. Richard Dyer, "Stars as Signs," in *Popular Television and Film* (London: BFI, 1981), 236–269, and John Fiske, *Television Culture* (New York: Methuen, 1987), 149–178.

31. Note that although the Sunday interview programs were shot in "real time," the purpose of Friendly's editing technique was to construct the appearance of a contiguous set of responses from disparate bits of footage culled from hours of exposed film. Thus the notion of temporal continuity within the interview itself is largely a fabrication designed to achieve dramatic effect. Similarly, spatial continuity was often implied even though juxtaposing different points of view often meant cutting back and forth across space.

32. Quoted in Yellin, *Special*, 164. Also note that Oppenheimer was a favorite interview subject of Murrow's and Friendly's. See Friendly, *Due to Circumstances*, 69–75.

33. Quoted in Yellin, *Special*, 165.

34. Ibid.

35. Tuchman argues in her study of news in the 1970s that the close-up and the extreme close-up are not acceptable for "straight, hard news" coverage because they are associated with moments of drama. She also notes that it is highly unacceptable to shoot reporters at this range because that might imply involvement. Rather, they are framed by a more neutral middle shot that is conventional both for news readers and for official spokespeople. Tuchman, *Making News*, 118–119.

36. Hackett, "Decline of a Paradigm?" 251. On the ideological implications of news photography, also see Stuart Hall, "Determinations of News Photographs," in *The Manufacture of News*, ed. Stanley Cohen and Jock Young (Beverly Hills: Sage, 1973), 188. Furthermore, it is important to point out that even though claims that film "documented" reality were quite common, we also have seen in regard to Friendly's shooting techniques that documentarists were well aware that the filmic representation, like narrative, was highly malleable. Although the claim was often made that film footage was the guarantor of validity, the fact was that few considered it an unimpeachable source. Thus I would argue that the narrative had to work just as hard to guarantee the validity of the image as the reverse.

37. Clipping, *New York Herald Tribune*, January 9, 1961; also see Gitlin quoted on same topic in *Variety*, July 27, 1960, Gitlin file, BRTC.

38. CBS News Clinic, p. 64.

39. I am not arguing that television documentary adopted all or even most of the conventions of Hollywood style. However, the influence of these conventions was strong. My understanding of Hollywood style derives from the work of Bordwell, Staiger, and Thompson, *Classical Hollywood Cinema*.

40. Yellin, *Special*, 132, 233.

41. CBS News Clinic, p. 49; italics are mine.

42. Ibid., 44.

43. Yellin, *Special*, 82.

44. Bordwell, Staiger, and Thompson, *Classical Hollywood Cinema*.

45. Memo to "The Correspondents" from Bob Asman, September 13, 1962.

Also see CBS News, *Television News Reporting* (New York: McGraw-Hill, 1958), 63–78.

These conventions were not adopted with the sole purpose of conforming to Hollywood style. Other factors, such as the social relations of production, are important as well. A conventional style facilitated the integration of operations by dispersed groups of news workers. One person might shoot footage on location in Africa, but another would edit in New York. Technical personnel did not always follow their work through to completion. Therefore the social relations of production encouraged an aversion to idiosyncratic styles. Even though the producer worked with a project from beginning to end, this was not necessarily true for the camera operator, the sound recordist, or the editor. Thus conventions were a means of extending managerial control in order to coordinate production activities.

Gaye Tuchman has observed, "One can change the written word, but cannot easily alter the recorded spoken word to insert a new phrase. Nor can one change the distance between camera and speaker, the framing of the picture, short of filming again. . . . Those limits mean that the rules governing the visual language of news film must be more explicit." See *Making News*, 107.

It can therefore be argued that conventions make it possible for news workers to operate within a corporate framework. But given the variety of filming situations that documentary workers confronted, the boundaries had to be broad enough to allow a certain amount of discretion. These conventions were not framed in terms of inviolable rules that subjected the transgressor to disciplinary action; rather, they were framed in terms of professionalism. Those who observed the codes of the profession made it possible for executives such as Richard Salant to defend their expertise. And, not coincidentally, they were rewarded with career advancement. They became the senior producers and unit managers.

46. Tuchman, *Making News*, 110.
47. Clipping, *Variety*, March 14, 1962, Gitlin file, BRTC.
48. Rosenthal, *Documentary Conscience*, 92.
49. Ibid., 94; clipping, *New York Times*, November 17, 1965, Gitlin file, BRTC.
50. *Variety*, September 20, 1961, 21, and clipping, *New York Times*, September 23, 1962, Webster file, BRTC.
51. Bluem, *Documentary in American Television*, 134–136.
52. Clipping, *New York World Telegram and Sun*, October 2, 1963, Webster file, BRTC. Another documentary producer who worked at both ABC and CBS during this period was Stephen Fleischman, who got his start in Hollywood as well, working as a film editor at Columbia Pictures. CBS press release, January 16, 1959, Fleischman file, BRTC.
53. Network report, "CBS News on the CBS TV Network," September 1965, 21, "CBS Reports PR and Reviews" file, CNL.

54. Clipping, *Newark Evening News*, September 25, 1965, David Lowe file, BRTC, and Madison, Wisconsin, *Capital Times*, August 17, 1989, 43.
55. See Winter, "Differential."
56. See, for example, Brian Winston, "Documentary: I Think We Are in Trouble" and "The Tradition of the Victim in Griersonian Documentary," both in *New Challenges for Documentary*, ed. Alan Rosenthal (Berkeley and Los Angeles: University of California Press, 1988), 21–33, 269–287.

Eight. The Overdetermined Text

1. Stuart Hall, interviewed by Lawrence Grossberg, "On Postmodernism and Articulation," *Journal of Communication Inquiry* 10 (summer 1986): 45–60, and Hall, "Signification, Representation, Ideology: Althusser and the Post-Structuralist Debates," *Critical Studies in Mass Communication* 2 (June 1985): 91–114.
2. Broadcast February 14, 1961.
3. NBC Television Network News Release, January 18, 1961, "NBC White Paper" file, CNL.
4. Note that these characters are social groups rather than individuals. Although this would be unusual for the Hollywood cinema, the notion of narrative tension between human actors is nevertheless very much in keeping with the storytelling style of entertainment television during this period.
5. Walt W. Rostow, *Stages of Economic Growth: A Non-Communist Manifesto* (Cambridge: Cambridge University Press, 1960).

Nine. The Missing Audience

1. Gary A. Steiner, *The People Look at Television: A Study of Audience Attitudes* (New York: Alfred A. Knopf, 1963), 4.
2. Part of this may have been due to scheduling. Documentaries were often given marginal time slots. Network programmers contended, for example, that 10:00 was a good time for documentaries because they were primarily targeted at an adult audience. Yet this was also a time when fewer sets were in use and when many adults opted for relaxing entertainment before retiring for the evening. An earlier time clearly had advantages, as became clear in the 1962–1963 season when *CBS Reports* switched from Thursday nights at 10:00 to Wednesdays at 7:30 and saw its average rating rise from 6.4 to 9.8. This still left the program third behind its rivals, *Wagon Train* and *The Virginian*, each of which drew an audience of twice the size. See memo from Market Planning and Development to May Dowell, April 9, 1963, "CBS Reports" file, CNL. For the ratings of the competing entertainment fare, see Brooks and Marsh, *Complete Directory*, 925–926.
3. "TV's 'Quiet Revolution' Investigated," *Broadcasting*, March 5, 1962, 53,

and "Sponsorship Brightest Spot in Public Affairs," *Sponsor*, March 26, 1962, 31.

4. N. W. Ayers and Sons, *Directory of Newspapers and Periodicals* (Philadelphia: N. W. Ayers and Sons, 1962).

5. This is a product of the "pass-along" phenomenon whereby those who pick up an issue while waiting at the dentist's office are listed as readers as well as multiple users in a single home. As a result, it is very difficult to know how many of these readers actually pay substantial attention to each issue. Furthermore, one study of *subscribers* (those who clearly had the option to spend the most time with the magazine) showed that fewer than half read the national or international sections with any regularity. The most commonly read sections were those that dealt with personalities and entertainment. See Gans, *Deciding What's News*, 221–225.

6. A comprehensive study of attitudes about the Cold War showed strong and continuing public concern about the Soviet challenge. Yet these concerns about Communism did not translate into public endorsement for a more vigorous involvement in Third World countries. See Benton and Bowles, Inc., "A Series of Seven 'Measurements' of Public Concern over Selected Cold War Issues and Certain Other National Problems, July 1960 through April 1963," staff files, Arthur Schlesinger, box WH-3, JFK.

7. Terry Eagleton, *Literary Theory: An Introduction* (Minneapolis: University of Minnesota Press, 1983), 28.

8. BBC radio had a similar mission during its early days. See David Cardiff and Paddy Scannell, "Broadcasting and National Unity," in *Impacts and Influences: Essays on Media Power in the Twentieth Century*, ed. James Curran, Anthony Smith, and Pauline Wingate (London: Methuen, 1987). Also see Scannell, "Public Service Broadcasting," 135–166, and Morley and Robins, "Spaces of Identity."

9. Memo from Arthur Schlesinger Jr. to Newton N. Minow, September 15, 1961, accompanied by a report entitled "National Cultural Policy," which was drafted by Max Isenberg of the State Department, NMP, box 56, White House file. Also see Schlesinger, "How Television Can Meet Its Responsibilities."

10. For an insightful discussion of the relationships between home, family, media, and leisure in twentieth-century America, see Spigel, *Make Room for TV*.

11. In fact, during this period, network news divisions became increasingly aware of the importance of personality in the production of news audiences. NBC linked the success of its growing news operation to the audience appeal of its star anchors Chet Huntley and David Brinkley. CBS responded by easing out Douglas Edwards in favor of Walter Cronkite and actively promoting his status as a personality. Meanwhile, ABC was openly pursuing a news figure with starlike charisma to take over the anchor duties of its nightly news program. See Mickelson, "Some notes from Eisenberg analysis"; promotional memo for *Chet Huntley Reporting*, March 1, 1962,

Reuven Frank Papers, box 292, file 26; clipping, "Huntley-Brinkley Scores 1–2 Punch in TV Q's 1963 Home-Test Polling," *Variety*, August 21, 1963, Charles Collingwood Papers, box 1, file 3, SHSW. Regarding TV Q-ratings, it should also be noted that news personalities were not only compared with their peers but also with entertainment personalities.

12. Lisa A. Lewis, ed., *The Adoring Audience: Fan Culture and Popular Media* (New York: Routledge, 1992).

13. Memo from Sig Mickelson to Frank Stanton, February 1, 1955, with attached report "Objectivity in Radio News and News Analysis," and Westley, "Objectivity Study," and memo from Mickelson to Stanton, December 6, 1955, Mickelson Papers, box 1, file 11.

14. Regarding television and the move to the suburbs, see Spigel, *Make Room for TV*, and George Lipsitz, *Time Passages: Collective Memory and American Popular Culture* (Minneapolis: University of Minnesota Press, 1990), 39–75.

15. Winston, "Racial Consciousness," 171–182.

16. This concern about what the individual could do to affect foreign policy was the focus of a campaign mounted in the early 1960s by the Advertising Council, an organization that included the heads of all three networks along with top executives from the advertising field. See correspondence between Theodore S. Repplier, president of the Advertising Council, and top administration officials, central subject file, box 209, JFK.

17. *New York Times*, September 19, 1961, 72.

18. Jack Gould, "TV: An Intelligent Study," *New York Times*, November 12, 1959, 71.

19. "The Population Explosion," November 11, 1959, in *Variety Television Reviews*, vol. 6, ed. Howard H. Prouty (New York: Garland, 1989).

20. *New York Times*, September 28, 1962, 68.

21. Fred M. Hechinger, "TV: Russian Education," *New York Times*, September 29, 1962, 47.

22. "Meet Comrade Student," October 3, 1962, in *Variety Television Reviews*, vol. 7.

23. The *Star* did not begin reviewing television programs in its daily edition until 1963. Most discussion of the medium took place in the weekly program guide, which provided station schedules and viewing tips. Here too, entertainment was the overwhelming focus.

24. *Indianapolis Star*, September 28, 1962, 19.

25. Gary A. Steiner's research during this period shows that before their bedtime hour, children were generally most influential in shaping family program choices. He also found that only 11 percent of his respondents chose adult information shows when asked which programs were best for their children. See Steiner, *The People*, 174–184, 104. It should also be pointed out that Steiner's research on television audiences was partially funded by CBS.

26. One CBS network study concurred with this interpretation: "Most of the support comes from people who were calling for more and better news and

educational types of programs and were most vocal in expressing opinions that everybody *ought to watch* these when they were made available." Memo from Sig Mickelson to Files, January 12, 1961, Mickelson Papers, box 1.

27. Steiner, *The People*, 159.

28. Ibid., 233.

29. Cited in Yellin, *Special*, 275.

30. Tore Hallonquist, CBS Research Department, Program Analysis Division, "What We Have Learned about Documentary and Educational Programs."

31. George E. Pitts, "Jim Crow Rampant in TV, Films, and Publishing," *Pittsburgh Courier*, February 28, 1961, sec. 2, p. 21.

32. "What's on TV?" and "Congressional Committee Hears How TV Ignores Negroes," *Amsterdam News*, February 24, 1962, 15.

33. For example, this was the reason African American political leaders punctured President Kennedy's trial balloon regarding the appointment of J. William Fulbright as secretary of state. They charged that Fulbright's record on race issues disqualified him despite his touted abilities in foreign policy. See Enoc P. Waters, "JFK Couldn't Act on Fulbright as FDR Did on Black in 1937," *Amsterdam News*, December 24, 1960, 2.

34. *Amsterdam News*, October 1, 1960, 1.

35. *Amsterdam News*, September 24, 1960, 1.

36. *Amsterdam News*, October 1, 1960, 1.

37. Ibid., 3.

38. Ibid. It should be noted, however, that the National Baptist Ministers' Conference (the "largest Negro organization in the world" with a membership of five million) was itself deeply divided between a conservative leadership and the growing power of activists such as Martin Luther King. These activists, though publicly focused on the issue of integration, were often privately critical of American foreign policy. See *Amsterdam News*, September 16, 1961, 1, 11. Also see editorial, "A Disgrace," in the same issue, 10.

39. "Playing It Cool," *Amsterdam News*, October 1, 1960, 10.

40. "A Mistake," *Amsterdam News*, October 1, 1960, 10.

41. P. L. Prattis, "Why Berlin?" *Pittsburgh Courier*, September 23, 1961, 9. It should also be pointed out, however, that around the same time the *Chicago Defender* sampled opinion among its African American readership and concluded, "Chicagoans Would Fight over Berlin If Necessary," *Chicago Defender* September 16, 1961, 1.

42. "Lumumba!" "He Hailed U.S. Negroes," "Becomes Martyr in Death," *Pittsburgh Courier*, February 25, 1961, 1, and "Strange," an editorial, *Amsterdam News*, February 18, 1961, 31.

43. James L. Hicks, "Patrice Lumumba," *Amsterdam News*, February 18, 1961, 8. On the same page is an editorial cartoon with the likeness of Lumumba and Lincoln side by side and a smoking revolver in the foreground. It is captioned, "Price of Leadership?"

44. *Amsterdam News*, February 18, 1961, 1.

45. *Chicago Defender*, October 15, 1960, 18.

46. *Amsterdam News*, March 18, 1961, 17.

47. *Pittsburgh Courier*, September 30, 1961, sec. 2, p. 21.

48. *Amsterdam News*, December 24, 1960, 8; *Pittsburgh Courier*, September 30, 1961, sec. 2, p. 21.

49. *Pittsburgh Courier*, September 30, 1961, sec. 2, p. 21.

50. *Amsterdam News*, December 10, 1960, 9.

51. "Malcolm X Rips JFK Advisor," *Pittsburgh Courier*, February 4, 1961, sec. 2, p. 10.

52. Poppy Cannon White, "Temper Tantrum," *Amsterdam News*, December 21, 1963, 13.

53. Although it has not been possible for me to pursue research regarding the reception of network documentaries in international distribution, these African American newspapers suggest some of the alternative reading strategies that may have been employed by audiences in other parts of the Free World.

54. Joan Landes shows how feminist scholars have interrogated the gender politics of the public sphere in "Jurgen Habermas, the Structural Transformation of the Public Sphere: A Feminist Inquiry," *Praxis International* 12 (April 1992): 106–127.

55. Clipping, *TV Guide*, March 12, 1960, Helen Jean Rogers file, BRTC.

56. Clipping, *New York Times*, January 8, 1961, Helen Jean Rogers file, BRTC.

57. Andreas Huyssen, "Mass Culture as Woman: Modernism's Other," in *Studies in Entertainment: Critical Approaches to Mass Culture*, ed. Tania Modleski (Bloomington: Indiana University Press, 1986), 188–207; Patrice Petro, "Mass Culture and the Feminine: The 'Place' of Television in Film Studies," *Cinema Journal* 25 (spring 1986): 5–21; and Tania Modleski, "Femininity as Mas(s)querade: A Feminist Approach to Mass Culture," in *High Theory/Low Culture: Analyzing Popular Television and Film*, ed. Colin McCabe (New York: St. Martin's Press, 1986), 37–52.

58. This does not mean that the networks were not interested in women as viewers. Rather, the primary address of these programs was to the father–decision maker as the head of the household. Certainly women were encouraged to watch, but the discourse of these programs was the discourse of the public sphere, a domain dominated by men. It was often suggested that the reason women watched documentaries was because it freed them from the isolation of suburban domestic life and enlightened them so as to make them interesting companions for their husbands. As one CBS study of documentaries argued, "There was surprisingly high favorable response from younger married women who apparently feel that their household duties keep them from sufficient contact with news matters of importance and they enjoy the show as a means of contact with the important issues of the day." Memo from Sig Mickelson to Files, January 12, 1961, Mickelson Papers, box 1. Furthermore, children were encouraged to watch documen-

taries in the hope that the programs would serve an educational function. Nevertheless, the target audience for network documentary was the father–decision maker. See memo to May Dowell from Market Planning and Development, April 9, 1963; memo to Miss May Dowell from Charles Steinberg with attached study guides for children regarding specific episodes of *CBS Reports*, October 10, 1962, "CBS Reports, 1962" file, CNL; and promotional memo regarding NBC documentary series *Chet Huntley Reporting*, March 1, 1962, Reuven Frank Papers, box 292, file 26.

59. Modleski, "Femininity as Mas(s)querade," 41.
60. *TV Guide*, December 10, 1960, 6.
61. Curtin, "Packaging Reality."
62. *Variety*, June 28, 1961, 31.
63. This policy was formalized in a speech by CBS president Frank Stanton in the fall of 1959 when the quiz scandals were beginning to heat up. One of the key criticisms of the quiz genre was that audience emotions and critical faculties were being manipulated by producers who tampered with reality. Dubbed laughter and applause were two of the key culprits. Consequently, Stanton announced that henceforth all CBS programs would refrain from manipulations of the sound track. Friendly, *Due to Circumstances*, 109.
64. Clipping, *New York Morning Telegram*, July 28, 1964, Friendly file, BRTC. This prohibition and its relationship to criticisms of entertainment television calls to mind Laura Mulvey's discussion of the distinction between nineteenth-century British melodrama (which used music to heighten dramatic impact) and "legitimate theatre." It also reminds us of Lynn Joyrich's claim that one of the defining characteristics of television melodrama is the use of music to evoke an affective response from viewers. Laura Mulvey, "Melodrama in and out of the Home," in McCabe, *High Theory*, 93, and Lynn Joyrich, "All That Television Allows: TV Melodrama, Postmodernism, and Consumer Culture," in *Private Screenings: Television and the Female Consumer*, ed. Lynn Spigel and Denise Mann (Minneapolis: University of Minnesota Press, 1992), 229.
65. *Variety*, May 1, 1963, 35.
66. May, *Homeward Bound*, 208–226.
67. During the early sixties Jacqueline Kennedy was the focus of dozens of articles in women's magazines—such as *McCall's*, *Redbook*, and *Cosmopolitan*. At the same time, these magazines featured stories about women's increasing role in public life.
68. Ratings data come from Bailey, *Examination of Prime Time Network Television Special Programs*, 261–294.
69. See, for example, *New York Times*, February 28, 1962, 67, December 1, 1962, 51, and October 7, 1963, 63.
70. Ien Ang, "Melodramatic Identifications: Television Fiction and Women's Fantasy," in *Television and Women's Culture*, ed. Mary Ellen Brown (Newbury Park, Calif.: Sage, 1990), 85.

71. Samuel Grafton, "Women in Politics: The Coming Breakthrough," *Mc-Call's*, September 1962, 102–103ff.; Milton J. E. Senn, "Child Care in Russia: Better than Ours?" *McCall's*, March 1963, 40–41ff.; and Betty Friedan, "The Fraud of Femininity," *McCall's*, March 1963, 47ff.

72. NBC ad entitled "Who Cares?" *McCall's*, November 1960, 190–191. There were nine installments of the *Purex Specials for Women* broadcast in daytime hours between 1960 and 1962. Irving Gitlin, the executive producer of these docudramas, earlier produced a similar series of four programs at CBS under the series title *Woman!* The CBS series was so popular and the sponsor, Purex, was so pleased with the results that it followed Gitlin when he moved from CBS to NBC. For reviews of these programs, see Prouty, *Variety Television Reviews*, vols. 6 and 7. Irving Gitlin discusses the popularity of the CBS series in a clipping from the *New York Herald Tribune*, May 1, 1960, Gitlin file, BRTC.

73. "The Soviet Woman" was broadcast December 10, 1963, and "The World's Girls" aired September 25, 1963. Both were special documentaries sponsored by Philco.

74. It is worth speculating that there may a be relationship between the ambivalent reception of the network documentary during the early 1960s and the emergence of what Lynn Spigel has referred to as the "fantastic sitcoms." Spigel suggests that the rising popularity of such programs as *The Beverly Hillbillies*, *My Favorite Martian*, and *Bewitched* was linked to changes in popular attitudes toward social conformity. In the late 1950s highly conventional images of suburbia were pervasive in situation comedies such as *Father Knows Best* and *Leave It to Beaver*. Spigel contends that their popularity diminished as criticism of middle-class conformity began to grow. At the same time, a new subgenre began to emerge that relentlessly parodied middle-class lifestyles and explicitly lampooned paranoia about threatening outsiders. It is therefore worth noting that the arrival of these extremely popular satires took place at the very moment that the Cold War documentaries of the three major networks were losing ground in prime time. If, as Elaine Tyler May argues, the ideology of suburban domesticity was intimately linked to the ideology of the Cold War, then it makes sense that network documentaries about the Cold War began to founder at the very moment that fantastic sitcoms began to gain popularity among television audiences. See Spigel, "From Domestic Space to Outer Space: The 1960s Fantastic Sit-Com," in *Close Encounters: Film, Feminism, and Science Fiction*, ed. Constance Penley, Elizabeth Lyon, Lynn Spigel, and Janet Bergstrom (Minneapolis: University of Minnesota Press, 1991): 205–235.

Conclusion

1. Sterling and Kittross, *Stay Tuned*, 502.

2. For example, see *Electronic Media*, February 1, 1988, 3, and Carter, "What Ever Happened," 42–46.

3. *Sponsor*, August 20, 1962, 33.

4. By 1962, 54 percent of the documentaries produced by the networks were broadcast during prime time. Ibid.

5. *Broadcasting*, January 16, 1961, 32, and October 23, 1961, 72.

6. *Variety*, December 21, 1960, 19, February 27, 1963, 27, and June 5, 1963, 21.

7. *Variety*, April 12, 1961, 17.

8. *Variety*, June 14, 1961, 19, and December 13, 1961, 25.

9. *Variety*, February 13, 1963, 23.

10. *Variety*, August 16, 1961, 27; *Sponsor*, March 25, 1963, 35.

11. *Variety*, March 29, 1961, 1.

12. *Variety*, June 20, 1962, 21.

13. *Variety*, June 6, 1962, 1, and July 31, 1963, 31; for an example of a program saturation cycle in another genre, see Allen, *Speaking of Soap Operas*, 121.

14. *Sponsor*, March 25, 1963, 75.

15. Indeed, one Cincinnati station even canceled its CBS affiliation because of the allegedly "leftist" bias of the news division and switched to ABC. *Variety*, May 10, 1961, 25. Also note Friendly's comments regarding pressures from affiliates in *Due to Circumstances*, 134.

16. *Variety*, July 19, 1961, 29. ABC did not have as much trouble with advertising sales on its flagship series, since it was fully sponsored by Bell and Howell through the end of the 1961–1962 season.

17. *Variety*, April 10, 1963, 26.

18. The italics are mine. *New York Times*, August 12, 1962, clipping, "CBS Reports—Reviews and PR, 1962" file, CNL.

19. *TV Guide*, February 9, 1963, 21; also see remarks by Richard Salant in CBS Annual Report, 1961, p. 5, BRTC.

20. *New York Times*, December 20, 1964, BRTC; also see *Variety*, May 1, 1963, 35, and *TV Guide*, May 6, 1967, 8.

21. *Business Week*, June 9, 1962, 52.

22. *Variety*, March 7, 1962, 1.

23. Ibid.

24. *Variety*, December 19, 1962, 25.

25. Friendly, *Due to Circumstances*, 120, 2157.

26. At the time, the $2.50 "cost-per-thousand" viewers of the NBC nightly news was one of the best ad rates in both entertainment and news programming. *Business Week*, June 9, 1962, 50ff.; *Variety*, May 31, 1961, 20.

27. *Variety*, January 30, 1963, 1, August 21, 1963, 21, and September 4, 1963, 22.

28. *Variety*, March 13, 1963, 39.

29. *Sponsor*, September 17, 1962, 29.

30. *Reporter*, January 3, 1963, Hagerty clipping file, BRTC.

31. *New York World Telegram and Sun*, May 8, 1963, "television documentary" clipping file, BRTC.

32. See, for example, Chafe, *Unfinished Journey*, 202–217.

33. Hallin, *Uncensored War*, 13–59.

34. *Variety*, April 10, 1963, 35.

35. See, for example, the longitudinal study conducted for the administration by the advertising firm Benton and Bowles, Inc., "Series of Seven 'Measurements.'"

36. Memo from Murrow to Kennedy, June 30, 1962, president's office files, box 91, JFK. Murrow entitled the memo "Foreign policy on secondary roads . . . casual conversations in Virginia, Western North Carolina, Tennessee and Missouri with assorted truck drivers, motel operators, farm equipment salesmen, farmers, service station operators, and others . . . a personal unscientific poll by a one-time reporter."

37. Auletta, "Look What They've Done," 7. Also see Ken Auletta, *Three Blind Mice: How the TV Networks Lost Their Way* (New York: Random House, 1991).

38. Auletta, "Look What They've Done," 5.

Index

About the Author

Michael Curtin teaches in the Department of Telecommunications and is director of the Cultural Studies program at Indiana University. After graduating from Brown University in 1977 with a history degree, Curtin worked in radio and television news in the United States and Japan before earning a doctorate in communication arts at the University of Wisconsin in 1990. Along with Lynn Spigel, he is coeditor of the forthcoming anthology *Sixties Television and Social Transition*.